W9-AGB-540

An
Acre
of
Time

Bird's Eye View of the City of Ottawa, 1876

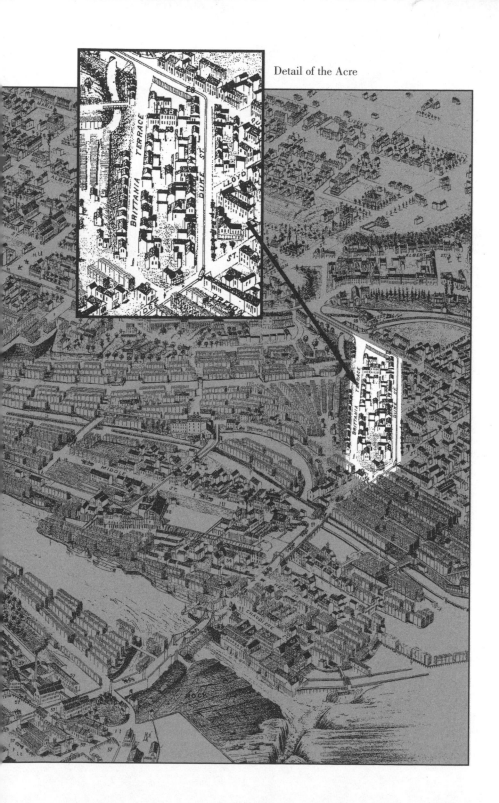

Detail of the Acre

An Acre *of* Time

Phil Jenkins

Macfarlane Walter & Ross
Toronto

Copyright © 2001 Phil Jenkins

All rights reserved. No part of this book may be reproduced, transmitted in
any form or by any means, electronic, mechanical, photocopying, recording,
or otherwise, without written permission from the publisher (or in the case of
photocopying or other reprographic copying, a licence from a licensing body
such as the Canadian Copyright Licensing Agency), except by a reviewer, who
may quote brief passages in a review.

Macfarlane Walter & Ross
An Affiliate of McClelland & Stewart Ltd.
37A Hazelton Avenue
Toronto, Canada M5R 2E3

National Library of Canada Cataloguing in Publication Data

Jenkins, Phil, 1951-
    An acre of time

Includes index.
ISBN 1-55199-002-4

1. LeBreton Flats (Ottawa, Ont.) – History.   2. Ottawa (Ont.) – History.
I. Title.

FC3096.52.J45 2001   971.3'84   C96-931863-4
F1059.5.O9 2001

Macfarlane Walter & Ross gratefully acknowledges support for its publishing
program from the Canada Council for the Arts, the Ontario Arts Council, and
the Government of Canada through the Book Publishing Industry
Development Program.

Printed and Bound in Canada

To my mother, Anne,
for the acres of time we've spent together, and
in memory of my two fathers, Eric and Jack.

Contents

Days of Occupation

Days of Speculation

Sunset

Acknowledgments

You can't get here from there, especially when dealing with history, without many a helping hand. For the pleasure of their acquaintance, knowledge, and kindness let me thank the following.

For showing how the rocks roll, Don Hogarth and Sandy McCracken. For giving me the dirt on flora and fauna, Dan Brunton (special big thanks) and Kris Pirozynski. For letting me borrow their memories, Harry Munro, Gerry Perrault, Dolores Beriault, Harvey and Louise Glatt, Mel Baker, Eli Baker, Betty Kotzer, Albert de Champlain, Viola Milks, John Miles, Glen Burton, and Al Cohen. For showing me where the lines are drawn, Karen Bergsteinsson at the Archives of Ontario, and Alan Day at Crown Land Surveys. At the National Capital Commission, for flexibility in a strait-jacket, Lori Thornton, Barbara McMullen, and Johanne Fortier. For lessons in aboriginal history, Peter Hessel, Harvey McCue, Janet Harper, John Lesley, Joan Holmes, and for showing me just cause, Greg Sarazin. For the dance steps, Paul Gravoline, John and Rita Albert, Armand Vanasse, and Fay Charron. For facts and voices, Shirley Berman, John Almstedt, Joe Legris, and Dave Lemkay (best of luck with your acres, Dave). At the City of Ottawa Archives, thanks to David Bullock and Serge Barbe for showing me the real keys to the city; and thanks to all the staff at the Ottawa Room of the Ottawa Public Library.

For the gift of guidance, Charlie Lewis, Derek Diorio, Ken Ginn (thanks for waiting, I owe you one), E. Annie Proulx, Francis Lionnet from far and near, and everyone who asked me, "When are you going to finish that book?" And to Liette, for grace under the pressure of book widowhood, and steadfast loyalty to a wobbly cause, an everlasting kiss. Ta, love.

Franc Van Oort, the illustrator, boarded late and delivered. Thanks Franc, for giving the story eyes. For permission to subvert their intentions to my drift, thanks to Canadian poets John Barton, Lorna Crozier, David M. Baird, Gary Geddes, Clive Doucet, and Michel-Ange Hyppolite.

My thanks to the Canadians and Ontarians who pay tax; their money, via the Canada Council and the Ontario Arts Council, partially funded the making of this book. And to Barbara Czarnecki, gratitude for her vigilance in editing my humble copy.

Gary Ross — my editor — took a leap of faith in my idea, stayed aloft even when I weighed him down, applied carrots and nudges, and came up with the perfect title. What more could a writer ask? Jan Walter launched the ship with a bottle, and listened when I whined. Glad I found you guys.

Sunrise
June 21, 1993

I'd grab hold of earth
and give her
a robe of moonlight
two round eyes
a pair of golden wings
so that she can fly
making loop-the-loops
and somersaults
until she lands all lit up
on the island of men's conscience

Michel-Ange Hyppolite
from "Zile Nou"

The Business of Respect

Leave where you are and come stand beside me. It is dark, a few minutes before the dawn of the summer solstice, the beginning of the longest day of the year. I am facing north, towards the top of Canada. Looking up, I can just make out a low line of trees, a black, erratic horizon that is beginning to fill with birdsong. The sound of running water burbles behind the trees. Rising above the treeline, a modern city is slowly coming awake. Some office towers, a hotel or two, and a few downtown high-rises appear as columns of lighted windows, like giant crossword puzzles. The streets are fault lines between concrete outcrops.

To the west, where it is darker, traffic signals are rehearsing for the day's game of catch and release. But something is not quite right. The growing dawn shows up a strange, half-finished landscape. There are roads, scruffy grey runways laid out across the grass, but the houses and stores that should go with them are gone, vanished. It's as though someone started building a town in the middle of a city, got the roads finished, then ran out of money.

The hum of cars climbs to a basso continuo beneath the birdsong, while the strengthening dawn starts to colour in the greys. A mile to the north, across a steel bridge that spans a big river, another city in another province punches clear of the dark. Behind that city there are soft, low hills. River, city, hills — the ancient trinity of settlement.

I've come here from my home in those hills to unearth a story, a

3

rolling tale of lava and glaciers, of tropical seas and waterfalls, of whales and white-tailed deer, of Indians and pioneers, millionaires and paupers, firestorms and bulldozers, railways and lumber mills, facts and gossip. It's the story, the biography, of the field beneath my feet. Every story has its borders; the borders of this story are the four sides of the acre I'm standing on, a single page from the book of land.

Before the invention of agriculture, a field needed no man-made borders. It was as wide as a savannah, or as narrow as a canyon floor. But the spread of farming forced the taming of the landscape. The taming was done by measurement. To make measurements everyone could agree on, the cultivators turned to what was at hand, and foot. The thumb, the palm, and the foot were already used to measure cloth. Three barleycorns made a thumb, three thumbs to the palm, four palms to the foot. When the argument turned to the broader loom of the ploughed field, the foot was tediously small. Something bigger was needed. The solution was the acre, a word descended from *ajer*, the Sanskrit word for field.

On their sunny Mediterranean estates the Romans used the *actus*, which was the amount of land ploughed after a day's work by a yoke of oxen. It was about two-thirds of a modern acre. Later the Celts and the Germanic tribes grudgingly adopted the actus when there was a Roman nearby, but at home they kept their own system. After the Roman empire had retreated, the Germanic tribes took over the job of attacking Britain. They imported their own foot as a standard of measure, slightly bigger than the British foot. For a while there was a foot-fight; eventually the Germans won.

The Germans used a rod to measure land. Probably the first rod was just that, a straight branch cut to the length of five steps, or fifteen feet. It also made an ideal fishing pole. The British called it a perch, which, to add to the delightful confusion, is now the name of a fish caught with a rod. When the rod was used to trace out the area ploughed by Germanic oxen between sunrise and sunset, the acre worked out to be forty rods long and four rods wide. And that is exactly what an acre is today, a dozen centuries later, apart from one small hiccup. At the beginning of the fourteenth century a royal decree moved Britain back to the Roman foot. The rod, once a tidy fifteen German feet, was now an awkward sixteen and a half feet. But a royal decree is a royal decree, and it stuck. Surveyors and foresters still use a sixteen-and-a-half-foot rod, and so will I to measure out the acre.

When the Europeans, this continent's first boat people, came to Canada they brought, along with their guns and germs, their feet, rods, and acres. They imposed their acres on a land that before they arrived had flowed from sea to sea, joyfully free of measurement.

A Definite Edge

The day before I go down to the acre I find a young fallen maple tree in the woods behind my house. With a bow saw I cut the greying trunk down to a rod, five and a half yards from the thick end to the thinner, including the slight bend where the prevailing wind has begun to get the better of it. When I go to the acre, I take the rod with me, strapped to the top of the car.

Standing on the edge of the acre, rod in hand, like a pole vaulter waiting his turn, I look around in the newday sunlight. Across the street a camping-ground with more tents than trees is waking up. The fence around the campsite is as high as I can reach, so there is a captive air about it, a compound for refugees on holiday. It is called, according to the sign, LeBreton Camping. In a hut by the camp gate Tony, the night-shift security guard, turns the pages of his book and sips from a Thermos.

Next to the campsite, down in a narrow valley, is an old stone building, built in 1874, flat-roofed, fashioned with civic, Christian pride. Water running through it is pumped into the city's veins. The stream leaving it at the front passes under the arches of a run-down bridge and drops thirty feet into a gully, then sprints for the river behind the trees. Kayakers use the white water, slaloming between suspended hockey sticks. The bridge was once twice as wide and carried a street. A fence halves it now, and posts painted in bee colours allow only cyclists and walkers through.

At the far, northern end of the acre, a couple of hundred yards away, an embankment carries cars past in a slow curve. One passes now, the lone driver bouncing his hand on the wheel to a rhythm I can't hear. A horn of land coming off the embankment intrudes into the otherwise flat field I'm standing on, like a foot pushed under the edge of a carpet. The embankment blocks the view of all but the tallest buildings in the city on the other side of the big river. The city is Hull, and the other side of the river is Quebec. The river is a scaled-down version of the English Channel; it separates by water an English from a French culture. Fish setting out from shore become *poissons* at the halfway point.

On my left, a street runs diagonally a quarter-mile until it meets another, grey scars on a grassy skin-graft, and together they disappear through a low bridge under the embankment. Two tour buses are parked at this end of the street, one from Vermont and the other from Manitoba. The tourists they have ferried to this part of the world are sleeping in a hotel somewhere in the city, nomads with cameras and itineraries.

Just as I am about to lay the rod down and start defining the acre, a small blue car parks at the far end of the diagonal street and distracts me. A bald older man gets out, in pale purple shorts and a white cotton shirt, gold chains and a thin white beard; he opens the passenger door and a black Staffordshire terrier jumps out. They seem the same age. They play fetch the ball, and then the man gets back in his car and drives towards me, the dog running behind. He introduces himself as Victor Garcia, and the dog as Maja Noir, who understands, he tells me proudly, French, English, Spanish, and sign language. Victor and Maja have visited here every day for four and a half years, sun and snow. Victor is a Mexican Indian, mother Aztec, father Topak, brought to Ottawa from California by an affair of the heart. He's the guardian of the eggs laid on the field by a bird called a killdeer.

Killdeer are named after their cry, which I hear now. It is loud and long, like nails dragging down a blackboard. Killdeer usually lay four eggs that look like speckled pebbles, on the ground in short grass. The eggs' only protection is their camouflage, and so the killdeer has evolved a pantomime, a theatrical bit of business to further guard them. Victor asks me to walk towards the eggs. As I do, a bird the size of a robin settles near her latent chicks and begs for my attention. Then she folds a wing awkwardly, as if her arm were being invisibly twisted, and waddles away, a crippled decoy.

Sometimes the bluff is not enough. Victor lost eighteen nests last year, all trampled. Several thousand Canadians, in a mood similar to that of pre-liberation Czechs, assembled here and then marched the mile east to Parliament Hill to pass on their opinions. Victor went out the day before the rally and managed to save four nests from the consequences of democracy in action.

Victor leaves, Maja's silhouette in the passenger seat alongside him. This is a man whose ancestors were conquered by land speculators, whose heart was conquered by a tourist, who crossed a continent, and who now protects the squatters' rights of the latest in a long line of inhabitants who have raised their kids on this acre.

Weave and Spin

To work. I lay the rod down on the first corner, pointing it at the river, and roll it to lie northwest, parallel to the street on my left. I mark this point with a horseshoe nail. It was once the site of a fire station, the only fire station in Ottawa that burnt down this century. Now I flip the rod end over end, forty times. Forty days in the desert, forty days and nights of rain, forty thieves.

As I hem the acre, the rod comes down on a variety of its tenants. There is viper's bugloss, once used as a cure for snakebite in Europe. Bees make blue honey from its blossoms. Little brooches of love-me, love-me-not white daisies are also in the mix, and bladder campion, and mountain sandwort, and oyster plants. The rod crushes a sprig of butter-and-eggs; mixed with milk, the juice can be used as a fly poison. Scattered about are the clover cousins — yellow sweet, hop, and red. Also wild indigo, purple bracelets of cow vetch, and chicory.

At the end of forty turns, I mark the corner with a beer coaster. I'm standing on the edge of the first tavern in Ottawa, run by Mrs. Isaac Firth. Upriver I can hear the Chaudière Falls, harnessed long ago as the tireless servant of a paper mill. The falls are hidden now by a bland collection of industrial buildings. Directly in front of me is a cluster of islands, giant stepping-stones dotted with stone buildings, most of them abandoned. Downriver I can see a bay, once called Sleigh Bay because a winter wedding was held on its ice. Rising up from the bay is a limestone escarpment, almost vertical; atop it are the Parliament Buildings, their backs to the view, a Gothic palisade of stone walls and copper-clad spires.

I right-angle the rod towards the east, make a mere four turns, and plant a wooden stake in this corner, to commemorate the stacks of lumber once piled here from John Rudolphus Booth's sawmills, in their time the biggest in the world. From here I can appreciate the full flow of the Ottawa River, already six hundred miles long on its way to the St. Lawrence. Right-angle again, to the south, and forty turns to complete the third side. A railway rivet marks this corner. I can see the rusty, long-abandoned tracks breaking through the icing of asphalt. Right-angle again to the west, four turns, and the narrow box — the acre — is complete, the tip of the rod resting on the horseshoe nail.

My canvas is stretched and ready. A long, thin rectangle, 4,840 square yards, a field of research, a dance floor for the feet of history. And it is not just a floor, it's also a ceiling for a world beneath. This pool of ground will be my Walden. One of the wondrous properties of holographic plates, those 3-D pictures on glass, is that if you break a plate, pick up one piece, and look into it at an angle, the rest of the picture is visible stretching out into the thickness of the glass. This acre will be like that shard of glass, and the picture is the history of attitudes the acre has endured.

On a whim, I walk to the acre's centre and raise the rod flat over my head. I spin it like a spoke, and in my mind's eye the wheel of time begins to wind back. Summer, spring, winter, fall. Years, decades. Tall buildings vanish, while others, smaller, rise up around me, age from old to new, and are replaced like teeth. Trains change their minds, leave and arrive. Stacks of lumber increase and decline like poker chips. Then, in a wink, the storm of human activity subsides into calm forest, with only a slight rustle of humanity along the river's edge.

Centuries fly by, millennia, and the forest yields to a sea that deepens, fills with life, and grows shallow. Then a tidal wave of pure ice passes over and retreats, then another and another. Millions of years, and the land grows warm and disturbed. A vast wedge of rock rises suddenly back into place and the river valley disappears. A huge basin, ringed by hills and folds, is washed and dried several times; life itself simplifies to a single cell, as the basin rises and falls as though breathing, shedding layers of rock like coats of varnish stripped back.

Eras and ages. The land buckles and bends, cracking and healing. Rock flows like candle wax, boils appear and burst, showers of rock, movement on a grand scale even as life becomes infinitesimal. Cycles of freeze and fire, while the continent itself begins to drift, one of the vast scales on the skin of the earth, colliding with others. Millions to billions. Water gone, life gone, and back, all the way to myth.

Early Days
YEAR 0–1613

But stay to
Witness what has
Gone on so long
And sure to be here
Thousands of years more,
Until the sands,
That move from my decay,
Move on down
To the distant sea,
To become another stone
In another verse
In earth's renewal song

DAVID M. BAIRD
FROM "BOULDER ON A RIDGE"

The Inside Story

In this century, satellites have driven the last dragons from the edges of the map; we fly casually over continents between dinner and breakfast. We understand the width of the world, but its age is beyond our grasp. How can I, who grow impatient in the few moments it takes my computer to save what I've just written, appreciate the span of even the Cretaceous period, the era of dinosaurs that lasted 70 million years, and ended 65 million years ago? Geological time makes the brain go boom. But it's crucial to understand the span of time that arches between the acre's formative years and now. Time puts us, the latest architects at work on the acre, into perspective. There are, for instance, rocks within the acre that have passed their billionth birthday.

An analogy: the acre felt its first footstep, the pad of an eastern woodlander, as recently as five thousand years ago. Recast that five thousand years as the top foot of an ocean of time, and I would have to dive almost a hundred miles down into the dark water of history to reach the moment when the acre's oldest rocks were formed.

Another analogy: I stand at the centre of the acre and walk west. Each step represents a century. I will reach Vancouver, twenty-five hundred miles away, by the time I have paced out the age, 450 million years, of a primitive sponge found fossilized in the acre.

Third and last analogy: I spread my arms like wings. I take a nail file and pass it lightly over the nail of my right index finger. I have just shaved off the entire history of European occupation from the wing-span of the life of the acre.

I am not a geologist, so I cannot casually reach for a million years as they do, the way a carpenter reaches for a handful of nails. Talking to geologists, asking them for a rock autopsy of the acre, I realized that they are detectives who search for the truth of rocks by wielding blunt instruments, chipping away in search of clues. The clues are the size of a boulder, or of a microscopic crystal. And always in the back of their minds is the golden rule of geology: sooner or later, everything moves.

There is a piece of the acre on my desk, plucked the first time I visited there. I use it to hold down piles of research papers. It is a plain thing, a chunk of limestone, the kind a child would throw into the water to see the splash. In a previous incarnation it was alive, a colony of ancient coral and molluscs; four inches tall, it took eight thousand years to grow. My paperweight was a piece of the compacted bottom of a sea called the Champlain that has now vanished.

The drama of the geology of the acre is a play-cycle written on rock, divided into four acts: the Proterozoic, the Palaeozoic, the Mesozoic, and the Cenozoic. Parts of the play — call it *Ages of Rock* — were written so long ago that they have faded from the page. We can only guess from the faint, remaining traces how they appeared at the time. However, there are phrases and sometimes whole scenes of the drama — a fossil here, a fault there — written clearly on the acre.

Act I. The Proterozoic. (Meaning the age before life. In fact, life was there, but it left almost no trace.) This first act in the life of the acre is the longest, the most spectacular, and the hardest to decipher. It is set in the vast forge that was once our solar system. In the forge, a spinning ball is fashioned. The ball has a super-hot and -dense centre, surrounded by liquid nickel and iron. The centre is wrapped in a mantle of plastic, tacky rock, and then plunged into the cold, cosmic bucket of space. A crust forms, a combination of oxygen and silicon that crackles with youthful energy. The crust is set in the vise of gravity and pressure is applied. The crust cracks and the mantle breaks through.

For a billion years there are tempests of volcanic activity, sheets of magma flowing across the stage. The spotlight from the sun is weak, but gradually the ball gains an atmosphere of carbon dioxide and water vapour, as gases fume up from the volcanoes and bleed through cracks in the crust. The planet insulates itself and begins to warm. More water vapour is squeezed from the pressured rocks, forming vast clouds that drop rain into the depressions, irrigating the land with oceans (visions of a gigantic laundry). It is a noiseless world, with no ears to hear the first fall of rain, the birth of volcanoes, the breathing of the wind.

The crust of the ball divides into blocks of land, giant scales, that crawl about the mantle. The blocks migrate randomly to the poles, are covered with ice, then strike out for the equator and thaw. En route they bump into one another, unmatched pieces of a vast jigsaw, slipping under or over one another to form gigantic steps, or crumpling up at the edges to form mountains. Sometimes they link up to make rafts, multi-continents, with stray islands milling around like lagging ducklings.

Then, lost in the swirl, comes the spark of life, more than 3 billion years ago. The first actors on the acre's stage are bacteria, single cells. (When I pluck a pinch of soil from the acre today they are still there, in their billions, virtually unchanged.) They do not breathe, they ferment. The bacteria evolve, in no great hurry, into algae; the algae multiply into huge blue-green pads, floating on the oceans. The atmosphere begins to fill with oxygen, enough to rust the iron in the rocks, putting rouge on the planet's face.

The air grows more complex and chews the rocks. The rivers swill the lighter crumbs of stone down to the seas where they are broken down further, a planetary digestive system. The minerals, the silicates and the carbonates, fall to the bottom to make sediments. In time, the sediments harden to rock again — sandstones, limestones. Meanwhile, the igneous fires of the forge have not gone out. They invade the sediments from below and alter the character of the rocks, messing with their minerals.

At the close of the first act, a vast upheaval lifts the Canadian Shield, the acre embedded somewhere within it, above the water, forming the Laurentian highlands. The rest of the block remains submerged, so that the continent is like a ramp. Where later the Rocky and Appalachian mountain ranges will enter, stage right and stage left, there are two gigantic trenches filled with sea water.

Act II. The Palaeozoic. (Meaning the age of ancient life. It brings the earliest appearance of fish, corals, insects with and without wings, plants on land, reptiles in and out of the water.) Till this time, 800 million years ago, the single-celled organisms have ruled. Now, through a trap door in history, a creature with a nucleus and chromosomes emerges. It doesn't clone itself; it reproduces according to the instructions housed in its genetic library. Evolution has entered the plot, and the plot thickens as life becomes the raw material for future stone. The seas fill with primitive evolutionary life-doodles, shelled and unshelled. On the seabed where they die, they leave their hardened outlines locked in rock. They are like signed and dated postcards from the acre's past.

Act II closes with the Atlantic provinces rising, 350 million years ago, from the ocean. A prodigal island surfs into the mainland and attaches to it like a bow-tie: Nova Scotia.

Act III. The Mesozoic. (Meaning the age of middle life. The "terrible lizards," the dinosaurs, begin their conquest, while underfoot the plants begin to flower. Feathers and fur make their first appearance.) The epic is calm now, lulled by the steady chorus of erosion. To the south of the acre, mountains begin to form. As the Appalachians shoulder their way up, like a giant body turning beneath a sheet, the acre feels the movement. Along parallel cracks in the Canadian Shield the land drops to form a rift valley, a natural trough. The acre lies, like a speck of dirt, at the bottom of this trough.

One wall of the trough lies just to the north of the acre, at the edge of an ancient mountain range. These mountains are slowly eaten down by the elements, reduced from Himalayan adolescence to gentle, round-shouldered maturity. They are now called the Gatineau Hills, the hills I live in.

A tail of the Canadian Shield curls down to the west of the acre (by what is now Gananoque, Ontario) and joins the Appalachians. A box is forming; it has three sides so far. On the remaining, open side, one hundred miles to the acre's east, a solid wave appears in the land, running north-south like a low dam. The box is complete. To the north, the Gatineau Hills. To the south, the Appalachians. To the west, the tail of the Canadian Shield. To the east, a gentle fold.

Within this stone fencing, the field of bedrock granite begins to rise and fall, inhaling and exhaling as many as four times. Each breath is millions of years long. When it inhales, the field is flooded with sea water pouring over the low fold to the east, and the raw material of future sandstones and limestones, like the piece on my desk, is set down in layers on the acre, crumb by crumb. When the land exhales, the layers are exposed to the relentless weather, which acts as a giant eraser.

In the bigger picture, there is much continental activity. The supercontinent of Laurasia, big as all outdoors in the northern hemisphere, undergoes geological revolution and breaks in two. North America is now recognizable, a cousin of its modern outline. It moves away from its neighbours, and the Atlantic Ocean flows in to fill the gap. A mere 65 million years ago the Rocky Mountains push up like sharks' teeth along the western edge of the new continent.

Act IV. The Cenozoic. (Meaning the age of recent life.) Around 65 million years ago a meteor hits the earth. All foliage dies beneath the dust cloud thrown out by the crash. This is too much for the dinosaurs, and there is mass extinction. The mammals, however, survive and begin to dominate. The grasses, the earliest lawns, spring up.

The land around the acre continues to find fault with itself. It slips and slides. (The area is still restless today; thirty earthquakes a year, most of them miles below the surface and too small to shake houses. But every three years or so there is one with enough rock and roll to put cracks in bedroom walls.)

One fault caused by the rattle runs directly alongside the acre, creating the limestone cliffs that will become the site of the Parliament

Buildings. A chunk falls from these cliffs, like a slice of bread cut from a loaf, and lands on the acre. It is so level that when the area is given a nickname by its first settlers, it is called the Flats. Along the fault line, a necklace of volcanoes erupt to the east. The volcano nearest the acre eventually dies and is weathered down. A few million years later a town, Montreal, will grow at the foot of the old volcano, and in the bowl of its old funnel the townspeople will make a park.

Somewhere within this rhythm of pitch and yaw and continental migration, a river begins to whittle its way across the rift valley, passing just in front of the acre. A cat's cradle of faults near the acre creates rapids in the river; a stubborn lip of limestone forces the river to spill over it. This waterfall will prove an obstacle for a species yet to come, in canoes; they will have to get out and walk around it. Later, another branch of the species from Europe will disembark here and make a city.

Intermission: Two Million Years Ago

During the intermission there is an ice age lasting over a million years. Each successive winter makes more snow than summer can melt, and a vast tide of ice begins to flow south and whitewash Canada, shaving it like a razor blade. Much of the gathered stubble ends up in the northern United States. Scenery from the acre winds up in what will be New York State.

Like a continent-wide snowplough, the glaciers, advancing on several fronts, deposit great ridges of earth like Long Island and Cape Cod where they stop. The glacial tide reaches as far as contemporary Wisconsin, after which state this ice age is named. It isn't the first age of ice to cross the acre, and it won't be the last. The next one is due in about ninety thousand years, when it might crawl all the way to what will then be California Island.

End of Intermission

The ice recedes. Wilting under the heat, it deposits the debris it has stored in its belly, stuccoing the landscape with glacial till. The melt water leaking from the retreating ice gathers in the basin, which has been pushed down by the weight of an icy hand. The melt water forms a lake, and then, yet again, twelve thousand years ago (recent history!), salt water washes in from the east.

The acre becomes part of a seabed. Geologists, who give names to the ghosts of seas, continents, and mountains, call it the Champlain Sea, after the French explorer who never saw it but who will travel along its old bed ten thousand years after it has dried up. In its heyday, the Champlain Sea rose six hundred feet above the acre, level with the proudest Ottawa skyscraper. Every time I stand on the acre, I am haunted by the fact that over my head, where now there are seagulls, bowhead whales, belugas, and ring seals once swam.

With the weight of the ice taken from its shoulders, the land rebounds, the bed of the Champlain Sea rising through a storey each century, then slowing down until the rise is imperceptible. The outline of the river valley begins to re-emerge. A hundred miles upriver from the acre a stubborn, gigantic ice dam holds back the water of the Great Lakes. In the course of time the dam breaks, perhaps in an afternoon (imagine!), perhaps over a century, and the valley is flooded with silt and sand, adding the latest layer of topsoil to the acre. A glorious finale to this geological opera.

Going Up

In the early afternoon of the solstice, after I've finished measuring out the acre, a thundercloud builds up overhead. Serious rain will soon pour down. I move under a tree, one of only three that now grow on the acre. These three trees remind me of stubborn tenants who refuse to leave, long after the others have relocated. I slide down the trunk of one of them and put my backside on the earth. The clouds darken; I feel below me the chronicle of stone, air, heat, and water that fashioned this calm platform.

Closing my eyes for a moment, I fall into a geological daydream. The day before, I rode an elevator with fake marble walls, down through the floors of the National Archives building, which overlooks the acre. I find myself back in this elevator; in my hand, a black-and-white diagram by a local geologist, showing the geological layers beneath Ottawa, drawn in separate strata, abrupt pencil-line boundaries between the strata.

With the kind of heroic engineering that daydreams easily accomplish, the archival elevator shaft now extends down into the acre, all the way to the Canadian Shield — the basement floor — a fifth of a mile below and sixteen degrees centigrade warmer. (If I were to drill on through to the other side of the world I would emerge on the opposing acre, in one of the few spots on earth that can truly be called the middle of nowhere — on the seabed two thousand miles off the west shore of Australia and an equal distance north of the Antarctic coast.)

My dream of rising from a granite cellar, up past neatly divided floors of rock, is exactly like the imaginary journey stratigraphers make when mapping the land beneath our feet. To understand the acre's thick skin, we can picture in our minds' eyes rising through the strata in a glass-doored elevator.

Before embarking on this Jules Vernian journey, however, a word about the father of stratigraphy, William Smith. Smith was born in England in 1769. As he grew to employable age, he felt the clanking of the Industrial Revolution around him. He trained as a surveyor and civil engineer, which led him to the growing profession of builder of canals. In digging his canals, Smith noticed that he was cutting through rock that had layers, like books piled on a table, and that the pattern of layers would repeat when he dug elsewhere. Studying this pattern of layers became his hobby.

Smith noticed that certain strata and certain fossils cohabited. In fact, he was looking at evidence of the process of selective evolution, the trials and errors of nature that lead to a bankable mutation. These fossils, Smith realized, provided a second opinion in the diagnosis of a particular stratum. He filled notebooks tracking these highways of rock running beneath the surface, continuing to hold his job as a drainer of swamps and excavator of canals. He illustrated the notebooks with drawings of the relevant fossils. In 1815, as Napoleon's brief era was fading, Smith published the first large-scale geological map, a rock-picture of England, Wales, and part of Scotland, a map the size of half a bedsheet. Along with the map, he published plates of fossils, and in doing so gave birth to the science of stratigraphy. His work, and the work of the honourable guild of stratigraphers over the next 190 years, permits me to have my rocky daydream, push the elevator button marked ROOF, and watch the rock show go by.

First floor. Sandstone; petrified beach, from 570 million years ago. This is Cambrian rock, first identified by a man called the Reverend Adam Sedgwick, Cambria being the Roman word for Wales. It's a creamy colour, around three hundred feet thick. The acre was beneath a shallow sea when it was laid down. Tiny tunnels in the rock show where worms have gone by, probably the acre's earliest residents visible to the naked eye. The general term for these worms is vermes, from the Latin, as in vermicelli noodles.

Second floor. Sandstone and blue-grey dolomite. When this layer was deposited the acre was just below the equator. The seas were getting deeper, and the rate of sedimentation was accelerating.

Third floor. Dolomite, which is limestone mixed with magnesium. We're in the Ordovician era of rock-building now. The Ordovices were an ancient British tribe. The acre rose out of the sea for a while, and the rock was thinned by atmospheric erosion.

Fourth floor. Back came the sea, from the east. Shale and sandstone. A trip to the Bahamas would give you an idea of how the region around the acre looked then. The acre just managed to get its head above water at the end of this period.

Fifth floor. Limestone, some six hundred feet of it, laid down 450 million years ago. Limestone is the alchemic result of organic matter turning into rock. The warm sea invaded from the south this time. Life had not yet mounted dry land, and the oceans teemed with variety. The latest and biggest life forms looked like a squid jammed into a thin ice cream cone. During this era the acre underwent a series of "rinse and dry" cycles.

Sixth floor. Black and brown shale, 250 feet of it. The shift to shale, which shows that the sediments were finer-grained than sandstone, occurred because the acre was under a large, cool, shallow sea that spread down from the north. You can break a piece of this petrified clay between two fingers.

Seventh floor. Grey shale. The flooding this time came from the Gulf of Mexico.

Eighth floor. A mixture of grey shale and dolomite. The Appalachian Mountains were beginning to flex their muscles.

Ninth floor. Red shale. The acre had moved above the equator. At the end of this era the acre lifted above the water and stayed there. Life got busy. Plants took to the land; their cumulative deaths deposited soil on the acre for the first time. As the millennia went by, dinosaurs appeared, but there is no bone-record of any around the acre. Many of the older houses in Ottawa have bricks that contain this shale.

Tenth floor. Glacial deposit from the Wisconsin Ice Age. The ice acted as a sort of Cuisinart, chopping and dicing boulders. These were dumped on the acre as till when the glacier backed off. Clay was laid — like asphalt on gravel — over the till.

Eleventh floor. A layer of marine deposits from the Champlain Sea, sifted out twelve thousand years ago. Dotted throughout, like chocolate chips in a cookie, are barnacles that fed by opening two little triangular doors at the top of their shells so that tentacles could wave nourishing water in.

Twelfth floor. The roof, and I step out of the elevator into the daylight of the very day when the acre, for the first time in a million years, feels the sun on its back. It is nine thousand years ago, and after two thousand waterlogged years the acre has risen clear of the postglacial sea. The acre has changed beds — from seabed to lakebed, from swampbed to riverbed, and out into the fresh, cool, sunlit air. Sun and wind will now give the roof a garden.

Life Story

Nine thousand years ago, the world's winds blow across the acre much as they do today. They airmail in dust and moisture from elsewhere, and each spring they assist the seeds, insects, and birds in their migrations, in the annual list of chores involved in the gardening of the acre.

On such a spring day, a hundred miles east of the acre, a flock of passenger pigeons, a tiny segment of the vast clouds of passengers that moved then on the winds, has reached the end of its spring flight. Tired and hungry, they settle into a stand of budding oak trees where two rivers meet, the northern edge of their summer territory. Some of the weakened branches break off under the sheer mass of bird. Greedy for space, some of the pigeons double-park, actually standing on one another in pigeon pyramids. Hungrily, the flock gorges on the rich menu of last season's berries, still hanging on the south-facing slopes: cherry, juniper, red pine, and jack pine. Half a million heads bob and swallow.

At dawn they feed again, and begin to nest. A layer of droppings thicker than autumn leaves builds up on the ground. Hawks pick off the easiest, weakest travellers. Then, like a bad joke, a thunderstorm rolls through, plucking loose the late arrivals perched on the outer branches.

The unlucky thousands are forced to fly another day, a hundred miles past their summer home, following the river that traces a silvery line to the west. By twilight the storm is spent and the exhausted flock comes down off the air. As they pour down, a skyriver of pigeon, they flow past limestone cliffs and into the noise of a waterfall. They settle onto the southern riverbank, in a colony of alder trees that has taken root along the eastern edge of the acre.

Having at last found a parking spot, the confused legions of pigeons drop the spoils of that morning's feast. The seeds from the berries are glued to the land; a shower of rain a few days later triggers germination. And in this way, perhaps, a cherry seed from a day downwind lands on the soil and becomes the first of its kind to colonize the acre.

For the next nine millennia, the acre will be a construction site of organic architecture, bustling with ingenuity and survival, reproduction and extinction. Skylines will grow, forest fires will level those, and new skylines will rise in their place. Water and sun are the architects, the materials flown in by birds and breezes. The settling of the acre by generations of flora will proceed unhindered until, to be precise, 1818, when the lordly trees will feel the first predator: a man with an axe.

The Circus of Unfamiliar Wonders

Nature is organized like a neighbourhood. It is full of new arrivals and reluctant departures. In each neighbourhood there are ground rules, biological by-laws. Amicable, suburban coexistence is continually threatened by outsiders. Nature is also a conservative community, caught up in a dress code that admits genes designed to survive and excludes others. A single trillium can take hold, multiply, and eventually take over the lot occupied by a cherry tree that has lived there hundreds of years. On the acre, it's often the determined exceptions that write the rules.

The first postglacial coat of vegetation on the emergent acre is amphibious. Sometimes, in the dryness of summer, it rises above the swamp; sometimes, in the spring thaw, it sinks beneath it. Breeds of plants arrive that tolerate the shift from under water to over water. Others fail. One family of seeds happens on the trick of hibernation, lying dormant in the swampbed for decades until a drop in moisture level triggers germination.

Growth on the acre is at first a silent pageant; there is no crack when the bud opens, no hum as the leaves push up to the sun. Eventually, the stems and leaves bend with the wind and provide a gentle percussion. Frogs and turtles add the timpani of movement. There is the melody of birdsong, the drone of insects. The sound of the waterfall roars on in the background.

Over the decades, as the acre dries out, the amphibious plants yield to a tough, independent breed of squatters. The thin soil is like an unfurnished apartment, low in nitrogen, sparse in humus. It can support only plants that move in quickly and stake their claim with the minimum of organic fuss: herbs, lavenders, mosses, heathers. Some of the plants even hunt, trapping insects and relieving them of their nitrogen.

As the soil is furnished with recycled life, it becomes richer; the new settlers it can support become bigger, taller. Speckled alders and dogwoods drop in. Willows fountain up from the spring pools. Solitary robins heading north after winter are taxis for new seeds, foraging under sodden leaves as soon as the sun banishes the snow cover. Arctic terns, the greatest of the migrants, pass over the acre, following their ancient meridian from the top to the bottom of the world. Caribou bring their big feet and a more diverse cocktail of seeds, in copious piles of caribou crap.

The forest grows taller. The hardier trees take hold, at first just the poplars and birches and the smaller pines, country cousins of the great northern forests. But then, around eight thousand years ago, a southern warmth comes into the region, warmer even than now, like a blanket thrown over the acre's shoulders, transforming it into a likeness of the southern landscape.

Stoked by a warmer sun, with its added solar carbon, life makes a quantum leap forward. The maples arrive and erect a summer canopy, a leafy roof of broad five-pointed shingles, supported on columns five feet round and sixty feet tall. The canopy is thick enough to block out the sunlight and choke much of the undergrowth, forcing "low-life," such as the trilliums, spring's first flowers, to bloom and broadcast their seeds quickly, before the shade descends. Dotted among the maples, in singular towers, are the white pines, coniferous titans, manoeuvred by the maple canopy into withholding their branches until they reach the sunlight. Their trunks run smooth, break free of the shade, and seize the day, rising another fifty feet above the tallest maples. (This feat of ingenuity will be the pine's death warrant. Its tubular near-perfection will one day make it the answer to a shipwright's prayer.)

The warming land entices the southern wildlife. Deer roam north into the river valley, pulling cougars down from the hills to hunt them. Elk and bear leave their prints on the acre as they seek the riverbank to drink and fish. A well-ordered neighbourhood is established. The only dramatic variable is the cycle of fire, sparked by lightning, raging every century or so, passing through the wilderness like a comet. For the forest it is an extra season of black between green and white. It is also a time of rejuvenation. There are pine cones, for instance, that open only when they feel intense heat, and their seeds are cannoned out. Some forest fires clear only the herbs and grasses, the lower orders, hardly touching the trees. After the fire, the rains come and the charred, cleared neighbourhood reinvents itself, a green phoenix in a world without men.

The acre's residents, the plants, trees, and animals, are familiar miracles. If I had stood alone on the acre since its birth, through millions of years of stone and ice, their arrival would be a joy to witness. But while their story unfolds above ground, there is another running concurrently, in the soil, in the world beneath vision — the microscopic, solarless system of bacteria, fungi, and tiny invertebrates in their billions. This is the circus of unfamiliar wonders lying beneath our feet.

To go into soil, the real thing, not the sterile tool that modern agriculture has turned into a parking lot for crops, is to step inside the word *land*. Soil is a living mat. An ounce of the acre's dirt, hardly enough to cover a child's palm, is a nation of relationships that we no more understand than we know the people in a city we fly over. There is no such thing as an individual in nature. Inside every seeming bit of independence, life is a colony of co-dependants.

First and foremost, the unfamiliar wonders are wonders of mathematics, the sheer numbers of things. Calculating the number of bacteria thriving inside the acre means reaching for a computer. Take a pinch of fungus, unravel its filaments, lay them end to end, and they would wrap the earth like the string on a pile of old newspapers.

The smallest of all the wonders are the bacteria. They are the original inhabitants of the acre, its first tenants. They move in 4 billion years ago, and make a lifeless world come alive. (They ruled it then, and nothing has arrived in billions of years to oust them. They rule it still.) For a long while, they are all there is of life. In the beginning there are bacteria. Then there are fungi, the acre's second tenant. Acting together, the bacteria and the fungi brush the veneer of life onto the rock at the edge of the sea. They are a double act, feeding off each other, a mutual fund of life striving blindly to stave off extinction and multiply.

Half a billion years after the arrival of the fungi, plants perform the alchemic feat of turning sunlight into carbon. The colour green is born, and the greening of the world occurs in an explosion of plant forms 400 million years ago. The fungi and the bacteria are the foremen of this green breakthrough; four-fifths of plants are dependent for survival on fungi performing an inside job in their roots. Fungi scavenge the ground for phosphate, which is hard for plants to swallow, and spoon-feed it to them in exchange for carbon. Even in the most primitive plants, plants that felt the wind 350 million years ago, there are fungi in the fossils.

The third ring that opens up in the circus of unfamiliar wonders, a few million years after the fungi, is of little round worms called nematodes. (*Nema* is the Greek word for thread.) They are the length of a fingernail, the distant ancestors of modern hookworms. They are also among the earliest mobile tenants of the acre visible to the naked eye, and they live there still, in numbers that would choke a calculator. Zoologists believe that there are half a million variations of the nematode; a mere thirty thousand have been named.

These groundworkers are present nine thousand years ago when the first colonizing seeds settle on the acre. With the basement of the acre stocked with microbiota, the ground floor becomes a rooming-house for a succession of boarders that grow taller and taller. Above and below ground, the visible and the invisible gracefully conspire to build a garden on the rock.

Wishful Thinking

At the beginning of this story, when I stood on the acre in the dark, waiting for the sun, I was filled with a sense of being out of time, of being sometime else. Selfishly, I wanted to be on the acre before humans got there, a ghost from a book written centuries ahead. I'd pick a tall, strong maple at the north end of the acre closest to the river and climb it. Then, swinging into the green periscope of a pine tree, I'd scramble through the porous, leafy umbrella of maple leaves and find a comfortable bark bench with a good wide view.

The vista from my pine perch is spectacular, an indifferent, humbling Eden. Everywhere I look the tree is master, each trunk a foot-soldier in an arboreal army camped wherever it chooses. The only thing it gives way for is water, the battalions of lakes and rivers. My grandmother used to use the word *awful* to mean full of awe. The view from the acre that no one ever saw is awful, the kind you can stare into forever.

The view begins to change, irreparably, when it includes, for the first time, a human being.

The New Tenant

The imagination is a hard thing to rein in, once it gets started. Ask it to go eighty feet up a pine tree, in a world before humans, and it asks why humans have to arrive at all. Did the gods get lonely? Did they create a pleasure park for themselves that needed fresh amusements? Or is it the other way around? As the first animal to become aware of its own certain death (and write about it), perhaps we consoled ourselves by filling the park with gods who would live forever. Or are we just a small part of the divinely invented quest for balance in a fragile mechanism?

Whatever the reason, the acre is about to suffer a major shift in occupancy. Here comes a biped with an ability to adapt that is frightening. It combines a limitless curiosity with the skill of manufacture. It possesses a brain that grasps solutions and hands that can grasp anything. It has a prodigious memory, and it very much enjoys breeding. It is determined, sooner or later, to go everywhere and, once there, to stay.

Arrive the new tenant surely did, but how the human race reached the acre has two answers, depending on who you talk to. If I had shouted down from my perch a thousand years ago and asked some passing woodlanders where they had come from, they would have assured me that people didn't come to the acre at all; they were here all along. Nowhere in the myths of the first inhabitants of this region is there any mention of their being a people from elsewhere. Their myths are of a race that evolved here, in the forests and snow. The blood descendants of those first people, the native peoples, are linked to their origins by a chain of mouths, a relay of stories stretching back beyond the earshot of history. That chain, they would say, is anchored here, as the trees are anchored by their roots.

The other answer to the question of how humans came to the acre is less than a hundred years old, and it is based not on stories but on clues. The clues suggest that the people of the woodlands came here from away; that they started walking out of the rift valleys of Africa a million years earlier. They were always on their way; it was just a question of when they would get here. The first people here were thus peregrines, a word that originally meant wanderers from other lands. Thirty thousand years ago, give or take an educated guess, the continent now called North America was joined at the shoulder to its westward twin, now called Asia. (How times change! Sixty million years earlier it had been joined along its entire eastern flank.) The great glaciers of the Ice Age had siphoned water out of the oceans. Sea level dropped, and land level rose. A grassy boom of tundra, hundreds of miles wide, linked west and east.

There were people on the western, Asian, side of the tundra bridge. They were big-game hunters, experienced, capable nomads. They were peregrines, picking off meals from the herds of prehistoric animals that strolled over the bridge from both directions, unaware that they were continent-hopping. These herds of animals now hunt only in our imaginations. Some were ferociously dental — sabre-tooths, mammoths; others were overblown, larger than life — sloths the size of bears, bison as big as minivans, with horns of Viking magnificence. There were tapirs, horses, and even one-humped camels. (The horse and camel travelled from east to west, deserting the continent even as the nomads were coming into it.)

Once across the land bridge, the nomads subdivided. Some stayed in the north; others funnelled down an alley that ran between the ice caps. They chose, like the herds moving ahead of them, the path of least resistance, the mountain pass and the river valley. They left traces, sharpened stone and the bones of a kill, twelve thousand years old and seven hundred miles from the continental crossing point. As I was researching this chapter, a cliff face near Calgary showed signs of human activity twenty thousand years ago. The footprints of this migration have melted into history and the exact route can't be mapped, only suggested. For sure it went south, each generation a stepping-stone along the trail, a trail that emerged from the glacial alleyways and fanned out in the southlands, a delta of nomadic hunters.

As these hunters moved into fresh killing grounds, their prey was already shrinking, first in number and then, quite dramatically, in diversity. There's a tar pit in California that has had dredged from its bowels, at a depth corresponding to fifteen thousand years ago, the carcasses of thirty-five different species of mammal. The same pit shows that by six thousand years ago all thirty-five species were history, including the horse, which would next return on a boat from Europe. As a mass extinction, it rivalled the exit of the dinosaurs. The reason is still unknown, but it may well have been helped along by bipeds, with sharp sticks, by the waterhole.

In the eastern woodlands of North America, ten thousand years ago, when the acre was still under the sea, the cold forests were fit only for caribou. The nomads remained hunters, but as the summers became warmer and longer, and the winters milder and shorter, the woodlanders were given a new lease on life, and over the next eight thousand years they took it. Climate was destiny. Gradually the landscape altered with the rise in temperature until it resembled the more lively southern forests. The soil changed character, setting in motion a chain reaction through fungi, plants, insects, birds, and mammals. Deer moved in, tracking the migrating grasses and bushes. Fish multiplied in the rivers.

The woodlanders were faced with an entirely new concept: enough. There was enough food, and it was close enough to kill easily. The business of killing was easier, and so loosened its hold on daily life. Fishing nets could harvest enough fish. Because there was enough, the woodlanders settled, commuting through the forest and along the rivers. They were no longer nomads. Now they were territorials. Their lives had grown borders.

When I measured out the acre, I noticed the campsite that operates alongside it. Today, the campers seem a polite impersonation of lives in the woods that were lived around here long ago. For the campers, it's recreation — they are actors re-creating a redundant way of life. For the original woodlanders, in their shelters, it was creation in action. Modern campers are going back to nature. The woodlanders were already there.

There's little evidence of how these early woodlanders went about life. Clothes, homes, and tools were all-natural, organic. Discarded, they reverted back into the natural scheme of things. Likewise, the facts of the woodlanders' lives returned to dust. As far as we know, they wrote nothing down, drew no pictures, until much later. Their voice is gone. Perhaps only the belief that life is uniquely precious and finite provides the motive to record it. The written history of Canada is a book that starts only five centuries ago.

The spiritual life of these people must have been plural. They lived in a world filled with many: many trees, many rivers, many lakes — many spirits. The granite boulders, the white pines, the foraging deer, the ever-running waterfall, these were all spiritual equals, part of nature's congregation. Humans were related to them, not separate from them. To bundle those spirits up into one almighty pile, as the Christians do, one singular, isolated spirit, would have denied reality. The turning wheel of the seasons, white to green to white, the reappearing foliage on the same tree-body, would have made the case for reincarnation, the continuity of spirit.

And if prayer involves talking to a spirit unseen but believed, then no doubt the woodlanders spoke directly to boulders, deer, waterfalls, and trees. Thousands of years later, I stand on the acre, mute. I know I'd feel silly addressing it, even though I routinely greet cats and curse combustion engines.

Back up on my pine perch, I'm the silent witness, scanning the horizon for the first woodlander to make it here, as it were, all the way from the continent next door. And there it is, a smudge on the horizon, moving in an odd fashion on the river — against the current, parallel to the riverbank. As it draws closer, the smudge resolves into a birchbark canoe, the tool the woodlanders used to shrink distance. The birchbark canoe conveyed the first human eyes that looked on the acre. It is the first of so many artifacts that will profoundly alter the acre's future.

The birchbark canoe was an echo of the forest. The basic shape seemed lifted from nature, a crescent moon reflected on the water. Midway through construction it resembled the backbone and ribs of a filleted fish. Birch, cedar, maple, white pine, white and black spruce, selected for their particular qualities, went into the canoe's making. The sheets of birch bark and the wooden framing were sewn tight with the split roots of black spruce or white pine. The gum used in waterproofing the joints and repairs was the boiled sap of spruce trees. The result was perfection. It was strong and flexible, like a moving river, and easily repaired when torn by the river's hidden threats. On land, overturned, it was shelter from the storm. Kneeling in it, the woodlanders faced, unlike Europeans in their rowboats, the way they were going.

Construction started with the skinning of a tree, as clothing began with the skinning of a carcass. The woodlanders hunted for a birch with unblemished bark, true and straight. A bend in the trunk resulted in a wrinkle in the skin of the canoe. It was easier to skin a birch in summer, when the bark is light brown. Blending that with the darker winter bark gave the canoe a two-tone effect. Winter bark also has a rind, like an orange, that can be scraped with a pattern, allowing the bands that paddled past the acre a way of customizing their canoes.

On a carefully selected, level piece of shady ground, with no rocks or roots sticking up, the canoe was assembled — shady because sunlight makes the bark stiff and hard to work with. The first step was to suggest the outline of the canoe with stakes, and then remove them, leaving a series of holes. The sheet of bark was laid out, bent up to resemble a pair of hands gathering water to drink, and the stakes were reinserted in the holes. The bark was used with its lining to the water. If several pieces were needed they were laid one over another, overlapping towards the back, so the canoe wouldn't get snagged by a rock edge. Next, the cedar ribs were steamed over boiling water, bent to form a horseshoe, and implanted to brace the skin. All that remained was to reinforce the bow and stern.

. The woodlanders in their canoes favoured certain waterways, the territorial backbones. On the riverbanks they found individual answers to the riddle of survival, like the tribe on the mighty river that ran past the acre. Their canoes were distinguished by noses that were straight and almost vertical, proud prows that cut the wind and pushed aside over-hanging branches. The acre thus became part of a territory without fences, defined by language and custom. Inside invisible borders they divided into scattered encampments on the rivers and tributaries. They had names like Kichesippirini, Matououescarini, and Otaguottouemin, names that are tiny stories in themselves. The names come to us through the filter of the conquerors, who, like Ellis Island clerks, wrote down what they thought they heard.

A segment of the arriving woodlanders settled only a couple of miles from the acre, on the opposite riverbank, in the delta of the Gatineau River. The recently uncovered six-acre site — in a park, near a gambling casino — is known to be at least five thousand years old. Part of it is under an old city dump, and there are signs of prehistoric quarrying on the shore of the lake in the park. The careful, delicate unveiling of the site's history started in 1991, and it already indicates what the archaeologists are call-ing a "constant and massive presence for over twenty centuries." Thousands of fragments of the daily life of these woodlanders have been lifted from their grave, and have again felt the touch of hands: arrow points, ceramic vases and pipes, scrapers, and copper artwork. Volunteers are being used to map the site and its treasures, and I'll be among them next summer, up to my elbows in history.

In this settlement, a range of utensils and weapons aided the kill (the whisper of bow and arrow), the meal, and later the gardens of maize, beans, peas, and squash. There was humour (laughter was a prized pharmaceu-tical), hospitality (showing a lack of it was criminal behaviour), fashion (body paint, shaved hair), sexual market research (women experimented freely before marriage), ritual (tobacco thrown into the river to influence spirits in waterfalls and rapids), and play (a rough ball game modern rugby players would have no trouble picking up). Death, when it came, was a stepping-stone. The vacated body went into the earth, staked out with a tombwood carved with the face of the buried. Male graves were marked with a weapon — plus feathers for a leader — and females were given a utensil; the division of labour carried into the next life.

The tribe on the acre's river also had a source of income — control of passage down the waterway. There were tribes to the left (Nipissing, Huron) and right of them (Montagnais, Malecite) who used the river as an expressway in a sophisticated trade route. By a fortunate stroke of geography, an island seventy miles upriver from the acre sits like a steep-sided lump in the throat of the route, alleys of water running either side. This island, called Morrison Island now, has also been occupied for thousands of years, latterly by the tribe called the Kichesippirini, which means, succinctly, people of the river. As the sitting tenants, they were also the gatekeepers of the river, able to demand a toll, a portion of the cargo: copper, obsidian, flint, tobacco, gourds, and corn.

So the human traffic past my perch in the pines grew with the centuries. It's hard to believe that in all those years, no one set foot on the acre. Curiosity, a chased deer, a couple's need for privacy, or maybe just a stroll — any of these could have brought the first visitor to the acre. The moment will remain forever inexact, just a small step for a man on a forest floor.

Boat People

The woodlanders, ancestors of the modern native peoples of eastern Canada, are sometimes referred to as the First Nations, or First Peoples. But they, as mentioned, were descendants of the nomads who had made a westerly, ten-thousand-year crossing of the continent to get to the acre.

Around four hundred years ago, explorers started heading towards the acre from the east, crossing the Atlantic Ocean. The Second Peoples, the Europeans, were on the move, "discovering" First Nations as they went. This business of being discovered by Europeans would become an occupational hazard for First Peoples everywhere. It may never have dawned on the European boat people that they were being discovered too.

Many days' canoeing from the acre towards the ocean, going east along the salty river filled with *adhothuys* — the small, white beluga whales that could be caught and eaten — at the edge of the woodlanders' world, the coastal natives were the first to begin dealing with the Second Peoples. These curious, overdressed, pale strangers appeared to have come from a land two full moons away, in huge, ugly cargo canoes that certainly looked up to the trip. They industriously loaded enormous feasts of fish into the big canoes, and sailed back with them to a territory called France.

These strange fishermen had many bad points — they stank for a start — and one good point: they understood trade. Even better, they made ridiculous bargains. Give them furs, used ones, already sleek and oiled from wear, and back came blades that didn't dull as quickly as bone or flint, cooking pots that would glow red in the fire but not break, and a new line of fashion accessories.

For a while this market remained a coastal enterprise, but then one spring (it was 1534) a man called Jacques Cartier came along. He was a different kettle of fish altogether, in fact not a fisherman at all; he seemed to be a full-time trader, eager to give and accept gifts, and even more eager to travel towards the sunset, to a great northern sea, and on to somewhere called China. Cartier was also on a mining expedition, sent by his king, François, to stake a gold claim, on the strength of glittering rumours brought back with the cod by French fishermen.

Cartier came three times from France to the woodlands, pushing his ships further west each time. On the first trip, the woodlanders whose territory he was invading watched him stop on a headland above a bay and plant a large, branchless tree with a crosspiece, as tall as five men. Then he knelt by it and intoned words that sounded like some sort of territorial claim. Cartier's antics were carefully observed by the tribal sagamore

Donnacona, his rank as senior elder denoted by his rich bearskin. Donnacona conferred with three of his sons and his brother; they all set after Cartier's ship, caught up with it, and went on board to explain that the territory was already spoken for. Cartier replied, inhospitably, by preventing them from leaving. There was a discussion, which led to an argument, which led to a truce, and a reluctant agreement that two of Donnacona's sons, Taignoaguy and Domagaya, would go back to France with Cartier when he left a few days later.

The next fall Cartier returned (with the two sons, who had picked up French, which made the defusing of arguments much easier). He weighed anchor at the mouth of the St. Charles River, in view of Donnacona's village, Stadacona. Here the two Stadaconan brothers on board ship, perhaps as a practical joke on the tribe, got Cartier to fire one of his cannons; the explosion was an unwitting starting pistol for a race down a fraught future the First Nations could not have predicted.

The Stadaconans were anxious to corner this new market that had sailed into their lap, and to prevent other tribes downriver from diluting their advantage. They shared pipes with Cartier, filled with the best southern tobacco, as a sign of their willingness to become trading partners. The Stadaconans tried the last-minute tactic of bad-mouthing the competitors downriver, but Cartier was restless, a front man with backers in France to pacify. He sailed west again, further upriver, taking his interpreters with him. Along the way the sons heard him refer to the river as the St. Lawrence, which seemed superfluous, since the river already had a name: Hochelaga.

Cartier reached an impasse at two sets of rapids that ran on either side of a large island in the river. On the island was a settlement, also called Hochelaga, on the present site of Montreal, walled with stakes, with a thousand people, members of the Iroquois nation, inside. Their day was enlivened when one of the foreign canoes they had heard about docked in the island harbour. They crowded round, passed comment on the outré appearance of the aliens, and escorted twenty-six of the French sailors inside the walls. Cartier gave the Iroquois sagamore two axes that were much harder than anything the Iroquois had, and a small, jewelled cross that Cartier apparently wanted the sagamore to kiss. This was a curious request but, lest Iroquois hospitality get a bad reputation, the sagamore graciously puckered up and did as asked.

Before letting Cartier return to his ship, the Iroquois walked him to the top of the mountain behind their village, an extinct volcano. He seemed impressed, took in the view, and pointed at the ground, saying, "Mont Royal," confirming for the Iroquois this odd French habit of renaming the already named. To the northwest of this marvellous lookout point Cartier saw a gold-coloured river (the Ottawa River appears yellow compared with the silvery St. Lawrence, which it meets at Montreal). This formidable waterway, he was informed, was controlled by the Iroquois' trading rivals. Along his line of sight, as he stared up this golden waterway, lay the acre. Cartier watched as the Iroquois did their best to sign some other information; whether he got his signs crossed or not is unknown, but Cartier decided that silver and lead lay ahead, and a tribe that walked on one leg.

Then, seemingly blocked by turbulent water from advancing into acre country, he headed back to Stadacona. The Iroquois never saw him again. The Stadaconans did. They took him and his men into the village for the winter, during which there was an outbreak of scurvy; the French needed fruit to get their vitamin C, which the natives got in other ways. In what may well have been the first act of medicine without frontiers, the bilingual Domagaya brewed up an elixir of evergreen needles and bark that arrested the death toll, after a quarter of the duplicitous Frenchmen had succumbed. Cartier repaid this life-saving act by kidnapping Donnacona, his two French-speaking sons, and seven others, taking them to France to use as human bargaining chips in his bid to get exclusive trading rights in "Nouvelle France." When he eventually returned five years later, on what was to be his final visit, these displaced natives didn't return with him. Cartier lied and said they had all become princes, and were rolling in wealth and acceptance. They had in fact all died but one, and were buried in Paris, their spirits forced to trek back across the ocean to rejoin their kin.

Cartier passed another lousy winter, losing more men to scurvy, and then departed for the last time to France, taking with him some mica chips that he thought were diamonds. The French had become seriously disenchanted with Canada and had also got embroiled in internal religious affairs. They didn't come sniffing after an inland trade route through Canada for sixty years. Meanwhile, the Iroquois at Hochelaga were driven south by the family of tribes, the Algonquins, who trapped and traded along the banks of the golden river, the Kichesippirini and the Weskarini. As controllers of the river, these tribes set up a toll booth opposite the abandoned Hochelaga stockade, the twin of the one on the island of the Kichesippirini several hundred miles upstream, past the acre at the gateway to Huron and Nipissing country. It seems likely that the Kichesippirini had jurisdiction over the main river, the Ottawa, and that other allied bands looked after the tributaries. In exchange for an untroubled right of passage into the main river trading system, the Kichesippirini took a percentage of the vegetable and mineral traffic with one hand, holding off the chafing Iroquois with the other. Canoes piled high with nourishment and raw materials wefted back and forth past the acre, on the busy loom of the golden river.

Then, when the demand for second-hand fur went way up, the French came again. This time they set up a trading post at Tadoussac, at the mouth of the Saguenay. The timing of their return was useful. The Kichesippirini and their allies, led by a one-eyed sagamore called Tessouat, were keen to enlist extra muscle in their ongoing scuffle with the Iroquois, especially since the muscle came armed with guns and cannons. Each spring they made a point of visiting, in their hundreds, the handful of French traders at the Tadoussac trading post, getting reacquainted, sowing sedition against the Iroquois, keeping the French in furs (which the French were apparently turning into hats), and conferring with their eastern allies, the Etchemin and the Montagnais.

As part of a general policy of harassing the Iroquois, the Kichesippirini were partial to guerrilla raids, like the one they mounted the year the

French returned. The raid went well, and Tessouat and the others went to Tadoussac to celebrate. It was a major party; these annual gatherings could attract a thousand people and more. While Tessouat sat in front of two poles, a row of scalps clotheslined between them, the Kichesippirini females stripped, sang and danced on the spot, shouted "Ho!" three times, rested, and did it again. The crowd gave them beads, hatchets, and moose-meat, and then the tribes held races, with prizes for the winners.

There was a particularly curious trader among the regular French at Tadoussac that year. His name was Samuel de Champlain. He was clearly an authority with the French, a robust, spiritual man given to gathering information about this wild land he found himself in. Intrigued by the uncatholic ritual and the al fresco nudity at the raiding party celebrations, Champlain eavesdropped on several Etchemin, who were gossiping beside him. He heard the word *algonquin* several times, and later recorded it in his journals as the name of the natives who had done the victory dance. *Allegon-kin* is actually an Etchemin word meaning dancer. And so the stewards of the acre were fixed with a name derived from an overheard misinterpretation: Algonquin.

A few days later, drawn as all French explorers were by the magnetic attraction of a trade route west to China, Champlain travelled upriver, retracing Cartier's keelprint. Since Champlain was headed in the direction of their toll booth, and as part of general operating procedure when dealing with the French, the Algonquins went with him, to keep an eye on things. Towards the end of the day the travelling party reached the same rapids that had stalled Cartier sixty years earlier. The men went ashore and Champlain continued his fact-finding. In the course of his questioning, mention was made of a golden river that ran to the west, and Champlain, an experienced cartographer, asked for a map. On a flattened piece of birch bark, using five lines to suggest a major river and its family of tributaries, the Algonquins sketched out their territory for him. The acre sat roughly in the middle of their sketch.

Change of Scene

Champlain, according to his Christian calendar, would describe the day he sees the map containing the acre as July 9, 1,603 years after the birth of Christ. While the Kichesippirini are making the acquaintance of the French cartographer, a new European century has opened its eyes. The telescope is three years old. The world has been round for only eighty years, and for another eight years the sun will continue to move around the earth. Queen Elizabeth I of England has been dead for two months, and Shakespeare has just finished *All's Well That Ends Well*. Work has started on the façade of St. Peter's in Rome.

Champlain's France is a powerful country. Paris is the largest European capital, lodging three hundred thousand people behind stone walls as tall as trees. Twenty million people call themselves French, making their country Europe's most populated. Seventeen million of them are farmers. The majority are comfortable with a Roman Catholic god, but the Protestants, the followers of Calvin, are making inroads. There have been religious massacres. The rivers of France, thirty thousand of them, are its highways (although France also has the most roadway in Europe). The boat is the engine of commerce. For almost one hundred years now, French fishermen have profited by crossing the ocean to the fish-thick waters off the shores of the new westlands. Two months' travel to get to work, two months' back.

The monarchs of Europe have begun to push their fingers deeper into what they hope is the plump belly of America. Champlain is thirty-six

41

years old in 1603. This is his second trip to the new lands — he has already walked the streets of Havana, gaped at Mexico City, and predicted the Panama Canal — but it is his first to what he calls Nouvelle France.

Who is this Frenchman, who will bring Europe and its values to the acre? He is a professional colonizer, an enthusiastic seeker and founder of settlements, an uneasy agent of big business, a spiritual man who hunts land for both his god and his country. Between 1599 and 1633 Champlain will cross the Atlantic twenty-nine times, averaging just over two months per crossing — five years of his life spent commuting. The number of crossings is uneven because he will die not on French soil but in Quebec, on Christmas Day, 1637, in a small settlement of two hundred souls on the cliffs above the St. Lawrence River.

If professions have lineages, Champlain's leads down four hundred years to the astronauts in the Apollo moon missions. On behalf of an imperial power, as part of a program of exploration with both political and financial agendas, he went to the edge of a frontier and extended it. He was a man of many skills, with a curriculum vitae ideally suited to the task. He was an expert seaman, a journalist, an illustrator, an urban planner, a diplomat, an administrator, and a brilliant, imaginative cartographer. In the course of his fifteen missions he tried many bold experiments, including making Canada into a French colony and its natives into Catholics. Champlain was a "terranaut," an ancestor of the shuttle pilots. But there was a vital difference between his job description and that of the modern astronauts. The frontier Champlain was contracted to explore was already inhabited.

China This Way

After the Kichesippirini have roughed out their map for him on birch bark, Champlain and his party, thwarted by the rapids, turn around and retrace their path to Tadoussac. Six weeks later they return to France. The map crosses the Atlantic with him. The accurate fixing of the acre on a

European map is a landmark. In Champlain's mind the acre is now part of his quarry, a place he will struggle to get to and ensnare for his king. If, through him, France captures the western passageway to the rich Eastern spice market, the golden fleece of the seventeenth century, his job will be secure; perhaps even a governorship is in the offing. In its turn, the acre, when the birchbark abstract is handed to Champlain, emigrates from one philosophy to another. The acre has begun to mutate from territory, part of a range of tribal movement, into property, a chip off a huge block. The word *territory* comes from *terra* — the earth. *Property* comes from *proprius*, meaning one's own. Look at it another way: if the Canadian wilderness is a body of land, and the acre a cell, the cell is about to meet a new virus.

In the forests of Canada, Champlain found his vocation, and he pursued it with enthusiasm. In ten years he criss-crossed the Atlantic three times, and in the spring of 1613 the rough huts of Tadoussac, his Canadian base camp, came again into view. Champlain was a veteran now, a known commodity in the colonizing business. In the decade since he first saw the naked dance of the Kichesippirini, he had charted a good deal of what would later become, ironically, the New England coast. Like Cartier, he had seen a Canadian winter kill half the men in a novice settlement, quartered on an island with insufficient vitamin C. He had become independently wealthy through an inheritance, and wedded a twelve-year-old French noblewoman, waiting two years to consummate the union, his energy flowing elsewhere. At a showcase skirmish with the Iroquois, designed, with the minimum of fuss, to fulfil his promise to back the Algonquins, he had killed two chiefs with one musket shot. The Iroquois had known a bad thing when they saw it, and retreated; in the next round, they had partial revenge when they almost killed Champlain — he collected an arrow's scar in the neck and ear.

Champlain had also founded Quebec City, on the site of Stadacona, planting Canada's first imported rosebushes there. Wearing his naturalist's hat, he had reported back to France the ugly wonder of the garfish, an eight-foot member of the pike family with an oboe for a nose. Feeding the French curiosity for all things agricultural, he had broadcast the native practice of burning off their corn fields, and using horseshoe crab shells as hand-ploughs. All the while he had not forgotten his regal commission — to develop the fur trade, to divine metal ore deposits worthy "to be digged and drawn from the earth," and, number one on his list, to discover the river route to the great northern sea that led to China. China was one of the major suppliers of pepper, used to preserve meat; open a westward passage to China, and you controlled the flow of pepper.

Throughout 1612, which Champlain had spent in France, he had been pumping out maps of Canada. They were not the dry sheets of topography that fill a modern atlas. They were much more like tourist guides, or chamber of commerce maps — stylized, loose in attention to scale, riddled with guesswork, and dotted with little cartoons of the fish and local inhabitants. They were also advertisements for French foreign achievement in general, and for Champlain's achievements in particular. They were visual aids in a sales pitch to attract investment.

Like maps of Eastern Europe at the end of the 1980s, Champlain's maps were rarely still. Late in 1612 he halted the printing of one map to include the "Grande Rivière des Algoumequins" — the Grand River of the Algonquins. That map was itself a revision of an earlier version, one that had deliberately not included the breakthrough into the great northern sea by the Englishman Henry Hudson. Hudson's getting there first had dismayed Champlain; he was like an athlete learning, after years of training for it, that the four-minute-mile barrier had just been broken by someone else. Hudson's sailing into the bay that now wears his name had consequences for the acre. It got Champlain revved up to see if the river the Kichesippirini had outlined for him reached all the way to the bay. If it did, England might control Hudson Bay, but France would control the easiest route to it.

The Kichesippirini, meanwhile, were ahead of Champlain on both counts. They knew the river didn't reach the bay; and they already had control of trade along the river. And so, on May 29, 1613, two canoes laden with five Frenchmen and an Algonquin guide, their guns (arquebuses; Champlain had three with him), camping gear, and plenty of spare paddles faced the swirling current at the mouth of the Grand River. Champlain was looking up a twisting valley that he hoped would lead to Hudson Bay: a horizontal mountaineer in search of a summit. The paddles were raised, like the legs of an insect, and the explorers pushed against the water. The water pushed back. There was white water at several stages on the journey. The canoes pinballed against the rocks, Champlain almost having a hand torn off by a rope twisted around it as he was rag-dolled between the outcrops. They made it through to calm water, and there met a trading canoe of Algonquins heading in the opposite direction; the canoeists all went ashore to talk over their separate agendas. The discussion ended with one of the Frenchmen getting into the Algonquin canoe, and an Algonquin taking his seat among the French. Champlain may have wanted one expert canoeist, with knowledge of the territory, per canoe. The transposed Frenchman was instructed to return, a human passenger pigeon, to Champlain's Quebec base, and report on how far they had got. Champlain, a non-swimmer, was perhaps fearful that this churning river was going to marinate him; he wanted posterity to know the extent of his forward progress.

The Algonquins, for their part, may well have been planting a spy. They knew that this Frenchman was keen to learn as much as he could about their trade routes. They wanted a pair of eyes close on Champlain, like an owl waiting for the mouse to move and betray itself; they agreed to his request for a guide. Champlain was now no more than a couple of days' paddling from the acre. But he probably would not be the first European to lay eyes on it. Two other Frenchmen had almost certainly already done so. Their names were Nicolas de Vignau and Étienne Brûlé.

Both Brûlé and de Vignau were, by the time Champlain made his move up the golden river, graduates of an exchange program between the French and native Canadians. By 1613, several young Frenchmen like Brûlé and de Vignau had lived the life of the woodland tribes for a year or more; they were willing clay, curious, and mindful of the fact that knowledge is power. Champlain, as chief negotiator for French business interests in Nouvelle France, had urgent need of people like Brûlé and de Vignau who had been over the mental topography of the tribes. Sixteenth- and seventeenth-century French high society had been equally titillated by the Canadian woodlanders who had crossed the Atlantic as exotic cargo. Cartier had kidnapped his exhibits, of course, but thereafter touring natives usually stayed for a year and then returned. Once in Paris the woodlanders were, in effect, put into a crash-course French immersion program, aimed at turning them into interpreters, able to explain the wealth and geography of their homelands. For their part, what must the woodlanders have made of the new world of Parisians? The overclothed women, the houses thicker than trees, the weird music, the horses, the competing smells, the claus- trophobia of the towns, and the formidable agriculture of the country.

The title for first European past the acre most likely sits on the intriguing head of Brûlé. Born of farmers just south of Paris, he was still a teenager when he put France behind him. When his turn came to live among the woodlanders, he revelled in the role of exotic outsider. He had the energy, the enthusiasm for the strange, of a punk musician, coupled with a gift for languages. He was allergic to fences, physical and mental. Moral codes made him yawn. After some arm-twisting by Champlain of his reluctant sponsors, Brûlé lived for a year with the Huron. He joined them in the summer of 1610, and they delivered him back to Champlain in June of the following year. The Huron knew themselves as the Ouendats, the "people in the islands" — the islands that cottaging Torontonians now sail around in Georgian Bay. *Huron* is a fourteenth-century French word that translates as something like "unkempt low-life." The contrast in hairstyles was one of many culture shocks between Europeans and the woodland tribes; the Ouendat clans were as adventurous in their coiffure and tattoos as shopping mall teens. On first sight, the description *huron* had sprung to the French mind.

The Ouendats were villagers, less nomadic than the Algonquins.

They lived on fertile soil by fecund water, but game was scarce. Brûlé ate well that first fall he lived with them: corn, squash, plums, raspberries, walnuts, strawberries, cherries, trout the size of muskets, sturgeon the size of cannon. In the winter, leaving the thirty-foot timber walls of the compound, he played a stick and ball game on ice; in the spring, lacrosse. He had no need to sleep alone. He shed his Frenchness as a water snake sloughs its skin and became a lapsed European, a consultant who traded on his native information, even as the natives used him as a guarantee against the fickleness of French support.

Brûlé was, then, at good odds, the first European I would have seen canoeing upriver past the acre, nearly four hundred years ago, on his way to the communal longhouses of the Ouendats. He was an intriguing anti-baptist for the more self-disciplined Champlain, whom we left in 1613 making the same journey Brûlé had made three years earlier. Brûlé's life stayed vigorously interesting until its end. He was the first European whose gaze fell on a panoply of Canadian lakes and rivers, including the greatest lake of all, Superior. He lost his fingernails in a mercenary excursion against the Iroquois.

In mid-career, he betrayed Champlain to the British in 1629, piloting the three Kirke brothers, colony speculators working for the English Merchant Adventurers, to a starving Fort Quebec. It was a Monopoly move; the Kirkes landed on Quebec and took it. Three years later King Charles I of England, running a little low in the royal coffers, sold the entire colony back to the French. After that escapade, Brûlé returned to the Ouendats until June 1633, when, for any one of several reasons, he was executed by them. He had betrayed his own people and, a moody drunk, abused the tribe he had adopted. They cannibalized him, as they sometimes did with band members who had changed sides in battle. Brûlé's errant spirit thus stayed within the Ouendats, his flesh reconstituted into theirs.

Brûlé was still ensconced with the Ouendats when Champlain set out in that summer of 1613 to ascend the river of the Algonquins to Hudson Bay, so Champlain employed Brûlé's stand-in, de Vignau. Though he was class of 1611, the year after Brûlé, de Vignau too had gone upriver, past the acre, for immersion with the Kichesippirini. When his year was up, in the fall of 1612, he had returned to France, reporting directly to Champlain, who, as mentioned, had skipped going to Canada that year. De Vignau got Champlain's attention with the news that he had personally seen an English ship, wrecked on the shore of Hudson Bay, and the eighty scalps of its crew. He had gone, so he said, the length of the Grand River, in the company of the various bands along the way, in a mere seventeen days. De Vignau's report fired up Champlain's urge up to get back to Canada *tout de suite*, and there chart the watery path that would take him past mountains full of copper, to the stolen bay, and on at last to China.

Close, But No Tobacco

Champlain's daily journal reveals that the day he came closest to the acre, and actually looked upon it, was June 13, a week before the solstice. He describes the territory in front of the acre. "Here are many small islands which are nothing more than rough, steep rocks, covered with poor, scrubby wood." Then he turns his attention to the falls, "that the savages call Asticou," which translates as kettle in English, *chaudière* in French. He mentions that "this waterfall makes such a noise in this basin that it can be heard for more than two leagues away." (The later claim for Niagara Falls was seven.) The guide with them also seems to have explained in detail the ceremony the Kichesippirini performed at waterfalls, which involved throwing tobacco into the churning water. A gift of tobacco was known to calm angered woodlanders, so it was logical to assume it likewise calmed an angry water spirit that had no doubt claimed lives.

Before he reached the falls, which only a salmon could have vaulted, Champlain put to shore on the bank opposite the acre, the side the Algonquins used, where the ground was firm and level and the portage back to canoe-able water shortest. There "the savages took up the canoes, and our Frenchmen and myself our arms, provisions, and other articles, to carry them over the rough rocks for about a quarter of a league [a mile] which is the length of the fall. Then we had to get into our canoes and then land again to walk for about three hundred yards through some underbrush."

Across the river, from my perch in the pine tree, I see four Frenchmen and two Algonquins set ashore, put their canoes over their heads, and centipede along the riverbank, following a trail already etched by the footsteps of centuries of previous portagers. They pass through the spray of the Asticou Falls and almost out of sight. Back in his canoe, with the acre over his left shoulder, Champlain raises his paddle and prepares to baptize it again in the river water.

This Land Is My Land

The acre now lies behind Champlain, in the wake of his progress towards China. According to European exploring tradition, that gives the country he serves claim to it. When Champlain resumes his paddle stroke, the acre will, to his way of thinking, have been grafted onto the territory of France, a country sixty days away.

On this June morning in 1613, Champlain is one of a hundred or so Frenchmen on the move in Canada. None of the hundred was born here. These trespassers are vastly outnumbered by the hundreds of thousands of people who were born — and reborn — on land fertilized by the flesh and bone of their ancestors. Yet Champlain's head is suffused with a sense of discovery and annexation. Into the muscle of this new-found land he wishes to inject a Christian Frenchness. Viewed down the telescope of history, that is a monumental conceit. But in his own mind, the part devoted to notions of God, country, and commerce, it is a simple tenet of belief. How did that belief get there? What is it founded on?

Equally important, what is in the mind of the man sitting in the canoe with Champlain, an unknown member of the Kichesippirini tribe? These two men are passing through the same immensity of trees and hills, their heads are less than a paddle length apart, yet the Algonquin and the Frenchman are oases of separate histories and beliefs. They are worlds apart. Each man has a word for land in his vocabulary — the French *terre*, the Algonquin *ndakim* — but these words do not trigger the same response at all.

Unfinished Business

To understand Champlain's response to the word, we need to take a core sample of his historical foundation, to drill down through the strata of his attitude. By performing this philosophical archaeology, perhaps we can make sense of his penchant for annexing acres on behalf of distant kings.

Champlain's vein of thought goes down through the Bible to the bedrock of the Greek philosophers. About two thousand years before Champlain's birth, men such as Xenophon, Aristotle, and Cicero began to ponder the relative position of humans and the rest of nature. Not surprisingly, the view they arrived at put them at the top. Humans, they decided, possess a "common sense," a sense over and above the other five that mere animals have. Humans, in other words, have soul, and to the Greeks having soul implied having been outfitted for a special purpose. Nature, they decided, is a machine, a thing of interlocking purposes and motives, set in motion by a godly committee of designers. Humans in general, and Greeks in particular, were the machine's mechanics.

To support these views, the Greeks had the evidence of their own achievements. Raw rock had been arranged into temples of mathematical perfection, chaotic wilderness subverted into cities glorious enough to be called states. Thought itself, hitherto a wild thing, had been tidied up into a neat philosophy of debate. This superiority complex, put into action, led directly to Alexander the Great, who had been taught by Aristotle and became one of history's most successful land-grabbers. Alexander was even able to rewire himself in such a way as to become certain of his own divinity.

The Romans, a pragmatic people willing to forgo developing a philosophy when there was one to hand, agreed with the Greeks. Whereas Alexander had been all forward motion, burnt out by the time he was thirty, the Romans gave the business of empiring a solid, enduring structure. They took the Greek fascination with the straight line and invented the geometry of colonization — roads built for speed that overruled topography; townships laid out in neat bundles of square lots; lines of power running back to Rome. The Romans seemed to be working to an ordained blueprint, backed by godly planning permission.

Eight hundred years after Alexander had set the standard for world domination, Christianity became the official religion of the Roman empire, and the sedimentary layer of Judeo-Christian attitudes to land began to deposit itself on the Greco-Roman bedrock. In the Psalms, Christians are informed, "The Heavens are the Lord's heavens, but the earth he has given to the sons of men." The Christians were the shop stewards of life on earth, in other words, subject to only one spiritual employer. All God's acres, including the one at hand, were unfinished, in need of the Christian touch to make them complete.

By the sixth century, the Christian thinkers were underlining the unique destiny of Christians. A man with the marvellous name of Cosmas Indicopleustas, in an essay with the apt title "Christian Topography," reassured every man of God that he was "the king of all things on earth." But certain people were more kingly than others. One person in particular, the Pope, was the king of all souls. Surrounding him, one step down, were the European kings of countries. Both forms of kingdom were rarely stable, and souls and nations were frequently devastated by the true pox of history — the family feud. The extended family of European monarchs has an amazingly dysfunctional history; they went at it hammer and tongs right up until the First World War. These feuds, given edifying titles such as the Hundred Years War and the Wars of the Roses, were not unlike full-contact Hollywood movies: they required huge budgets, tricky financing, deadly stunts, and state-of-the-art technology.

The continual search for the financing of the great European feuds eventually launched an era of oceanic exploration; the kings started looking for offshore assets, in the same way that corporate nations now look for oil. Often with the tacit backing of the Pope, which gave their missions a divine sanction, freelance sea captains began roving the oceans hoping to net fresh sources of wealth, and eventually they sailed towards the acre. The Vikings got within two thousand miles of it in the year 1000, but the era that would have a direct effect on the acre began after 1400. It was the era when the native respect for land had to give way to the Christian, European respect for business.

First away from the European marina were the Portuguese, hop-scotching down the coast of Africa. In 1483 they made a tactical error when they turned down a request for funding from Christopher Columbus. Columbus went next door to the Spanish who, by default, gained exclusive rights to the lucrative South American concession that he opened up. The Portuguese tried to make up for lost ground by lobbying the Pope, a Borgia called Alexander VI. Using a page from Solomon's book, Alexander VI drew an imaginary line down a map of the known and the unknown worlds, assigning the left half to Spain, the right to Portugal. Technically, the acre was in the Portuguese half.

The Pope's new world order lasted as long as it took the rest of Europe to ignore it, and the freelance captains began pouring out of seaports and crossing the oceans; men like Bartholomeu Dias and Vasco da Gama. In 1496, King Henry VII of England gave John Cabot, an Italian colony-hunter, a note saying he could take possession of any countries he happened on that were "then unknown to all Christian people." What Henry really meant was that Cabot should take possession of any countries that were then known to unchristian people, in this case Canadian woodlanders. A year later Cabot did just that when, on his way to Asia, he bumped into Newfoundland, in the middle of the ocean. Cabot promptly labelled as English every non-Christian acre to which it may have been attached.

The French, as we have seen, were not far behind; in 1535 Jacques Cartier made a boast similar to Cabot's, planting a cross and claiming with impunity a vastness it would take other men almost five hundred years to chart. It was Champlain, armed with quill and crucifix, who turned Cartier's rhetoric into reality.

Time Out of Mind

One can trace Champlain's attitude to territory through the centuries, in the same way that the stratigrapher William Smith traced out his geological strata. The attitude of his fellow canoeist, however, is more of a mystery. Canadian anthropologists didn't start asking questions about how the woodlanders related to their territories until almost three centuries after Champlain had overruled them. What the anthropologists did learn was got mostly from talking to old men, and from researching the journals of early explorers and missionaries, looking for observations made in passing. For instance, a man called Chadwallader Colden, in 1764, noted that the Algonquin families had "parcels of land" which they had had since "time out of mind." The anthropologists bundled these snippets of information together, added in what the modern woodlanders had told them, and came up with a basketful of theories.

The most elegant of the theories on hunting territories starts at the hunting end of things and works forward to the territory end. Basically, form followed content, the content in this case being food. In the woods, the Algonquin diet was dominated by smaller mammals: the beaver, the otter, and the hare. The beaver, *amik*, was the easiest to trap. Beaver lodges were all too obvious, beaver lived in families, and a lot of the time they were home. Furthermore, they advertised where they were by chewing down trees.

In hunting the beaver, the Algonquins effectively mimicked them. The Algonquin family, which might be a few or many, and hold within it brothers, widows, children of former husbands, and aunts, was the centre of allegiance. The Algonquins were not gregarious, except in the spring, when they would gather and enjoy the benefits of a wider community — gossip, games, seeing who had survived the winter, looking for a mate. In winter they would set up permanent lodges, and use those as the hub of their traplines. In summer they moved around their territories, returning year after year to the same riverside campsites.

Unlike the Plains tribes, who had to become herds themselves to tackle the vast herds of buffalo, and go where the buffalo went, the Algonquin families had no need to pack up their belongings to hunt. Their hunting territories, compared with a modern suburban lot, were not subject to much in the way of regulations. (The area just west of the acre Champlain paddled past in 1613 is now a suburb called Kanata. Among the municipal regulations in force in Kanata are: no washing to be hung outside, cats must be on leashes, and only certain colours of front door are permitted.) The acre was part of one family's territory, operating under unwritten guidelines. The guidelines were tools, whittled from experience, designed to ensure long-term survival.

To show how these guidelines worked, let's reverse the flow of history. Imagine that Champlain is not here to impose Frenchness. Instead, he is here as a guest, in another's home. Anxious not to offend, and looking to settle in the area, he wants to learn the ropes as quickly as possible. What, he asks his companion in the canoe, do I need to know to make a go of it? In his journal that night, Champlain writes down what he can remember.

• The border of a family's territory, *nokiwaki*, isn't marked out with fences or stone walls; it is understood. A river, a ridge, a lakeshore, a swamp, a clump of cedar or pine may mark the perimeter of understanding. A territory is defined by the ability to sustain the family, its yield, not by its acreage. If disease, fire, or natural cycle reduces the yield, the understanding will grow accordingly.

• The seasons have shown that, on average, one hunter can provide for three non-hunters.

• The family with a large territory stands in no more regard than the family with less. Bigger than, and smaller than, bear no relation to status or wealth.

• One hunter can manage only so much trapline. To extend a trapline beyond what a hunter can harvest makes no sense.

• The islands are common territory. Hunting on islands is a

communal affair, done by driving the animals from the centre to the edges, where hunters wait in canoes.

- The territory around the summer camp is reserved for older hunters, whose horizons are closer than those of younger men.

- There are times of abundance and times of scarcity, and no one escapes them. A family experiencing scarcity turns to a family in abundance and asks for territory to be shared.

- Someone from another territory, passing through, may be hungry and make a kill. So be it. The resulting pelt is given or delivered to the host family. The open invitation by the visiting hunter to make a reciprocal kill on his territory is understood.

- On a good day, a moose or caribou will be taken. The antlers are placed on a trimmed tree stump, the skull in the branches of a nearby tree. Forget to do this, or show lack of respect, and the next kill will be harder, or fail. On a very good day, a bear will die. Paint the skull with two stripes at right angles, making four quadrants. Put a dot in each quadrant. Trim the bark from a spruce tree, hoop the trunk with red painted stripes, and tie the skull to the tree. Attach ribbons to the treetop.

- Sometimes hunters kill without respect. To kill a beaver in another family's territory, and then try to keep it secret, is the greatest disrespect. The wronged family will undoubtedly ask the shaman to make the hunter suffer illness.

- Eating a slice of the kill at the moment its spirit leaves, but not before, will ensure further kills.

- The discovery of a new beaver lodge is celebrated by putting a blaze on a nearby tree.

- No more than two-thirds of the adult beaver in a lodge should be taken from one spring to the next.

- The family territory should have a nucleus that is left unhunted, in case of emergency. The remainder should be divided in four, and each quarter hunted in turn.

- There are some gifts of the forest that never know scarcity, such as berries and birch bark. These are for common harvest, by anyone who needs them.
- A white animal coming into the territory is bad luck.

There is, naturally, no way Champlain could abandon centuries of hardened attitude, and see the acre — all the acres — from the other man's point of view, any more than the woodlander can see the river and hills from Champlain's. They cannot change places in the canoe.

Time-Space Discontinuum

The introduction of the Christian god into the woodlands, where he had not been before, caused a seismic shift in attitudes to land. Whereas the Greeks and Romans had positioned their gods no higher than the tops of mountains, the Christians borrowed from the Jews and lifted their god clear into the heavens, there to reside as a sort of absentee but watchful landlord. The creative spirit was transplanted by Christians out of the land and hung in the sky.

The European Christians, with only one life to live before they depart for eternity, think in terms of acreage. God's kingdom, and the kingdom of man, were meant to be as wide as possible. The woodlanders, with many lives to live, think in terms of time: they, after all, will be back to ask the same land to support them again. Examples of each line of thought sit only a few feet apart in a birchbark canoe on this summer's day in 1613, but a deep fault lies between them.

This spiritual separation will echo down the history of the acre for the next three hundred years, and beyond. Indeed, the crisis at Oka in the summer of 1992 resonated with the separation. Oka is a small village in Quebec, in territory once hunted by Algonquins and Mohawks. It is on the present border of a Mohawk reserve. The crisis ignited when the town council wanted to expand the local golf course, a metaphor for controlled acreage if ever there was one, from nine to eighteen holes. The extra nine holes, however, would have overlaid a Mohawk burial ground. At the deepest level, it was a clash not about by-laws and zoning, but about space and time. The echo sent out by the collision of two worlds centuries ago was still reverberating the day I first stepped onto the acre.

Days of Transition
1614–1819

Each life leaves its shadowy remnant
of light on the soft clay
of time, every breath a living
history of the earth
inside
outside our skins

JOHN BARTON
FROM "ACADIA NOTEBOOK"

Getting Closer

The road that today runs along the north end of the acre lies on top of a dyke. The dyke supports four lanes of traffic and obscures any view of the river; nowhere on the acre can you glimpse water. To see the Ottawa River, you have to walk to the dyke and scramble up onto it. From there, you can see the grey-backed river on its way to Montreal. Stand there all day and you won't see a single working boat go by.

All the commercial traffic goes by road now; the canoes, the passenger and cargo boats, and the log rafts of earlier eras have grown wheels and climbed on land. The modern voyageurs, the truckers and the sales reps, travel along the Trans-Canada Highway, a mile or so south of the acre. The Ottawa River, apart from a few ferries and pleasure craft, has lapsed into disuse.

For at least a millennium before Champlain "drove" the three hundred miles from Hochelaga up to Lake Nipissing, the golden river was the highway for the woodlanders, the senior member in a family of trading routes reaching from Lake Huron down to Florida. The beavers on the acre were used to sharing the calm water below the falls with canoes hauling copper, corn, flint, whalebone, obsidian, and tobacco.

After Champlain seconded the acre to Nouvelle France, the river traffic increased and the Grande Rivière des Algoumequins — later the Ottawa — became the major Canadian commercial route, the Trans-Canada of its day. The Kichesippirini at first treated Champlain as an exotic, intrusive purchasing agent from a market called France, a market with a sizeable demand for two lines: furs and souls. For the next 150 years the French soul and fur reps who passed through Algonquin territory sought control of the traffic in these two commodities. The acre, like a hunter in a blind, witnessed the sailing by of most of Nouvelle France's star explorers, missionaries, and mercenaries.

The fur trade came first, souls later. In 1611, when Champlain got as far as the Lachine Rapids (*la Chine* is French for China) at the mouth of the golden river, he met Hurons, on their way to the St. Lawrence, intent on trading with the eastern Algonquins. The Hurons perennially travelled downriver in spring in large convoys, up to sixty transport canoes, swapping excess agricultural produce for beaver pelts from northern Algonquin traplines. They took the furs down to Hochelaga (Montreal) and bartered for beads and cloth for the return journey. Champlain, interrupting this flow, bargained for some of the Hurons' furs, as samples of an item he figured he could move back home.

Hats made from Canadian beaver fur became a fashion rage throughout Europe, similar to rages yet to come for the fedora in the 1940s and the baseball cap in the 1990s. Nurtured in the wet, cold woodlands, beaver made for the best, most expensive hats. The marshy conditions gave the fur a lustre, the severe winters made it thick, and the tree canopy provided the shade that kept it dark. The saying "If you want to get ahead, get a hat" was in full force in the seventeenth century, and the best heads required a full-furred, dark, shiny hat from Nouvelle France. To meet the demand, the woodlanders went into high gear. Then, in the blink of a beaver's eye, the native traffic along the river was infiltrated by freelance French fur traders, who went around the native middlemen and made deals at source, deals of spectacular profitability.

In 1615, two years after Champlain first made his way past the acre, he passed by again, and paddled and portaged all the way to Lake Nipissing. In his wake was Father Joseph Le Caron, a frail but determined agent for Christianity. Le Caron was from the Récollets order, a branch of the Franciscans. The God of Europe was on the move in the woodlands, seeking converts. Le Caron made the journey barefoot, and the long days of paddling almost ruined him. He reported being mightily tested by "pestiferous" mosquitoes; he had wrapped a cloth around his face to thwart them. Blistered and bitten, Le Caron quickly went back down the river, waited eight years, then set out on another tour of duty in 1623.

He was accompanied this time by Father Gabriel Sagard. Sagard kept a log of the journey, which was published in Europe in 1632 and became a bestseller. In it he described the Kichesippirini as the most uncivil "Sauuvages" he had ever met, and the best dressed. The Hurons, he informed his readers, were "shameless belchers."

After Sagard's travel book was published, the Récollets, till then the sole agents of soul in Nouvelle France, realized that the Canadian franchise needed better financing. They called in the Jesuits. In 1626 two Jesuits, Father Jean de Brébeuf and Father Anne de Noue, in their black robes, went upriver. Brébeuf was a big man with sickly lungs and a gift for languages, laterally transferred to Canada from his position as treasurer of the Jesuit College in Rouen. These advance Jesuits infiltrated the Hurons and began the serious usurpation of the Great Spirit. The Jesuit work schedule was interrupted in 1629, when the English Kirke brothers captured Quebec. The fur and soul trade was put on hold until the French got Quebec back, in 1632.

A few years later, the Dutch arrived late and crashed the party. At first they colluded with the Iroquois, but quickly they realized they could deal directly with western native fur suppliers. They cut the Iroquois out as middlemen. Determined to keep themselves in the manner to which they had rapidly become accustomed, the Iroquois were forced to displace their rival middlemen, the Kichesippirini. Iroquois raiding parties went higher and higher into Algonquin territory and began wiping the Algonquins out. Democratic in their raiding, the Six Nations of the Iroquois also attacked the Huron and French commercial canoes.

After 1643, to avoid the Iroquois raiders, the Huron fur convoys began turning left just past the acre and going up the Gatineau River, the river I swim in each day in summer. The Iroquois promptly countered the Huron detour by stationing small but effective patrol bands at the mouths of all rivers flowing into the Grande Rivière des Algoumequins; they succeeded in choking the flow of furs to a trickle.

Eventually, with raids on camps and villages in the woods either side of the river, raids that would have involved crossing the acre, the Iroquois completely shut down the river. In 1652 not one beaver skin went downriver. Checkmate. The banks of the Grande Rivière were, for the first time in a thousand years, devoid of Algonquins, who moved back into the hills and stayed nearer the French trading posts for protection. The riverbanks remained Algonquin-less for decades, and as a consequence the French name for the river lapsed.

With the river cleared of their adversaries, the Iroquois left a skeleton crew along the banks and returned south to cultivate the British. This left a trade vacuum on the river; a tribe called the Ottawa, from well northwest of the acre, near Manitoulin Island, took up the slack and transported furs bartered from Michigan tribes to the French at Quebec. They slipped easily past the understaffed Iroquois river patrols.

Realizing that all this trouble and strife was bad for business on both sides, the Iroquois and the French fashioned a truce. The river got busy again and soon afterwards two woodsmen in their early twenties, Pierre-Esprit Radisson and his brother-in-law, Médard Chouart, Sieur Des Groseilliers, canoed past the acre and into the great lakes to the west. Once there they did some serious fur wholesaling and assembled a canoe convoy loaded with more than 140,000 pounds of beaver pelts, hauled by over a hundred Ottawas. When this convoy, the biggest ever to pass the acre, reached Montreal, it persuaded the traders there, who were about to call it quits, to unpack their sea trunks and stay on. As a side effect, the river got a new alias — the Ottawa. The name was given the seal of posterity when it appeared on maps, and it remains so named to this day, making the Ottawa a river named after a tribe that neither settled nor hunted along it.

Unsettled Waters

The river traffic now gained a steady rhythm. The French put several small supply stations along the way, and business picked up, although the river banks remained uninhabited. The coureurs de bois, who were the French seventeenth-century equivalent of outlaw bikers (with canoes instead of motor bikes and furs substituting for drugs), took over the fast lane. Resisted at first as too wild by the Montreal establishment (who had been there all of sixty years) they were eventually tolerated and given financial support; if you can't beat 'em, back 'em.

In both the fur and soul businesses, no money was changing hands. The coureurs were using beads and bits of glass, cheap tools, and, increasingly, brandy to pay for the beaver pelts. Likewise the pockets of the Jesuits' black robes were filled with Christian paraphernalia, rosaries and crucifixes, and even medals, to entice natives to make the leap after death from earthly haven to celestial heaven.

There was also an invisible exchange taking place between the Europeans and the woodlanders. Diseases were swapped, with the natives getting the worst of the deal. Most likely, the coureurs de bois were the main agents, since they had taken no vows of chastity and frequently found themselves drunk and lonely in the vast forests. Smallpox, influenza, and tuberculosis, collectively known as the white death, joined the bacteria and viruses in the acre's soil and set about clear-cutting the native population.

While the acre stood vacant, with neither pelts nor pagans to offer to the passing trade, a turf war that would last 150 years was developing between the English and the French. The English had Hudson Bay and the French the St. Lawrence; both were looking to extend their territory west. To make sure that the Ottawa River stayed French, a party of a hundred mercenaries, headed by the French warrior Chevalier Pierre de Troyes, went upriver in 1686. Their mission was to destroy the English trading posts up on James Bay and Hudson Bay, which were starting to have an adverse, trickle-down effect on the French monopoly. Among the hundred was the "expansionist" Pierre Le Moyne d'Iberville, later a founder of Louisiana. The mission was successful, and de Troyes's party returned past the acre with thirty thousand furs and thirty English prisoners.

Around 1693, the fragile Iroquois-French truce broke down, and the Iroquois resumed their guerrilla tactics. Some bands, anxious to get in on the action, risked ambush and paddled hard downriver. One such band from the headwaters of the Ottawa River, called the Têtes de Boule (in English, the Round Heads), made it to Montreal, but asked for an armed escort back up the Ottawa. They got past the acre, but were attacked further west and turned back. When word got around that the Iroquois were at it again, the fur trade started to atrophy, and Montreal's reason for being was again threatened.

This time, the French had had enough. A SWAT team went upriver to Huron territory in the summer of 1693. That fall two hundred protected canoes packed with furs made it back to Montreal unharmed. The French built a substantial fort on the future site of Kingston on Lake Ontario, and installed a small patrol fleet. The Iroquois, who had successfully disrupted the dividends of the merchants of Nouvelle France for half a century, decided discretion was the better part of valour; they withdrew to the south.

With the turn of the century, the slow fuse that had been burning between France and England reached the powder. A series of territorial wars in Europe that took up the whole century gave the two rivals, like heavyweight boxers on the comeback trail, the chance to clash again. These clashes were mimicked across the Atlantic in the colonies, New England versus Nouvelle France. The subtext of the colonial battles was control of the fur trade and the constant itch for more territory, which received some serious scratching.

The French began to extend the belly of Nouvelle France out into the great plains to the west. In 1701, the year the slave trade between Africa and America began, Antoine Cadillac set up a fort and trading post at Detroit, the future home of the industry that eventually replaced the canoe and created the car named after him.

The acre witnessed the last French military search-and-destroy mission to go up the Ottawa in 1728. Forty-five soldiers teamed up with a major war party of seven hundred native allies. The objective of this hit squad was the Ourgaimis, who had been disrupting trade around Lake Michigan. Three years later, the greatest French expansionist of them all, Pierre Gaultier de La Vérendrye, passed the acre on his way to, he hoped, the Pacific Ocean. La Vérendrye was a one-man fort industry, setting up a string of them as far west as Lake Winnipeg and poaching trade with the Plains natives from the Hudson's Bay Company. The French seem to have been better at exploring and relating to the natives than the British. It was French explorers who first trespassed on all ten future Canadian provinces, and twenty-three American states, and who provided one-half of the input for a new tribe, the Métis.

Despite all this turmoil, the waters of the Ottawa River were relatively calm in the early decades of the eighteenth century. The Algonquin bands were able, gradually, to return to their hunting territories. Meanwhile, the French took a belated interest in the other possibilities for wealth extraction from the Ottawa River valley. A road commissioner, Jean-Eustache Lanoullier de Boisclerc, spent several months on the river in 1734 and reported some lead deposits, and two German engineers on contract to the French passed by the acre looking for minerals. They found some copper, but there was no time to extract it; the era of French control of the Ottawa River valley was coming to a close.

In 1758, a fleet of 108 British ships, carrying forty thousand men, dropped anchor off Cape Breton Island; they had come to take Nouvelle France. Under General James Wolfe, they went ashore on June 8, and, after a brutal siege, the fortress at Louisbourg gave in. It was the beginning of the end for the French. A year later Quebec fell, after Wolfe and his French counterpart Louis-Joseph de Montcalm fought to their deaths on the Plains of Abraham — named not after the Hebrew prophet but after the farmer on whose land the battle was waged. Montreal fell a year later. That put the British in charge of either end of the Ottawa River and, by proxy, of the acre. They, not the French, would be the ones to turn its trees into homes. Ironically, most of the inhabitants of those homes would turn out to be French Canadians.

So it is in 1760. In the New England colonies, Benjamin Franklin has perfected the harmonica. In London, they have begun the practice of giving the houses street numbers. The acre is still trees, still part of Algonquin hunting territory, but that won't last; it's now under new management.

Naming Names

On February 10, 1763, the victorious British and the defeated French signed a treaty in Paris. Great Britain now considered itself greater by millions of acres, and Nouvelle France would never grow old. As the last signature dried on the parchment, the acre formally became subject to the British way of land. Three and a half thousand miles from Paris, deep under a monochrome quilt of snow, the worms in the acre did not turn. For the acre, it was merely an unwitting change of address.

No piece of land knows which flag it is flying, or the nation that flag represents. Putting name tags on soil is a matter of convenience, so we can find one another, and state where we are from. Place names, sprayed on maps, street corners, and garden gates like graffiti, let history know who has passed this way, but they are not etched in stone. Landlords, as they arrive, mark their territory not by leaving scent on a tree, but by changing the title of the ground the tree stands on.

If you assemble a chronological series of maps of a region, and lay them one on top of another, like layers of paint on an old piece of furniture, you can track the changes of address. Today, it is possible to pinpoint any home in four short lines; a number on a road, a town, a province, a country; that's all it takes. Beneath that bland formula, scribbled on an envelope, is the history of that plot of land.

The acre's first address, the first time it would have been referred to as part of a specific region, might have been a Kichesippirini word; they passed close by as they portaged past the falls. It seems likely, because they gave Champlain a map when he asked them, that the Algonquin peoples knew how to draw scaled-down pictures of their territory. Unfortunately, no Kichesippirini map has survived, and they didn't have a written language. The only guide we have to the way they referred to their own territory lies in the modern Algonkin language.

The Algonkin word *waka* means the area nearby, the land surrounding. The word for waterfall is *asticou*. Put those together, like one of those compound Welsh place names that accumulate to a descriptive paragraph, and you get *asticouwaka*, the land near the waterfall. It may have been something quite different, but one of the modern Algonquin reserves, Maniwaki (Mary's land), uses that sort of approach.

The first boat people to reach the continent from the east, taking Newfoundland to be part of the continent, were Norse. Extending their explorations from Greenland, the Vikings beached their longboats here around 1000 A.D. A settlement has been uncovered to prove it, at L'Anse-aux-Meadows, on the tip of Newfoundland's finger of land that points back towards Europe. That was as far as they got. The Vikings hung around long enough to have children, and to name the territory Markland, but the native Beothuks didn't appreciate the company; the Vikings cut their losses about five hundred years before the French came jigging for cod. The Viking name for North America didn't survive. If it had, 350 million people might now be called Markers.

When they arrived, the French brought with them an advanced system of cartography, with enduring paper, pen, and ink we can still look at. The business of cartography and the dispersal of names went hand in hand. In fact, the Europeans' maps were a reflection of their increasing opinion of themselves. In a couple of centuries their maps, which once put Jerusalem at the centre, like a bull's-eye, began putting Europe at the earth's heart. The first world map, drawn in 1500 by Juan de la Cosa, a shipmate of Columbus, put Europe smack in the middle, like a Hollywood kiss on a movie screen. The acre was included in the vague mass off to the left, in the less important west wing.

The Europeans, with their geographical ego, were quite happy to slap a new name over an old one. In 1507, fifteen years after Columbus bumped into the continent, the German cartographer Martin Waldsee-muller suggested calling the western discoveries America, after the Italian explorer Amerigo Vespucci. Vespucci had by then made a couple of trips here, and concluded he was dealing with a continent separate from India. Despite Vespucci's correct hunch, the Europeans continued to call the natives Indians. Until recently the natives went along with the misnomer, presumably grateful that Columbus hadn't been aiming for Turkey. North America started appearing on maps around 1538, but by then the French had got a toehold in the St. Lawrence valley and were using appellations of their own.

The French expeditions across the Atlantic in search of territory rather than fish had started after François I had had a delayed fit over the Pope's division of America between Portugal and Spain. "I would like to see the clause in Father Adam's will bequeathing that vast inheritance to them," François said, and dispatched Giovanni da Verrazano to the coast of America and staked a claim of his own. Father Adam hadn't sanctioned that manoeuvre either, but royalty are not known for acknowledging their contradictions.

Canada was a name the French sailors picked up from people who lived there. There was a river valley off the one Cartier had renamed the St. Lawrence. Pointing up the tributary, someone no doubt asked the standard question — What do you call this? — and was told Canada, or Kanata. The word is there on a 1537 map drawn by one of Cartier's cartographers, which also shows the Ottawa River, rerouted to run due north. The name Canada expanded like an inflating balloon and now defines the second-largest country in the world. The first time it was officially mentioned was by François I in a 1540 written proclamation, wherein he made a favoured nobleman the "Viceroy and Lieutenant-General in Canada and

Hochelaga," which François called "the extremity of Asia." (The acre's first viceroy was assassinated shortly afterwards, on a night stroll in Paris.)

It was the cartography of Champlain, though, that really put the acre on the map. As much advertisements as navigational aids, his flyers were printed and distributed in the cities of Europe to entice people to sample the product, Nouvelle France. He was also the first cartographer of New England. By 1632, when he drew his last one, he was producing maps of some refinement, showing Nouvelle France with a simplified course for the Grande Rivière des Algoumequins, and the Chaudière Falls, with the acre right alongside.

Shortly after the Treaty of Paris, the British king, George III, put his seal on a proclamation designed to tie up several administrative loose ends in the North American colonies. The Royal Proclamation of 1763 relied on convoluted language still recognizable today as the work of lawyers, embellished with some royal jargon. Essentially, it was a statement by the chairman of the board to the new employees.

First, it tidied up the ragged borders of the colonies that George's generals had been collecting for him, from Hudson Bay to Florida. Second, it made it possible for George to pay soldiers who had won him that land with bits of it. This was standard practice, and it killed two birds with one stone; it tied a ready-made militia to the region and, since the land granted was free or ridiculously cheap, it saved the British treasury vast amounts in wages. The proclamation also sought to stroke the natives who had fought with the winning British, and to placate those who had backed the losing French. Finally, it put a stop to the independent operators who had been pushing a booze-and-baubles-for-land deal with the natives.

All four measures affected the acre's address. The British, as they usually did after a conquering, got out their rulers and started drawing lines all over the maps. Two such lines were pinned to the corner of the lake at the head of the Ottawa River, Lake Nipissing. One line headed northeast towards Greenland, and the other almost due east, ignoring the meandering path of the Ottawa River and passing about ten miles below the acre, the two lines forming the borders of the Province of Quebec, the acre's new address. Land on the western side of the two lines was deemed to be "Indian Territory," which was another way of saying, "Temporarily surplus to requirements."

The British in Canada set about implementing the other measures in the Royal Proclamation. Forts, like pins in a hat, were built onto the landscape. Squatters were un-squatted. The bureaucracy required to distribute parcels of land to the military, anywhere from one hundred to five thousand acres depending on rank, was installed in the forts. The first of several centuries of negotiations with the natives began.

Meanwhile, the acre kept getting new names. In 1774, two Englishmen chatting on a street corner in the swelling town of Montreal would still have included the acre when they referred to the Province of Quebec, but by then the province had grown like a wasp's nest as far north as Hudson Bay, as far south as the Ohio River, and as far west as the Mississippi, taking a large bite out of Indian Territory. Two years later this vast province was bisected, moving the acre into the District of Montreal. This district had an undefined western border, since the British had no clear idea of how far west "west" went. The District of Montreal, they imagined, went all the way to the Pacific Ocean.

Setting up and holding on to colonies is a fluid enterprise. Having dealt with the French, the British almost immediately had to deal, badly, with a rebellion in the American colonies. They lost, and the result was the sudden need to house people who had been on the blunt end of the war retreating north. One group was made up of Loyalists, people who preferred to live under an established monarchy rather than an emerging democracy. The second group was the natives, the Six Nations, who had signed up and fought against the Americans and were now *persona non grata* in their own territory. The land previously designated surplus to requirements was now required, and the order came down to negotiate with the relevant Indians and stock up on territory for the housing project.

Purchasing Order

There is a party game, involving a chain of people. The first person in the chain makes up a short story involving some false gossip, and tells it to the second. The second person tells the third, and the story moves on down the chain. When it reaches the end, the last person tells the first the version that got to her. Everyone laughs at how much the story has changed.

The chain of people passing on the story of the acre, its transition from hunting territory to British real estate, goes back two hundred years. The story comes to us from the letters and recorded speeches of men now dead, so we can never ask the first person what the real story was. Besides, there is no such thing as the real story. The most studied event in history is the assassination of John F. Kennedy, and we still don't know what happened.

The person who originated this particular story was Captain William Redford Crawford, a British soldier with war experience who had led native raiding parties. Crawford filed a report on October 9, 1783. In his report, Crawford tells the second person, Sir John Johnson, about some land he has purchased. Johnson was the first British superintendent of Indian affairs and his boss, the governor general, had landed him with the task of settling the Loyalists, native and otherwise.

Crawford told Johnson that the deal took place on an island in Lake Ontario called Carleton. He had dealt with chiefs of a tribe called the Mississaugas. In particular he mentioned Chief Menas. Menas, a very old man, had been staying at the French mission at Lake of Two Mountains, a wide part of the Ottawa River at the Montreal end, with the Algonquins, but he made it to Crawford's gathering. In his time Menas had been to Europe, and appears to have had extensive hunting territory. The British described him as being helpful in the negotiations.

In the next section of his report, Crawford drew a verbal sketch of the land he had bought from Menas and the other chiefs. It was rectangular, and ran along the shore of the lake, between two rivers, and included any islands within sight of that stretch of coast. Put in modern parlance, and interpreting the geography that was still a little fresh to the British, the Crawford Purchase incorporated a forty-five-mile stretch from Port Hope to Brockville, two towns on the Canadian side of Lake Ontario. Crawford said that his purchase extended "from the lake back as far as a man can travel in a day."

Exactly how far a fit Mississauga could travel on a given day in October 1783 is moot. A day's travel was indeed a unit of loose measurement (the only kind the woodlanders had) among natives, a way of circumscribing a family's hunting territory in discussion. Some things don't change, however; the shortest distance between the north shore of Lake Ontario and the south bank of the Ottawa River along that stretch was, and still is, ninety miles. No one could walk that in a day. In October 1783, then, the Crawford Purchase, according to Crawford himself, didn't include the acre.

Crawford called the price agreed on with the chiefs a "consideration" and he recorded it item by item, thus. "All families . . . shall be clothed and . . . those that have not fusee [guns] shall receive new ones, some powder and ball for their winter hunting, as much coarse red cloth as will make about a dozen coats, and as many laced hats." Later, Crawford says that Chief Menas (the name means hawberry) got some rum, which he was told to "manage with economy." He also received a small wampum belt; the other chiefs got a large one, as a receipt and a memorial of the day for their children.

This report is the only hard evidence of Crawford's deal. The rest of the paperwork, if there was any — and Johnson said later there never was — is lost to time. But Crawford, though muted by two centuries, is able to tell us indirectly that the acre wasn't any part of the bargain.

As the story moved down the chain, however, the acre, like an oddment picked up in a job lot at auction, somehow got thrown into the bargain. Maybe Crawford changed his story, or renegotiated the deal. The will was certainly there to make the entire scarf of land between Lake Ontario and the Ottawa River available for incoming Loyalists, because later, in November 1783, Sir John Johnson told the governor general that Chief

Menas had disposed of a whack of land "including all the Country between the River St. Laurence and the Grand River." (To confuse matters, the British sometimes referred to the river as both the Ottawa and the Grand, a hangover from French occupation. The practice lapsed after 1800.)

Next in the chain, separated from Johnson by eleven years, was an otherwise obscure bureaucrat, a commissary at Kingston called John Ferguson. In a statement he made in 1794, Ferguson recalled that seven years earlier he had overheard Crawford, at a meeting between Johnson and the Mississauga chiefs, describe his purchase as going all the way to the Ottawa River. After Ferguson, the possibility becomes fact. In all major history books thereafter the acre, indeed the whole carpet of land on which Ottawa now stands, is included in the Crawford Purchase. For the price of a wagonload of clothes, guns, and booze, Crawford had picked up about two and a quarter million acres.

By Any Other Name

The Crawford Purchase, along with a series of deals cut with the natives along the shores of Lake Ontario and Lake Erie, gave the British an enormous acreage to put names on. In 1788 Lord Dorchester (a title created to adorn the chief colonial administrator in Canada; the first was Sir Guy Carleton) decided to have the District of Montreal, the western half of the Province of Quebec, renamed Lancaster; it was drawn and quartered into four smaller districts. The acre became part of the Lunenburg District, the most easterly of the four. The use of German names for the four districts was flattery on Lord Dorchester's part, since the royal family then was German, from Hanover, of which Lunenburg was a part; moreover, loyal Germans from around the Mohawk River were coming out of the United States through Niagara, the first settlement in Lancaster.

On Boxing Day, 1791, an act of the English Parliament called the Constitutional Act became law. The Province of Quebec, hitherto vast, had its vastness reduced; it was divided into Upper and Lower Canada. On a map, the twin Canadas were not one above the other, but side by side. But if you were climbing the St. Lawrence River, Lower Canada was your first traverse. Once past Montreal, you were in Upper Canada. The border between Upper and Lower Canada ran down the middle of the Ottawa River. (Borderlines drawn on rivers always seem particularly incongruous, permanent markings affixed to the constantly moving.)

The acre, lying to the west of the Ottawa River, was in Upper Canada. But only just. The acre's address was now Upper Canada, district of Lunenburg (or Luneberg: old maps use both spellings). One of the perks of being a pooh-bah in colonial administration was that as the colony filled and the electoral districts were rejigged, an area got named after you. It was, and it remains, a kind of immortality. The British favoured this cult of personality, and used it extensively to overlay the native names that were more inclined to geographical and naturalist poetry. Often the names were chips off the old English block, transferred wholesale from the Thames valley. By 1800, you could leave London after breakfast, travel down the Thames River, and arrive in Stratford for dinner, all without leaving Upper Canada.

Besides a box full of names, the British had brought their system of governance; as the inventors of Parliament, their taxonomy of land was based on the voting district, a district being a catchment of voters (who could double as militiamen) that selected representatives, who held meetings on their behalf. In midsummer 1792, John Graves Simcoe, the first lieutenant-governor of Upper Canada, an elitist determined to create an English theme park for Loyalists coming into the area, decided to subdivide the districts into nineteen parliamentary counties. The voters hadn't arrived yet, but they would; the non-native population of Upper Canada went from fourteen thousand in 1791 to a million in sixty years, thanks in part to mass immigration from Britain.

With assistance from his wife, Elizabeth, a talented landscape artist and mapmaker, Simcoe pre-emptively mapped out Upper Canada like a country garden, planting the county names Dundas and Grenville on the region surrounding the acre. Mrs. Simcoe chose people's names for the eastern counties, and named the rest after the English counties surrounding London. By a whisker, the acre was in Dundas County, named after the home secretary of the time.

Meanwhile, in a triumph of the obvious, Simcoe, at the very first session of the Legislative Assembly of Upper Canada in 1792, erased the Germanic names of the four districts created in 1788, and renamed them Western, Home, Midland, and Eastern, Eastern being the new alias for Lunenburg. The acre's address now read Dundas County, Eastern District, Upper Canada. That lasted a few years, but by the turn of the century the number of districts had doubled to eight, and the number of counties increased again — the acre ended up in the District of Johnstown, in the County of Carleton. The county name honoured the aforementioned Sir Guy Carleton, Lord Dorchester. Sir Guy was a protégé of General Wolfe's who had been wounded in Quebec, Havana, and France. He was twice governor of British North America, arriving to take up the second term in 1786.

Efficient as ever, the British set about surveying a gaggle of townships, focal points of potential habitation inside the counties, all of them near water. The colonial authorities were preparing for a flood of refugees from the War of Independence, who would be handed parcels of land on arrival. After a survey in Carleton County in 1793, the acre was deemed part of Nepean Township. Sir Evan Nepean was an undersecretary at the Home Office who had handled the Canadian beat since 1782. He moved to another portfolio in 1794 and died in 1822, without ever having set foot in Canada. His successor at Canadian Affairs handled the paperwork that, in 1823, broke Johnstown District down into Bathurst and Johnstown. Lord Henry Bathurst was yet another British civil servant, the colonial secretary at the time of the division. In 1824, then, the acre was in Nepean Township, which was in Carleton County, which was in Bathurst District, which was in Upper Canada, in British North America.

By the time Bathurst District was created, there were a handful of settlers in Carleton County. Several of them lived within a few yards of the acre, at a place called Richmond Landing. There was also by that time a postal service along the Ottawa River, and one of those settlers could have received a letter bearing the acre's address. The history of the Canadian postal service is a fascination in itself; it was started in 1764 at Quebec by no less a person than Benjamin Franklin, deputy postmaster general, with a branch office at Montreal. In 1819 a steamer began doing regular runs up the Ottawa River with mailbags, and in 1829 the acre got its first postmaster, Matthew Connell, who would have walked the letter down to the acre himself from the post office in Bytown, on the hill above, after announcing the mail's arrival by blowing a horn.

British North America, though rapidly filling with settlers all this time, was not a settled place. The chemical mix of elitists and democrats, French and English, the poorly governed and the governors, the poor and the privileged, and the reformers and reactionaries, exploded in rebellion in the two Canadas in 1837. As a way of Band-Aiding the problem, an Act of Union was passed in 1840, and Upper and Lower were united in 1841, renamed West and East, and each given an assembly, a manoeuvre that changed the last line of the acre's address to Canada West.

By coincidence, 1840 was a year of major shake-up in the postal service. Stamps, the penny black and the twopenny blue, appeared for the first time, the rate was standardized, and the first steamer carrying mail between Liverpool and Halifax ran on July 1. A letter from Liverpool addressed to a resident of Richmond Landing, dated July 7, 1840, would have borne one shilling and two pence postage, and taken about three weeks to arrive.

In one final attack of district-itis two years later, Bathurst was reassigned as the District of Dalhousie, following the completion of the courthouse and the jail. The letter to Richmond Landing would have read Nepean Township, Carleton County, Dalhousie District, Canada West.

In 1850 the acre left Nepean Township to become a facet of Bytown, the forerunner to Ottawa; by 1855 it was part, as it is now, of the newly incorporated City of Ottawa. Duke Street ran alongside it, solid stone houses set back. A man called Perley, an American lumber merchant, lived at number 9. A letter coming to him from his folks in Vermont would have had a 15-cent stamp on it, arrived by mail train, gone to postmaster George Baker, and been hand-delivered for an extra two cents to Mr. Perley, 9 Duke Street, Ottawa, Canada West. From then on, until 1867, when Canada West became Ontario, that was the acre's permanent address.

We Beg to Differ

A fence runs through the middle of every story, giving it two sides. The white picket fence that bisects this one runs all the way back to the Royal Proclamation of 1763. On one side of the fence are the Algonquins, who in 1763 have never heard of fences. On the other side are the British governors, who eventually turn into the Canadian government.

The Algonquin side of the story begins in a time long before writing, when the acre was part of their hunting territory. It stayed that way, with a hiatus for the trouble with the Iroquois, until George III's Royal Proclamation of 1763, which was a conquerors' manifesto. Proclamations are meant to be proclaimed, and the first chore of the new administration was to broadcast the details; representatives of the Algonquins met with Sir William Johnson at the Lake of Two Mountains where, in his own fashion, Johnson explained the relevant parts of the proclamation. He assured the tribes that they would not be molested on their hunting grounds; that only the Crown could buy their land, after public consultation. The king, their new father, had said so. Then he asked the Algonquins exactly where those territories might be. Either side of the golden river, they said (the river the British referred to as the Grand or the Ottawa), back to the point where the sister rivers that fed it began flowing towards it; and from the rapids at its mouth to the lake at its end; from Long Sault upriver to Lake Nipissing. In other words, the Ottawa River watershed.

The man asking the questions, Sir William Johnson, was the Crown's first superintendent of Indian affairs. He was also one of the richest men in America, having made a fortune as a trader on the Mohawk River. He had used his position as paymaster of the Six Nations to run his store and pay his family. His landholdings were phenomenal, not least because it was his job to set the price per acre when the Crown bought land from the natives. As well as a grant of 130,000 acres he received for services rendered, he bought an additional 100,000 acres from the Mohawks and 40,000 from the Oneidas — at a bargain rate. He was a consummate diplomat and a one-man nation builder; in addition to the children from his marriage, he had eight with Mary Brant, older sister of Joseph Brant, the chief orator of the Six Nations.

Sir William was asking the Algonquins for the first time to put a definite border on what for them was a given; their sense of boundary was closer to that of a lynx than that of a surveyor. The British, for their part, took walls, fences, and borders for granted, forgetting that such devices were merely the solution to a historical problem the Algonquins had never had. After 1763, not only their land was slowly usurped; the Algonquins' very sense of land was being violated. The British were about to redefine the acre, to turn it from a mustang to a packhorse. They would call it part of Canada, and make it subject to the laws of property. But the Algonquins never did, never would, see it that way. In the many, many speeches they made over the next fifty years, they never named their collective territory. They never said it was part of Canada either, and they never signed anything that added it to the Canadian land bank.

The British came into the Algonquin *waki* (territory) by going upstream against the flow of its rivers, and against the flow of the Algonquins' philosophy of land. The momentum of the European style of settlement simply overwhelmed the natives. As you read through the transcripts of their complaints, petitions, and speeches, you see that they knew, probably from the first moment a hunter left with beaver furs and returned with British rum, that an act of sordid imbalance was being performed, that the neighbourhood was doomed. The Algonquins sensed at once that the British were a different calibre of disruption from the French.

Remarkably, the Ottawa River Algonquins never killed any of the trespassers or repaid the umpteenth bent or broken assurance with a broken head. In the years before 1800, they threatened several times to clear the area, and they repeatedly asked that the government regulate the substance abuse that was tearing at the fabric of their society. But their anguish never spilt over into violence. There was no blood on the acre, although they had camped in the area for many centuries.

The Algonquins usually filed their written complaints in July and August, when many of them assembled, as they had done since well before British occupation, in the region around Oka, on the Lake of Two Mountains. There was, and still is, a French monastery there, and a nearby fort. In these months they would gather stories and assemble them into an oral newspaper, outlining the increase in squatting, lumbering, poaching, and rumrunning through their waki. Then the older family heads would have a communiqué transcribed and presented at council to a representative from Indian Affairs.

One of the more eloquent of these communiqués, distressing to read two hundred years later, was made to Sir John Johnson in 1798. It speaks for itself. (I've brushed up the punctuation of a translation of the original document to give it the rhythm of a speech.)

My Father,

We thank the Master of Life to find you in perfect health as well as your Family. This is the first time that your children the Algonquins and Nipissings come to speak to you; we ask you to listen to what we have to say.

We come to speak to you for our lands, that have been taken on both sides of the grand river to the right and left. Some years ago we came to find Governor Carleton to complain to him that our lands were being taken; we spoke to him with a belt of wampum and the map of our lands. He seemed surprised to hear us complain, and he told us that he thought our lands had been paid for and told us that the King never took the land of his children without paying for them.

My father, you are always the master of taking our lands, but we beg you not to take more than forty arpents deep from the edge of the water. At least we will have the backlands for our hunting.

Since that time we have never received any reply and it is thought, my Father, that our Belt and our Map are lost; that you have never seen them. That is why we come to find you and we see, in seeing you, the representative of the King Our Father, and we place the map of our lands in your hands and we hope you will consider it and that you will have pity on your Algonquins and Nipissing children, because, my Father, since the world is the world, it is the master of Life who gave us these lands so that our families might live and survive.

My Father, we hope that you will do for us as you have done for your Indian children the Mississaugas — that you will pay us for our lands. We have found a good Father in finding you. You have a good heart. Our lands are infertile; we have almost no more game. The animals have fled. We find but little for our families to survive on.

Sir John Johnson — second in the chain of people who passed on the story of the acre — was William's son, and he too had an intriguing career. He fled the Mohawk River for Quebec in 1775 to avoid arrest, and with his knighthood, a promise kept by George III to his father, became a leading Loyalist. He had more respect for natives than did his father, fighting attempts to cease the annual giving of presents to them by the Crown. His landholdings were considerable, including four houses, a château in Montreal, and 150,000 acres in Lower Canada. When he died, in 1830, three hundred natives attended the funeral.

Forty-two years after the 1798 petition, in the spring of 1840, the Algonquins and Nipissings were still coming to the Lake of Two Mountains in summer. Once again they made the annual harvest of their grievances. The main complaint now was that none of their earlier petitions had even raised a royal eyebrow. They were unwittingly being snared in that old British schoolyard trick where one kid hands another a note; on one side it says, "How do you keep a petitioning Indian distracted for hours? Turn over." The paper says the same on the other side.

Still, despite this repeated insult, the natives kept on trying to get some attention, in an adopted language and in a style that remained an unsettling mix of dignity and obeisance, echoing the pleas of an innocent man resisting arrest. They kept their hand up, and wouldn't put it down. Their petition of 1840 was delivered March 9. Again the punctuation has been polished, and some repetition edited out.

Father,

We have frequently represented our grievances to our Father your predecessor, but we are sorry to say to very little effect. The only answer we received was that they were sent across the big salt lake to Our Great Father the King, who would pay attention to them and send us an answer.

We much fear that our Great Father and present Good Mother have never heard of or seen these writings in question, for from what we have heard of them they would certainly have sanctioned our demands that are but moderate and just, in conformity to the wishes and instructions of Our Great Father of Blessed Memory King George the Third. A copy of which we have in our possession, given to our tribes by our late good father Sir William Johnson, dated 24th December 1763, when our ancestors were told by him that we should always have the enjoyment of our hunting grounds, without being molested by any strangers, until we thought proper to sell them to the King for the use of our white brethren.

Father, we have always been good loyal subjects. We have fought and bled during the two last American Wars, and are ready to do so again, whenever called upon.

We were formerly rich and independent. Our hunting grounds embraced a vast territory. They abounded in rich furs of every description, our forests were alive with deer. We lived well, and had wherewith to clothe our wives and children comfortably, and we were happy.

About forty years ago, when the Whites first came amongst us to settle on our hunting grounds, they were good and grateful. We took pity on them, received them with open arms. We knew them to be the children of our great Father the King, as well as ourselves, therefore had no objection to them cultivating our land for the support of their families. Always bearing in mind that when our hunting grounds were ruined, destitute of furs, it was at our option to sell them to the representatives of Our Father for his disposal.

That day is now arrived which we never expected to see. Your red children the Nipissings and Algonquins have never been in the habit of tilling the ground. From time immemorial our chief and only dependence for a livelihood sprang from the chase from which we procured abundance. Not so now. Our beaver and other fur have been destroyed by the constant fires made by the lumber men in our majestic forests. Our deer have disappeared. Our timber to the amount of hundreds of thousands of pounds is annually taken, but from which we derived not the least benefit. We are starving, Father. Our wives and children are naked. Our traders will give us no more credit. Why? Because we can procure no furs and of course are unable to pay.

Father — For these many years past we your Children

have been in the habit of receiving certain annual rents from squatters and other individuals who have clandestinely taken possession of certain islands and divers lots of land on both banks of the Ottawa River. But, strange to say, on the eve of our departure for that purpose our Superintendent came and explained to us an extract of a report, which in manner prohibits us from doing so.

Father, we have only you, the representative of Our Good Mother across the Salt Lake, to look up to for protection. We are persuaded, when you are more acquainted with our deplorable situation, you will immediately listen to the prayers of Your Children, to be allowed to go and gather these small rents, and that you may be pleased to order one of your officers to accompany us with authority for doing so. We have made innumerable complaints against these intruders, as well as against lumber men; we received many promises from Government, but all turned out in smoke.

We can no longer depend on the chase for support. We must set ourselves to the hoe, or else starve.

Father, our brethren of Upper Canada receive a very handsome annual remuneration, in merchandise to a certain amount, for such part of their hunting grounds as has been sold by them to Government, and besides they have retained most tracts of their best lands for their own cultivation. While we, who possessed by far the most extensive and richest hunting grounds, have been deprived of the most valuable parts of the same, by the Upper Canada government.

We request of you further to be pleased to assume the whole of our hunting grounds in the name of Our Good Mother the Queen, with the exception of Isle aux Allumettes, which we have for these many years back reserved. Many squatters are settled thereon. We have no objection that they should remain by acre. But that no other strangers will be allowed to come and annoy us.

At the bottom of the petitions, the grand chiefs of the Algonquins and Nipissings would make their marks, and the scribe preparing the petition would put their names, spelt as he heard them.

One of the petitioners was Constant Penency, Penency being an English interpretation of the Algonquin word for partridge. Constant, of the Partridge band, was the Algonquin whose hunting territory included the acre.

9

The Ballad of Constant Penency

History is a cat's cradle of intersecting lives. With hindsight, it seems some lives were born to intersect, while others had intersections thrust upon them. The moment when one way of life crosses another can be a blessing or a curse, a tragedy or a comedy, a win or a loss.

Constant Penency was born in or around 1786. He fought in the War of 1812 with the British and then returned to the ways of the game hunter, spending his summers at the Lake of Two Mountains and his winters with his family upstream on the banks of the river. He was the father of at least four sons, two of whom died and left him young children to care for. The hunting grounds of Constant Penency had provided his ancestors with deer, beaver, and fish for many generations.

Because of a petition Constant made to the British Department of Indian Affairs in February 1830, when he was forty-four, we know where those hunting grounds were. In the document Constant said: "After several years the hunt has more and more diminished with the destruction and the distancing of the beaver and of game. The only means of subsistence of the supplicant whose hunting grounds, situated to the South of the Ottawa at the top of the Rideau, are almost all ruined by the incursions that were made and the numerous settlements that now run along them."

Constant dictated his notice of trespass in French, to a Frenchman with a fine florid hand. At the bottom he drew his band sign, a little

Egyptian-looking hieroglyphic the size of a thumbnail, the outline of a partridge, standing side-on and listening for danger.

The expanse of Constant's family territory can only be guessed at, but the average Algonquin grounds (a thing as average as the cloud cover on a given day) was one hundred square miles, or an area ten miles by ten. The acre lay a mere two miles to the west of the mouth of the Rideau as the partridge flies. Almost certainly, then, the acre lay within the territory on which the family of Pierre Louis Constant Penency laid their traps.

The "incursions" that Constant mentioned in his petition were the first stirrings of settlement, stirrings that, as we have seen, would divide, subdivide, and eventually become Bytown, then Ottawa, the capital city of the British invasion. Constant and his family were to be replaced, in six generations, by half a million people.

By 1830 Constant was a Great Chief of the Algonquins. He earned the description "very deserving and possessing the entire confidence of his tribe" in the memos his petition spawned in the Department of Indian Affairs. The British, in the person of Lieutenant-Colonel Duncan Campbell Napier, who had the corpulent title of "Right Arm to the Secretary of Indian Affairs," took Constant seriously. Napier backed the petition with an endorsement, and the advice that the rations and presents due to a chief who has been wounded in action should be forthcoming.

Within a couple of months of his petition, Constant got a form letter. It was a fancy-looking document dressed up as a certificate, with flourishes and filigreed edges, designed to impress the receiver. It came from Sir James Kempt, who was, as it said at the top of the paper, "Captain General and Governor-in-Chief in and over the provinces of Lower and Upper Canada," as well as of other glories. Sir James wanted Constant to know that "reposing especial trust and confidence in your courage and good conduct, and in your zealous and faithful attachment to His Britannic Majesty King George," Kempt was appointing him "a Grand Chief of the Tribe of Algonquins at the Lake of Two Mountains."

This could be looked on as a notice of promotion from Great to Grand, but it could also be viewed as roughly equal to the mayor of Ottawa deciding that a member of the New York City Council should be made governor of the state — in other words, as none of Sir James Kempt's business. Being upped to Grand Chief did entitle Constant to a better class of rifle and blanket in the annual handout of presents, as the British termed them, and as we would now call a settlement for damages — a bribe to stay ruly, to not make waves on the Ottawa River.

Four years after his appointment as Grand Chief, almost to the day, Constant, together with a Nipissing chief, went to visit James Hughes, an Indian Affairs agent in Montreal. Hughes later reported the meeting to his employers, giving his take on what the two chiefs had on their minds. An edited version of his letter reads:

Old Constant Pinaisais [French spelling] was here a few days ago. He brought a map made a few years past. These lands on the borders of the Ottawa are now almost all settled. They however have marked out a lot above the Grand Calumet Portage some distance above the last settlements. They would wish to have a township or a seigniorie given to them there, before these lands are granted.

It is on the south side [of the river]. There is an island before it which they would also like to have, to make hay thereon and place their cattle in summer. They say they have no encouragement to work on pieces of land that are in manner only lent to them, whereas were they masters of a certain tract that they could call their own, they would be happy and industrious. They would have it in their power to make better hunts — find more deer and catch plenty of fish.

The history of the British theft of the Algonquin way of living is right there in those few words. No one goes through life without great change, but Constant Penency found himself pushed over the edge of an era. He was born a free hunter's son, and by the age of fifty he was asking men born in another world for the right to relinquish any claim on his birthland, and to become a sharecropper and part-time trapper far away from their incursions.

Constant had felt the tide rush down his valley and push him under. He had shouted at the wave even as it drowned him, and now all he asked was a small space out of the current, on shore, to sink quietly from view. But this was a tide that could think and decide its own course. How it chose to deal with Constant Penency after he asked for safe haven in 1834 is almost completely submerged by history — but not quite. Forty-two years later, Constant bobbed up again, thirty miles west of the acre. His life had made one of its more ironic intersections.

John Rochester was one of the twenty-seven Americans sometimes referred to as the founders of Bytown. He brought enterprise and a wagon full of sons north with him from New York State, and he got wealthy from supplying the military with bread, beer, and butchered meat. He capped his prominence with the mayorship of Ottawa in 1870.

George Rochester was John's youngest son, born in 1820. With the family head start, he went into the lumber business, and his fortune rose as the forest fell. In 1849 he was persuaded to become an investor in a small Scottish settlement called Burnstown (after poet Robbie Burns) on the Madawaska River, then a feeding stop for lumbermen driving the shorn logs down the tributary to the Ottawa. George put up the money for a mill so that Burnstown could make its own flour, and he bought some real estate around it.

Though the rest of him may have wanted to go back to Ottawa, George's heart was felled by the Burnstown schoolteacher; he stayed on and built a home. As befitted a man of wealth, George consolidated his community standing with respectable sidelines, such as justice of the peace and agent for the Department of the Interior, Indian Branch.

It was as an Indian agent that his well-swept path crossed the broken trail of Constant Penency. "The Indian in question is about 90 years of age, and is in very destitute circumstances and dependent on his daughter." So Constant reappeared, in the paperwork of George Rochester, in late June 1876. George was trying to get a yearly allowance for Constant, whom he labelled in his request "an aged Indian, living on the Madawaska River." He succeeded. Within a month, the minister of the interior gave George a written nod, writing that "the aged Indian" should receive $60 per annum, in two half-yearly handouts. The paperwork ends almost as quickly as it started, with a note scrawled in the margin of a ministry letter, giving the number of the cheque (2684) issued to "an aged Indian" on August 9.

The irony in this intersection of two such disparate lives feels almost orchestrated. George Rochester was the son of the man who built the first industrial park in Ottawa, a separate suburb called Rochesterville until annexation in 1889, on the very hunting grounds that Constant had been forced to vacate.

On an unseasonably warm April day, I set out from the acre to find the grave of Constant Penency and pay my respects. An hour later I drove through Burnstown, past the thriving general store, and out on the highway that dogs the beautiful, narrow valley holding the Madawaska River. In a few moments, as I'd been advised, a boarded-up Roman Catholic church appeared, surrounded on all sides by a well-spaced regiment of tombstones rising from the rough grass, the majority with their inscriptions facing the river. If Constant was buried anywhere, it would be here, at the oldest Catholic church in the area. I had been told that an Algonquin woman called Meg, daughter of Simon Constant, was buried in the churchyard; the odds were that she was Constant's granddaughter.

I found no tomb bearing his name, or Meg's, even after I had fingered the moss and dirt from the oldest ones at the back, where the graveyard met the forest, and where a partridge made me laugh by rising and flapping deeper into the woods. But there was evidence nearby of the Constant family; to the north was a small lake called Constant, and a stream of the same name ran out of it. There was a Partridge Island in the lake. Further, around the time Constant had appealed for a pension, an Algonquin going by the name of Frank Partridge had died fishing in the lake.

Back in Ottawa, disappointed, I got a message that a lawyer who was part Algonquin (a small part) and lived in Renfrew, just north of Burnstown, had written to the local paper about the naming of Lake Constant. When I contacted him, he told me a story. The church I had visited, which closed during the Second World War, was once the concern of Father John Sullivan. In the construction of a path from his house to the church, the father had used some unmarked tombstones from the back of the churchyard. News of this reached the locals, who objected. Sullivan, a priest with a fighter's temper, had the stones pulled up and dumped at night from the Burnstown bridge.

The lawyer knew that the last part of the story was true, because his son had worked on the renovation of the bridge. Spotting something in the water under the bridge, the son had gone in, and come up to report that there was a graveyard below, a jumble of tombstones. I want to believe that one of those stones once marked the grave of Pierre Louis Constant Penency, that his body indeed lies undisturbed in the churchyard, and that I was standing on the very spot when the partridge startled me.

10

Setting the Net

B y the late 1780s, around the time Constant Penency was born, the British had more than enough land in the bank to meet the needs of the incoming Loyalists. Almost the day after they had made their various deals with the natives, they set about throwing a net over the wild topography, taming it with a grid of survey lines.

When the Romans conquered Britain, almost two thousand years earlier, their basic unit of occupation was the township — a square of land with sides ten miles long. As latter-day imperialists, the British used the same model. The ten-mile square was chequered into smaller squares, lots, like a gingham tablecloth, two hundred acres to a lot. Squares for the church, squares for the Loyalists still in the process of percolating up from the lost American colonies, bigger squares for the men of military rank being paid in property, and squares for the farmers who would cross the Atlantic Ocean from Europe, to plant new lives on land they could call their own.

Once surveyed, the townships could be checked out for townsites on the rivers: once occupied, the townsites became buffers of Britishness against foreign take-over. The townsites were modern castles, strongholds of settlers who, already displaced by Americans, would defend their new homes all the more fiercely if anyone attempted to conquer Canada.

By 1790, the Office of the Surveyor General — Orwell would have called it the Ministry of Land — was taking on deputies to cope with the huge workload. The job of land surveyor became a popular one in North

America, much as computer salesman is now. In their time, George Washington, Thomas Jefferson, and Henry Thoreau all worked the lines; Thoreau put out a handbill announcing: "Areas warranted accurate within almost any degree of exactness."

One of the men who applied for the job in Upper Canada, in October 1792, was John Stegmann. A cameo of him from two years earlier shows a wide-eyed young man, clean-chinned, nose as straight as a plumb-line, looks that would have put him in a daytime soap opera today. Stegmann stated in his letter of application for the job of surveyor that he had fought against the Americans right through the war until August 1783. Now retired from the military, he farmed with his wife and small family in a township on the Thames River. He said he had a commission in surveying from Lord Dorchester, despite admitting to being "intirely ingnorant" of the craft.

Stegmann seems to have done a little moonlighting before seeking a position with the surveyor general. In December 1790, a qualified surveyor complained that Stegmann had turned up in his neighbourhood foisting, as he put it, strange trapeziums on the already established parallelograms of the French seigniorial field system. David William Smith, the efficient, harried surveyor general, working out of Detroit (then still British), wrote back to the complainant saying he had never heard of Stegmann. (This is the second time we've met a William Smith; the other was the inventor of stratigraphy.)

A year later Smith had Stegmann's surveyor application sitting in the pile on his desk. Shortly before he got it, Smith had hustled Lieutenant-Governor Simcoe for extra funds (a perennial conundrum in Ontario, government funding) to map out a bunch of new townships. His drawings for these new settlements include four that would hang down from the shore of the Ottawa River like grapes. The acre was in the township to be called Nepean, the top right of the cluster.

At the end of November 1792, Stegmann got a brief note of congratulation; he was officially on the books as a deputy surveyor. Be patient, Smith told him, a work order will follow soon. Stegmann got his orders fifteen months later, hand-delivered by another deputy on his way to start work the other side of the Ottawa River. Stegmann had landed the job of tracing out the four townships that included the acre.

The job, like most government jobs in those days, was a mixture of paperwork and fieldwork. To the British, both were equally important; filling out forms, in triplicate, has long been the national sport of the British, as building straight roads was for the Romans. They needed clear chains of paperwork, and they feared the loose end; that might be where the Empire would start to unravel. Stegmann had a folder full of forms and memos from Surveyor General Smith by the time he assembled his survey team. Memos asking him to keep an eye out for any tasty morsels of geography that might have, as Smith put it, "singularity and value towards the public utility," such as waterfalls and fine stands of timber. The British referred to these unsurveyed regions as "wastelands," as in "going to waste." Stegmann got memos telling him not to cut down trees — an added expense and time-waster — unless absolutely necessary. And memos giving him licence to rename rivers and prominent landmarks that had "uncouth Indian names."

Stegmann's mission was to "mint" new land, land to serve as currency to foot the recent war's wage bill and pay off decommissioned militiamen like Butler's Rangers and the Detroit Volunteers. These golden landshakes were doled out according to a set schedule, in the following amounts: field officers got five thousand acres; captains, three thousand acres; subalterns, two thousand; non-commissioned officers, two hundred; private men, fifty. Many of the areas marked for survey had been rooted out by these knights errant, by men who had chosen to stay in Canada as potential big frogs in very big swamps, rather than go back to small puddles in England. They scouted the unsurveyed landscape with an eye to future holdings, knowing that the trick to successful colonizing was to get there first. Stake your claim early and you could set in motion the generational momentum that would eventually turn new territory into old money — rocky wasteland into Rockefeller-sized fortunes.

In the fever to get a piece of the action, some men claiming to act for a large group of speculators would petition the surveyor general for their very own township, site unseen. On his second blueprint for Nepean Township, done in October 1792, Surveyor General Smith had pencilled in the name George Hamilton, the head of such a consortium, supposedly of 143 men. Hamilton had obviously written Smith, asking to be considered for a hefty land grant, and Smith had redrawn the townships accordingly. These speculators would have been the acre's first overseers, but it didn't happen. One of the group wrote to Smith in 1795 to renege on the grant. They now felt that "finding it such a distance from any settlement without any road it has frightened them."

Line Drawing

Stegmann waited until January 1794 to start work. His first move was to assemble a team. The Surveyor General's Office had strict guidelines for the size of these teams — ten men — and fairly miserable rates of pay, one for rainy days, another for active days. The deputy surveyors kept field notes — Stegmann favoured a tall, thin, leather-bound notepad embossed with his name, and kept his notes to the minimum, in holiday postcard fashion. He began page one of each notebook with "Procured the necessaries." That was followed by a quick précis of each day's activity, as in "Very good going" or "Ran the North limit." If it "Rained all day" nothing got done, and on Sundays he would always write, "Lay still this day."

The team of ten broke down into a gaggle of functions. Surveying involved making the simplistic, geometric acquaintance of the wilderness. Large imaginary lines were tacked onto an area, then reduced and lifted onto a map in identical relation to one another. It was model-making. First up in any survey, then, were the axemen, usually five of them. They chopped and hacked and made tunnels in the foliage, like giant caterpillars, so that the surveyor had a clean line of sight.

Next a portable line, a chain sixty-six feet, or four rods, long, was laid along the tunnel. One hundred links to the chain. The chain was standardized in 1624, and it crops up here and there on the Canadian landscape. The main street of Niagara-on-the-Lake, for instance, is a chain wide. Coiled up, these chains were bulky things, and their care and transportation were the job of two chain bearers. Another bearer was sufficient for the instruments. Last to perform were the two picket planters.

The energy expended by this chain-gang was replaced with a fixed daily ration of half a pound of flour, a chunk of pork, and half a pint of pease, a do-it-yourself sort of stew. Stegmann sometimes hired natives as axemen, and complained that they ate twice the usual ration. This claim was made in reply to a terse query from head office about his expenses. Stegmann also whined about the lack of pencils, a constant complaint of all deputy surveyors, and asked for more.

In the early spring of 1794 Stegmann boated from Kingston down the Rideau River, and laid out the first of the four townships he had been assigned, Nepean. Stegmann and his team were servants of the straight line, the imaginary twine the British used to bind their empire and prove their ascendancy over the undisciplined curves of nature. Where the straight line wanted to go, it went — over wetland, through forest so thick a man had to squeeze between the trees, up rock faces, down slippery slopes. The notebooks of Canada's early surveyors read as though written by men gasping for breath at the end of a hellish obstacle course. Most of Nepean, Stegmann wrote in his notebook, was a "tedious swamp," the kind another surveyor called "not fit for culture" in his notes. The chains had to be laid out like runways, no matter what the terrain.

To mark out the new township, Stegmann probably started at the riverbank, a couple of miles west of the acre. Aligning his compass with the directions Smith required of him, he set up his circumferentor, essentially a rifle sight attached to a circular plate, on a tree stump or a flat rock, squatted down, and sent his axemen down his line of sight. The axemen used a picket to anchor the beginning of the chain, then went ahead, paying out links of chain as they went.

When the chain was taut, Stegmann waved to move his axemen to the left or right until they were back on the compass heading, and another picket went into the ground. Stegmann and his instruments walked, more likely squelched through the boggy ground, to the chain's end, selected another flat surface, and on it went. There might be a pause for note-taking — a fine stand of pine here, a cataract there — and a surreptitious sip of rum, and gradually the township was boxed in. The results were entered in precious pencil on graph paper pinned down like a picnic tablecloth to a portable plane table. Then the lots were laid out, running back from the river in long strips like planking on a deck, with a span of one chain left for a road after every fourth lot, and the lots numbered. The pickets stayed in the ground, leafless stems of a new weed in the forest that would attract settlers. The acre was in Lot 40, in a section marked A to denote that it contained broken waterfront. Stegmann took note of the power of the Chaudière Falls, and the quality and true straightness throughout the township of the soaring white pines.

By March of 1794, then, the acre had been fixed in the British web. Stegmann went home in April, picked up a letter that had arrived from Smith pushing the virtues of accuracy, and decided he had better go back. By October he was done and his report, in triplicate, was on Smith's desk.

After the four-township assignment, Stegmann carried on surveying for another ten years. He added many other townships to his bag, assisting on the ground plan of modern Toronto, among other things; and he laid out a village called Coote's Paradise (now Dundas) that was neatly bisected by the three-hundred-foot cliffs of the Niagara Escarpment, a mistake that gave new meaning to the labels upper and lower class.

Stegmann's final surveying assignment, in 1804, was the death of him. It all started when an unknown colonist murdered a man from the Mississauga tribe. Not much effort was made by the authorities to find the murderer, which tipped the brother of the dead Mississauga over the edge; he evened the score by killing a token colonist with the wonderful name Moody Farwell. At the time of his death, Farwell was manager of a trading post on an island in the centre of Lake Scugog, northeast of York, as Toronto was then known.

Moody's murderer got away clean, but later confessed under questioning by his chief, who handed him over to the British. When the brother's trial began, his lawyer played his opening gambit, which was to speculate that the murder had taken place not in York District, where the court was, but in Newcastle District, where the court wasn't. If the court would direct someone to find out in which district Farwell's home actually lay, then the proceedings could proceed in the correct jurisdiction.

The someone was Stegmann. Grabbing the chance to requisition two extra pencils, he went up to Lake Scugog in late August and discovered that the "exact and positive situation" of Farwell's place was in Newcastle District. This meant the court would have to move, and Stegmann would have to appear as a witness. To that end the entire court — the solicitor general, the judge, the lawyers, the prisoner, and witnesses like Stegmann — was put on a ship bound for Smithfield, in Newcastle District, via the port of Brighton, a day's sail to the east. The ship was called the *Speedy*, but it never reached Brighton. Sometime during the stormy night of October 8, 1804, it went to the bottom, with the entire courtly cargo. No one survived. Lake Ontario had exacted its own judgment on Moody Farwell's murderer.

This episode gave rise to the rumour that Stegmann had drowned in the Rideau River while surveying Nepean Township. He was said to have committed the Laurel-and-Hardy stunt of backing into his fate while taking a line of sight. The rumour made its way into the history books, but the true story is even better.

Three years later a young man from Maryland, a seeker of waterfalls, applied to become the first owner of the acre.

11

Possessed

Defined by surveyor John Stegmann's lines, packaged and delivered into the British family of property, the acre could now trace its ancestors back to the straight-edged fields of Norman England. The Normans, after their take-over of the Anglo-Saxons in 1066, implemented the first-generation model of the modern British landscape. The open fields of the Anglo-Saxon countryside were inscribed with ditches, regular fields, and roads; the era of enclosure had begun. The conquered natives of England dropped their notion of land as a communal, village asset and reassembled it as a patchwork of properties, berths for individual families, Thus the land was domesticated. English gardens, tiny fields with their crops of pedigree foliage, are tiny urban echoes of the closure of the countryside.

When they took over management of new land in their rash of colonization, the British exported the doctrine of enclosure. An unwitting recruit, the acre lost much of its spiritual wealth and respect in the process. Its essence no longer lay in its ability to provide food for a native family, but was inherent in its surface area and its proximity to a waterfall. It was primarily this latter virtue that first bestowed on the acre its market value.

Power comes to us these days — pours through the wires in our walls — but before the burst of ingenuity in electrical technology in the nineteenth century, we went to power. In 1800, power lay in the weight of water as it dropped over falls and was decanted through dams. The hearts of the first settlements in the eastern woodlands were the water-powered mills, and men looked for step-downs in the rivers the way they would later search for the click of uranium. John Stegmann, walking the lines of his tedious swamp, and mentioning the tumbling waters and the towering trees, was, in effect, creating a treasure map for woodland entrepreneurs, the pirates of property.

Land Ho

As the centuries fly by, as more human history accumulates, the more the rhythm of it becomes apparent, the point and counterpoint of the seizure and relinquishment of territory. To these two beats history marches; playing away above the rhythm section, in major and minor keys, is the refrain of politics. After 1750 the British began beating the drum of empire. For the next two hundred years it would be overwhelmingly loud in most parts of the world, but along the eastern seaboard, down through New England, it was drowned out by the snares of the American revolutionaries. By 1783 the thirteen colonies had left home, renamed themselves states, and united.

The aftermath of war is migration; the dispossessed Loyalists sought new ground, and waves of migrants went to the far side of the St. Lawrence and the Great Lakes. If we could send a historical surveillance satellite back in time and fly it over the eastern woodlands at the end of the eighteenth century, it would reveal a steady flow of human specks heading northward among the vast, uninhabited tracts. This new ground, as we have seen, was permanently borrowed from the natives. For the most part the natives were innocent, north of the St. Lawrence, of the difference between property and communal territory. The northern woodlanders continued to offer to share their territory, in return for what the British would have considered low-tech utensils and accessories, technology that would wear out long before the land they had lost. South of the St. Lawrence, the natives were beginning to catch on to who the "treat" in treaty was really for. In

1745, an Iroquois sachem told the British, "The white people think we do not know their [our lands'] value; but we are sensible that the land is everlasting, and the few goods we receive for it are soon worn out and gone."

As the war migrants and the emigrants from Europe began to pin their settlements to the Canadian map, the policy of land grants attracted other varieties of colonist. Unlike Champlain two hundred years earlier, these late arrivals at the land party were not in anyone's employ but their own. Their intention in travelling to Canada was to build up a capital of free land and convert it into wealth. They were land-mercenaries.

Our historical surveillance satellite, at high resolution, can now focus on one such mercenary. His name is Robert Randall. The year is 1795; Beethoven has just published his first opus. It is late fall and the thirty-year-old Randall, born in Maryland, is on the trail north. (Maryland, a colony named after the wife of Charles I, was one of the states that in 1788 had cut themselves off from notions of being ruled by absentee monarchs.)

Randall had already had a busy year. In September he achieved the honour of being the first American to get caught trying to bribe congressmen. Congress had met for the first time only in 1789. Randall and a consortium of merchants had offered the congressmen shares in a plan to buy a hefty chunk of Michigan from the government. As the clincher in the deal, Randall, 150 years before Hollywood agents perfected it, used the scam of claiming he already had big names (more than thirty congressmen) in the bag to entice others. Caught out, he got off with a reprimand and a few days in jail. With mud on his name in the United States, he headed for a clean start in Upper Canada. The government there was still making land grants to the "late Loyalists" — Americans who had first dithered and then decided to stick to being British. Randall made a beeline for Niagara, where the immense latent power of the falls was already being tamed, and mills were being stuccoed to the side of the Niagara River.

Over the next twelve years, Randall picked up and juggled several properties, using some for manufacturing, storing others like squirrel nuts for future use. After a false start on the Niagara, he dropped from history's sight, then reappeared in 1798, having somehow acquired a decent line of credit and letters of recommendation from wealthy men. He purchased the means to make iron, started a foundry, and quickly ran up heavy debt. Undaunted, he found new partners, switched to grinding wheat, and became, so he claimed, the first Canadian exporter of flour to Europe. When that enterprise also got into trouble, he unloaded all but a third of his Niagara holdings and hit the road again, going east. In debt in one pocket, and with borrowed Montreal money in the other, he bought land on either side of the St. Lawrence, at Cornwall. On the American side he put up a tannery, a potash factory, and a ferry across to Cornwall, where he set himself up as a merchant.

The image of Randall from here on is of a man running forward, juggling properties like beanbags, with a hole in his pocket out of which flows a steady trickle of money, faster than he can stuff it back in. Lined up between him and the jackpot were a pack of merchants, lawyers, and judges eager to de-bag him. He made headway in Cornwall, putting his seal on the place, in the fashion of the times, by building an Anglican church. But by 1807 he was back in debt, expenditure once again trotting ahead of income. He needed a big score, and some breathing time, to stay on his feet. Accordingly, he hired native guides and canoed up the Rideau River hunting for fresh properties. Pausing to make a note to acquire 450 choice acres along the way (which he later did), Randall reached the Ottawa River, turned left, and found what he was looking for — the Asticou Falls.

On the north shore of the river, he could see the fledgling settlement of Philemon Wright from Massachusetts, who had got there seven years earlier. The better flank was already gone, but Randall could see the potential on the acre's side. All he needed was some of the islands ahead of the falls, the waterfront, and the stretch of land behind — which included the acre. He checked the siting of the surveying pickets John Stegmann had left. He had heard that there was iron ore in the hills to the north. Harness the water-power, turn ore into saleable iron, add some grist mills and sawmills, and his problems would be solved.

Two years later, after some dancing with lawyers and bureaucrats in the land office, Randall had his lease on the land, 950 acres of it. He had retained a father-and-son tag team of lawyers, D'Arcy and Henry Boulton, to get it for him. In his first letter to them about the Chaudière property, in October 1807, he writes, "It will be a means of settling the wild lands on that river, that is at present a perfect wilderness." Randall started settling in, putting a small building just in front of the acre, on the shore of a little bay.

Randall was now, on paper, poised to join the big boys. He had the lease, by his reckoning, on 3,400 scattered acres of land in Canada that included a waterfall, some rapids, and an iron deposit. He was the owner of several businesses and the patron of a church. Unfortunately he still had creditors, and in the spring of 1809, while he was in Montreal assuaging some of them and arranging the development of his Chaudière property, the Niagara pack caught up to him. Randall was fingered and locked up in debtors' prison.

There were two ways out of debtors' prison in 1809. Pay the debt, not an easy thing to arrange from inside a cell, or have it forgiven. Business and forgiveness rarely walk together. Thomas Clark, who was now one of the leaseholders of the Niagara property, visited Randall after he had been in prison for a year and tried to squeeze his remaining share in the property out of him, at the same time as he was suing Randall for money owing on the same property. The evidence suggests that Thomas Clark was the nimble businessman who had fingered him; Randall was released from prison shortly after Clark wangled the entire freehold on the Niagara property into his own name. That was in October 1815. Randall had been in prison six and a half years.

While in prison, Randall, as often happened with debtors, was fed by the poor. He emerged one of them. (In his will, he left what little money he had to the people who had shown him compassion in his cell.) He remained relatively poor the rest of his life and, denied the straight route to wealth and property by the setback of his years in prison, went by the twisted route of the law to try to recover his property.

Lawyers and judges were much thinner on the ground in Upper Canada in the early 1800s than they are now. Six judges had been created in a single day in 1802, from the small pool of men of education and wealth, to make up the numbers. Then as now, holding the reins of the law was the way to political power. Real estate, the raw material of power, was cheap and abundant. The rich power-cake of the time was divided among a few men, who controlled the buying and selling of land. It was these men whom Robert Randall had to battle after he walked out of prison.

Landing Place

It was now almost two centuries since Champlain had paddled past the acre, and thirty years since it had been surreptitiously bargained away in the Crawford Purchase. Europeans, injected into the bloodstream of the continent through Quebec, had diffused through the veins of the woodlands, a restless infection attaching itself to riverbanks, moving between the dots of the nascent communities. Their excursions tended to start and finish at the town landing stage, the foundation stone of the woodland settlements. Landing meant just that, getting back on the sturdy earth from the uncertain water.

The acre, at the beginning of the nineteenth century, performed its first act of service as part of such a landing. When Robert Randall was given the grant of the lots containing the acre, in 1809, his first act, as we've seen, was to mark his territory with a building. Downriver from the falls, on the edge of a small bay, he put up a modest log storehouse. Randall made his mark at the spot where water-travellers coming up from Montreal to his factory would come ashore.

It takes only a couple of minutes to walk from the acre to the probable site of Randall's hut. When I did it, it was rush hour; single-occupant vehicles were stuttering like freight-train cars over the road bridge that separates the acre from the landing. On the other side of the road, a concrete path leads down a narrowing, manicured wedge of park to a ring of boulders. Each boulder is the size of a beanbag chair, and they can all be sat on, except one, which has a bronze plaque screwed onto it. The plaque announces that this is the start of an old pioneer trail leading to Kingston, and that Ottawa started here. No mention of Randall, or his hut, although it must have been close by. A few steps ahead of the ring of rocks, there's a fingernail of stony beach. When Randall stood here in 1809, the landscape would have been designed by only one architect, nature. Now the cliffs are crowded with palaces of government, art, justice, business, and tourism.

If I had stood here at the end of August 1818, and stared hard down-river, a convoy of sailboats would have hove into sight, loaded with four hundred people, soldiers and their families, making for this landing. The men on board were all from the Ninety-ninth Regiment of Foot. Most of them were Irish, men who had chosen active duty in the British army over inactive poverty at home. With them were the wives who had waited for them while they fought against Napoleon in Egypt from 1798 to 1801, and then against the Americans in 1812. For the last two years they had been calmly garrisoned in Quebec City, near the battlefield where Wolfe and Montcalm had died. Now the bill for all these wars had come in, and the military was cutting back. The Ninety-ninth had been given the choice of remaining in Canada or returning home, and most of them, not pleased with the prospects back in Ireland, had taken up the offer of a half-pay pension, and the grant of anywhere from a hundred to a thousand un-broken acres, according to rank.

The offer of land in Upper Canada had a military string attached. The colonial command had decided a settlement needed to be built, from scratch, in the woodlands between Lake Ontario and the Ottawa River. The settlers would be bound to act as an off-the-peg militia if the Americans got restless. To this same end, the military had financed the founding of Perth two years earlier, but Perth was already a pint-sized pot trying to hold a quart of emigrants, and the military had decided to bankroll another set-tlement between there and the Ottawa River.

This time, however, instead of going from Montreal to Kingston along the St. Lawrence, and thence to Perth, as previous settlers had done, the deputy quartermaster general for the Canadas, Lieutenant-Colonel Francis Cockburn, wanted the Ninety-ninth to go in by a different door: up the Ottawa from Montreal to the Chaudière Falls, then inland. This would create a second gateway in and out of the region.

Mission understood, the disbanded Ninety-ninth sailed from Quebec on July 28. On the way out of harbour they passed an incoming man-of-war carrying the new governor general, who had been appointed a few weeks earlier. He was Charles Lennox, the fourth Duke of Richmond, the first duke to represent the British Crown in the new colony. In his ducal career to date Richmond had fought a duel with the Duke of York (Richmond shot first and grazed York, who refused to shoot back) and started his own racetrack, called Goodwood, on his estate. To mark the governor general's arrival, there had been a flurry of naming things in his honour throughout the colony — a slew of taverns called the Duke, an epidemic of Richmond Roads. The settlement the Ninety-ninth were about to found would, in the spirit of things, be called Richmond.

For a while the regiment parked at Lachine, at the mouth of the Ottawa River. The stopover turned into a month; rations dwindled like cheese in a mousetrap. Finally thirty men, led by Colonel George Burke, set off as an advance party. Burke was a stolid career soldier of nineteen years who had sold his rank for £1,500 because of "embarrassment in my private affairs," the result of a bad land deal. Burke had fought the Americans at Queenston Heights and at Lundy's Lane. In his pocket he carried a silver snuffbox dented by a bullet in the Napoleonic Wars.

Burke's party came ashore at Randall's landing in mid-August. Robert Randall was not there to meet them; he was back in Cornwall, three years out of jail, fighting to get his stillborn estate back. The acre felt the weight of regimental footsteps as the soldiers wove their way several miles into the bush. Eventually they came to the river that would carry them to their latent settlement; they noted tree stumps cut by axe, the first teethmarks of the lumber trade that would soon dominate the valley. A couple of miles downriver they reached the rapids that marked the site of Richmond, and there they started building.

Two weeks later, the rest of the settlers followed on. This was the most human activity the acre had ever seen, as the bare necessities needed to make a village were unloaded at the wharf — which the migrants started calling Richmond Landing. The families spilt out onto the muddy, thickly treed flatlands, piling up stacks of boxes holding the basic army-issue kit for homestead makers. Philemon Wright was there to meet them, the American who had started a small colony on the opposite side of the river two decades earlier. Wright had been contracted by the British military to supply the settlers with wagons and "fresh beef and flour at the rate of a pound of each per day for each man and woman and in proportion for children, for eight or ten months."

Alongside the acre, the familiar jumble of pioneers in transit grew larger. When they reached Richmond, boxes would be broken open, and the families would receive one each of: the axes and saws needed to turn timber into lumber; the implements to ready soil for planting, and to harvest the rewards; stones for keeping these sharp; twelve panes of glass, combined as preferred to provide light with various opportunities to enter, using the one pound of putty provided; four pounds each of three sizes of nail; a one-size-cooks-all kettle, and some rudimentary bedding. For communal use there were two-handed saws, a grindstone, two sets of carpentry tools, and the promise of a schoolteacher and preacher under the direction of the Society for the Propagation of the Gospel in Foreign Parts, the head and soul respectively of the new Protestant order come to the woodlands.

On that first day, while there was daylight, new noises filtered among the trees. Orders were issued, comments made about the weather, and a word or two said about the beauty of the scenery. There was the rustle of canvas tents being pulled out of packing sacks, and the sound of axe blade biting into virgin trunk. That sound, axe head into living wood, was cousin to the tear of a saw, and hammerhead on nail, the percussive backbeat that marked a change of circumstance for the acre. What nature had packed into the acre for several thousand years was going to be unpacked, with a prolonged ferocity.

The settlers probably took out only a scattering óf trees in the few weeks spent at Richmond Landing, waiting for Burke's road-clearing party to return and announce that the route to the promised settlement was open. They wouldn't have felled the giant pines, just enough maples to clear a tent site and keep the cooking and night fires going. The hundred or so families made camp that first night beneath a new part of the sky. Imagine their dreams that night, and put them alongside the dreams of contemporary tourists asleep in their Gore-Tex tents in the camping ground by the acre.

A mural by the artist C.W. Jefferys fancifully shows the Richmond settlers building the trail they hacked out of the forest. (One of four historical paintings done for the Château Laurier Hotel in 1931, it hung in the bar there for many years but has since disappeared.) The painting has the air of revolutionary, heroic art, full of straining muscular male forearms and backs. In the foreground, an officer and a sergeant in decorated hats are studying plans, their backs to the shirt-sleeved strainers — probably Colonel Burke and a man called Andrew Hill, a grey-eyed Irishman who had enlisted thirteen years earlier. Behind them, women are cooking and washing outside a tent. One of the women may be Andrew Hill's wife, known as Mary or Maria, who was quite a story in her own right. She enlisted in the army as a soldier, trying to hide her gender. The camouflage was discovered, but she was allowed to stay on and nurse wounded soldiers during the war with the Americans.

Rising up from Jefferys's painting is the sound of two men in the background felling and notching trees. The natural empire of the forest is under siege as men move with bacterial progress down the tunnel they are cutting. The great green verticality of the landscape has started tumbling to the horizontal.

Autumn maple leaves, then winter's first snow, fell on the settlers in their haphazard arrangement of canvas tents. Then word came that Colonel Burke had reached the settlement site; gradually the pioneers peeled themselves free of Richmond Landing, family by family, and made the two-day trudge over twenty miles to their new homes. At first they stayed close to the Ottawa River, taking the bush path that led to Bell's farm and then dog-legged down to meet the river at Jerard Chapman's homestead. Chapman had worked for Philemon Wright, then gone off into the woodland to set up on his own.

After Chapman's, the Richmond settlers got onto rafts and went two or three miles by river to a set of rapids. There Burke and his men had raised storehouses to keep winter off the supplies; by late November most of the settlers had staked out their acreage, got four rough log walls around them and a sod roof over their heads, and begun clearing the land for next spring, when they would emerge from their snowbound cocoons, not as soldiers but as farm families.

In 1819 the town's namesake, the Duke of Richmond himself, visited. He dined well with the town's important folk in the brand-new inn. It turned out, however, to be a tragic visit. Bitten several days earlier by a rabid fox, the duke now took ill and died two days later, at Jerard Chapman's farm, on his way to Richmond Landing. His body was taken, in one of Philemon Wright's carts, down the Richmond Road, and he thus had the distinction of being the first dead European to pass the acre.

Over the next few years, the muddy, corrugated trail from Richmond Landing to Richmond itself, dotted with low stumps waiting to be burnt out, became a road. It's marked on a rough map drawn by a Major G.A. Eliot in 1824. The two schoolteachers bound for the Richmond school came down the road in the early 1820s. Their names were Mr. Read and Mr. Enough. At the acre's end of the road, habitation came slowly; at the other end the hamlet of Richmond, like sourdough in an oven, slowly swelled. There was some talk of making it the capital of Upper Canada, but that died away and Richmond never reached glory.

Richmond Landing, however, was now established as the gateway to the interior, an important stop on the growing timber trade route. It was only a matter of time before the acre came up for development.

Days of Occupation
1820–1965

What does a house want?
Laughter, sounds
of love-making, to strengthen
the walls;
> a house
wants people, a permit
to persevere

GARY GEDDES
FROM "WHAT DOES A HOUSE WANT?"

Matter for Speculation

It is a short distance nowadays between For Sale signs. The streets of any town or village wear them like accessories, as the housing lots work through rotating casts of owners. Leave a video camera running for a decade on the corner, play it back at super speed, and the average avenue will sprout For Sale signs like dandelions. Not too long ago, though, you could have hiked from ocean to ocean and never spotted such a sign. It is wondrous to think that the hunting territory of Constant Penency did not see its first For Sale notice until 1820, when my grandmother's grandmother was a young girl. The acre was part of that first sale.

Robert Randall had not been able to hold on to his purchase. For three years, from the moment he stood outside debtors' prison, he sought legal revenge on the men who had put him in. The implement of legal revenge is a lawyer. Randall had already employed the Boulton family, but in fact it was the son, Henry Boulton, who turned round the shotgun of the law that Randall had hoped to use on his enemies, and let off both barrels full in Randall's face. When the smoke cleared, Boulton had taken Randall's acres on the Ottawa River from him, in lieu of the legal fees Randall had racked up trying to hold on to the land.

The final blow came on November 1, 1819, even as the Richmond settlers moved off the acre, leaving behind a scarred landscape. A writ was issued that day by the sheriff of Johnstown District against Randall, stating that everything in Johnstown District that had been Randall's was now

Henry Boulton's. Robert Randall had paid the necessary fees to get a "patent," a grant, on his acreage. He did the paperwork, wrote the promissory note; it was granted to him as part of the great handing out of Canada. But he lost it unfairly.

Almost from the moment it landed in European hands, then, the acre was involved in a land scam, albeit one bearing the highest credentials. Randall was an ironic victim of this one; twenty-five years earlier he had tried bribing several United States congressmen in an attempt to pocket half of Michigan.

Boulton put Randall's former estate up for sale as soon as he was legally able, a year after he got it. When put on the market, land becomes real estate; a *real* was a Spanish coin; the phrase came into common use in the late 1600s. When land is transformed into real estate, the emphasis shifts from its natural gifts to its commercial potential; from greenery to greenbacks.

Any piece of land, be it in Brockville or Burkina Faso, experiences a moment when it is first owned, and a moment when it is first sold. Sometime deep in history this happened for the very first time — land first changed hands — and its frequency has been increasing exponentially ever since. Consider the area now clumsily called Ottawa-Carleton, the administrative corral in which the acre resides. In 1819 no land changed hands there, and there were no real estate brokers. During 1960, 1,088 For Sale signs appeared on the streets, and properties went for an average price of $17,687. In 1994, 7,630 For Sale signs went up, and ninety-nine different real estate firms put them there. The average sale price was $147,543.

The exact wording of the For Sale notice posted in 1820 for the acre is not known, although the notice certainly appeared in the newspaper and was stuck up in general-store windows throughout the region, including the store of William Morris of Perth. The successful buyer would get a mixed blessing. True, the estate had water-power that could be exploited; on the other hand, it wasn't very good farmland. Certainly it could be described as undeveloped, but there was plenty more virgin territory where that came from. They were giving it away free to the military.

At the time of sale, apart from the dock at Richmond Landing, there was not much to hold your attention around the acre. A night on the town would have consisted of a drink in the tavern run by Andrew Berry and the Firths. Maybe Ma Firth, who had come over from Scotland to keep the lumber boys in liquor, would have sold you one of her black otter hats. Then perhaps a visit to the other squatter, Mr. Torry; after that, once round Berry's garden (he had been "seven years a-gardening" in the Royal Artillery) and down to the wharf past the vacant government storehouse, for a stare at the water. A short walk into the woods to answer nature's call would have taken you onto the acre.

The nearest neighbours were the Billings and Dow families to the south on the Rideau. Upriver on the Ottawa six other families were barnacled. They were all fallout, one way or another, from the War of 1812, and they were almost all farming lumbermen or lumbering farmers. Word of the wealth of lumber along the Ottawa had by now floated down to the Americans, and they were increasingly on their way up, axes in hand. Across the river, Philemon Wright and his brood had been felling and squaring timber for twenty years.

The sale was scheduled for December 10, 1820, in the Court House at Brockville, a more developed town to the south on the St. Lawrence River. Some twenty-five people crowded in. No one from Richmond was there, although all the residents had a vital interest in Richmond Landing. Only one man from the neighbourhood of the acre turned out: John LeBreton.

LeBreton already had his eye on Randall's blighted investment. In May 1819 he had written to Randall asking for a couple of acres there, either by straight sale or lease. LeBreton was one of the six neighbours, five miles upriver from the landing. Those five miles, which had to be crossed with any stores that had come from Montreal, bugged him. LeBreton had gone ahead and set up a log storehouse at Richmond Landing and was asking Randall for retroactive control of the land around it. Six months after he sent the letter LeBreton's inquiry was moot, because Randall had had the land snatched from beneath him.

Travelling in the cold bite of early December, LeBreton left his six-hundred-acre land grant, dubbed Britannia (as a jab at the Americanism of Philemon Wright's little republic, Columbia, on the opposite shore), and headed for Brockville, via canoe and horseback. He arrived with sufficient will to buy the land, but insufficient money. He had left the army a captain, after being badly wounded at Lundy's Lane, so his pension was tolerable, but his liquidity was stretched by the investment he had sunk into building Britannia.

Liquidity was not a problem for the region's compact of lawyers, however, and LeBreton knew one — Livius P. Sherwood. Sherwood had the added stripe of being a member of the Upper Canada House of Assembly. A poker player with talent but not enough chips, LeBreton persuaded Sherwood to bankroll him. Sherwood would not attend the auction, but he would take a piece of the resulting action.

Only four men bid for the land, either directly or by proxy: two doctors, LeBreton, and William Morris, the Perth shopkeeper, who had walked the thirty miles to the acre pre-sale to view it. The two doctors dropped out early, and when the price hit £499 Morris backed down. LeBreton had his landing. In the new year, 1821, LeBreton divided the spoils across the middle, and Sherwood took the southern half, farthest from the river. The acre lay in LeBreton's half.

A Troubled Lot

From obscurity thirty years earlier, the acre soon occupied the minds of several famous Canadians. There developed a four-sided wrestling match, with Lot 40 as the prize. In the royal corner, acting as champion for His (new) Majesty George IV, was Lord Dalhousie, out of the Castle, Quebec City, the holder of several titles, including captain general, governor-in-chief of Upper and Lower Canada, and Order of the Bath. In the

I-was-robbed corner was the former American veteran Randall, who had once held the title, but had lost it when he left the ring for seven years to do time. In the present-holder corner, with his promoter Livius P. Sherwood, was the light but quick-tempered Captain John LeBreton. And in the conscientious-objector corner was the quiet man, Constant Penency, who had heard the bell toll but refused to come out and fight.

The first round, featuring Dalhousie and LeBreton, started when LeBreton went to Quebec City shortly after the sale, where Dalhousie lived in the Castle. LeBreton had got a letter issuing the challenge that Lot 40 was needed by the government, and that LeBreton should concede forthwith. Before LeBreton went in with Dalhousie, one of the governor's sidemen, Colonel Francis Cockburn (whose diary is the main record of the death of the Duke of Richmond), took LeBreton for a walk, and wondered if he would take some "wild lands" in lieu of Lot 40. LeBreton shrugged that off, so Cockburn asked him to name a price. LeBreton made the standard move of getting the buyer to name a price first. Cockburn pushed harder, and LeBreton mentioned £3,000, which would have given him a profit, in less than half a year, of 500 per cent.

LeBreton was shown into the Castle drawing room. Dalhousie accused LeBreton of having cheated: he had bought the land in a badly advertised sale, Dalhousie claimed, knowing the government needed it. Now he was flipping the property to make money. Dalhousie wanted it back, and he threatened to use his rank to get LeBreton's military pension cut off. LeBreton stormed out.

Next into the fray was Robert Randall. In July 1820 he was elected to the House of Assembly on a crusader's platform against, naturally, elitism and patronage. While in the assembly, in January 1821, he learnt that his property at the Chaudière had been sold. The man who told him was the representative for the district the acre lay in, none other than William Morris, unsuccessful bidder at the sale. This set Randall off on a round of court appearances.

As his seconds, Randall was able to get help from no less a person than William Lyon Mackenzie, then a rebellious newspaper publisher, and Robert Baldwin, who went on to become the Reformist head of government in Canada West in 1848. Mackenzie's printing press was wrecked one night by a gang that included Henry Sherwood, the son of LeBreton's partner Livius Sherwood. At one point Randall also petitioned Lord Dalhousie for help. It was a potentially interesting political alliance, Randall the Reformist opposed to elitism holding hands with a British lord, but Dalhousie saw in Randall an opening, a way to get Lot 40 into the hands of someone more pliable than LeBreton.

The contest between Dalhousie and LeBreton heated up in the mid-1820s. The spark was the arrival from England of Lieutenant-Colonel John By, a fifty-year-old unemployed military engineer. Lord Dalhousie, who was keen on canals, had plans to adapt the Rideau River, cutting it wider and deeper where necessary, and pasting locks on the various rapids, so that if it became a military necessity, soldiers and supplies could navigate from Kingston at the Lake Ontario end to "sometown" at the Ottawa River end. At that point "sometown" consisted of eighty-three cows, forty-seven horses, and a dozen people. Within a year, however, the citizens of what was already being called the Village of Bytown outnumbered the livestock.

By, who had worked in Canada before, on Quebec's fortifications and on the Les Cèdres canal, got together with Dalhousie in 1826 and did a tour of the area. The Rideau River emptied into the Ottawa via a forty-five-foot waterfall, which made a bypass canal necessary. They surveyed the landscape, trying to decide where to put the canal. There were several ways they could have gone, but the path of least resistance lay in incorporating a branch of the Rideau that cut across a bog and ran along the back of the acre, linking up with the Ottawa River just below the Chaudière Falls at Richmond Landing. Anywhere else would have involved a nasty set of locks and a tidy stretch of canal to get boats down off the cliff and into the river. The problem with taking the obvious route was that somebody already owned it: John LeBreton and Livius P. Sherwood, who wanted Dalhousie to cough up £3,000 for it.

Sticking in Lord Dalhousie's throat was LeBreton's stubborn contention that he hadn't known the government was going to want the acre, and the area around Richmond Landing. Dalhousie was sure that that was precisely why LeBreton had bought it. LeBreton fired off a belligerent, unrepentant letter to Dalhousie in March 1827. Dalhousie replied within five weeks, effectively blowing his lordly nose on LeBreton, accusing him of conduct "not becoming in a British officer." Dalhousie mentioned in the letter the dinner he had attended with the local gentry in Richmond, in 1820, when he'd been doing a lap of honour around the province. LeBreton had been at the meal. The chatter over pipe smoke had turned to the various ways Richmond could prosper. One of the keys to that prosperity was, yes, the building of a government storehouse at Richmond Landing.

Seized by either righteous indignation or guilt (which often look the same) at Dalhousie's slurs, LeBreton began haranguing the VIPs of Richmond, to get them to refute Dalhousie's charge that he was guilty of insider trading. He horsewhipped one of them, challenged another to a duel, and in the end got at least five of them to swear they had no recollection of such a conversation. Whether LeBreton actually had a specific or merely a general inkling that Richmond Landing was going to be boomland is buried with his bones in St. James's Cemetery in Toronto.

Meanwhile, in the same month LeBreton wrote to Dalhousie, 162 assorted military engineers and miners had arrived from England to start work on the canal. Like the Richmond settlers, they camped out, this time on the high ground where Parliament now stands. They were followed by the money to cover the canal expenses — it arrived in barrels, in birchbark canoes — and the purchase of the land needed to build it. A recent act of Parliament gave Colonel By the right to expropriate if he wanted to, so he could have forced LeBreton to hand over, but that must have seemed like an uphill battle. Besides, Dalhousie was loath to give LeBreton one penny; he preferred to get the courts to sort out the ownership question.

The Lot 40 affair came to a grand finale in a court case in 1828. LeBreton and Sherwood believed they had a good thing almost going, and they wanted rumours that their holdings were ill-gotten scotched. Throwing down a challenge to Dalhousie and Randall, they gave eviction notices to the Firths and Andrew Berry, the squatters running the tavern on the lot. The acre's future hung in the balance. Was it going to become Colonel By's canal, Randall's financial salvation, or LeBreton and Sherwood's money-maker?

Randall and Dalhousie reached for a lawyer to help Firth and Berry fight the eviction, a man called Thomas Radenhurst. The idea was to establish Randall's claim, thereby having the sale at Brockville declared illegal; Randall would then sell to the government at a nice price. Colonel By could build his canal, and the sun would shine down.

In Perth, in August 1828, the lawyer Radenhurst stood before temporary Judge Christopher Hagarman. Hagarman normally collected customs duties at Kingston, but the two judges who usually would have heard the case were Chief Justice Sir William Campbell, who was in London chasing down a pension, and Judge Livius P. Sherwood (he had been promoted in 1825), the same Sherwood who was trying to eject the Firths and Berry. On the reasonable assumption that Sherwood would not find against himself, Hagarman was made judge for a day and put in the big chair, for reasons that made impeccable political sense to the Upper Canada old boys' network, of which Sherwood was a member.

Throughout the trial, Hagarman seemed to be a man with a predetermined mission. He wouldn't allow a single sheet of Randall's trunkful of papers to be used as evidence, and he turned a proverbial deaf ear, something he perhaps acquired working for customs, to Radenhurst's plea that "Colonel By required the property for the Government use, for the purpose of the Rideau Canal." On the last day, Hagarman directed the jury to find for Sherwood, which they promptly did. Randall nudged the Firths into an appeal, which was duly heard by none other than Judge Hagarman, now permanent, who decided without too much thought that he had been right in the first place.

Sherwood and LeBreton thus had outright, undisputed title to Lot 40.

It was a hollow victory; a group of landowners made By an offer he couldn't refuse on the other side of town, and work began on the first of the eight locks that today transport the occasional luxury cruiser from Parliament Hill down to the Ottawa River.

Down but not out, Randall continued fighting for his trampled rights, even getting William Lyon Mackenzie to ask questions on his behalf in the assembly, where Randall held his seat till his death. Despite the fact the acre had some heavy-hitters batting for it, however, Randall never won his lands back. He died in 1834, a death that left him still seeking recompense. He is buried in the graveyard for Canadians killed in the Battle of Lundy's Lane, one of the bloodiest battles of the War of 1812. Randall's tombstone bore the inscription "The Victim of Colonial Misrule." With time, ironically, the inscription has faded to read just, "In memory of Robert RANDALL, Esq."

Within a week of Hagarman's decision, LeBreton did what thousands in Ottawa have done since: he put an advertisement in the newspaper, dated August 26, 1828, encouraging purchase of lots in his subdivision, the first such advertisement in Bytown. The subdivision was called the Town of Sherwood, and the wording of the advertisement was as contrived and inflated as the "Paradise Just Two Minutes from Downtown" style of today. The last paragraph read, "The situation is most beautiful and salubrious, being on the south side of the Chaudière Falls, with the Grand Union Bridge abutting on the centre of the front and leading through the main street. It is replete with mill sites, and for commerce no situation on the River Ottawa can equal it. The subscriber is determined as much as possible to confine his sales to persons of respectability."

It was three years after Colonel By's canal builders set up shop that Grand Chief Constant Penency, who had had a look at the advertised situation for commerce on the River Ottawa and didn't much care for what he saw, filed his petition concerning these "incursions." Constant's pleas were written on ice, of course; a thousand people were already living in Bytown. Progress had arrived, and progress is a train with no reverse gear.

Lumbering Along

The business the acre went into, the particular form of progress that afflicted it, was the Ottawa valley timber trade. The trade had been founded in 1800 by the previously mentioned Philemon Wright. Wright was the kind of man who wasn't comfortable in someone else's community; he needed one of his own to live in. By 1795, he had a large, fit family, ambition, and the energy needed to found a dynasty. Now he needed to root out a suitable, unsoiled, solitary piece of land, get his hands into it, and make his wealth.

From his hometown of Woburn, Massachusetts, Wright had made several forays into the Ottawa River valley, canoeing past indifferent woodlands that could be processed, he could see, into commercial potash. He reached the Chaudière Falls on his first foray, knew at first sight he'd found his spot, went home, and tracked down the man who held the grant for the land to the north of the falls. On his 1799 expedition, half the grant now his, Wright and two accompanying Woburners gave the area a serious going over. Assessing the lay of the land wasn't easy: he couldn't see for the trees, so he went up into them. In this extract from his papers, Wright described his aerial surveillance. "I should think we climbed to the top of one hundred or more trees to view the situation of the country." To reach each treetop, they hacked down an adjacent smaller one, organizing its fall so it rested like a ladder against the taller. From their hundred temporary nests, the three men sat as though at table, and

124

discussed — loudly, to cut through the various forces of nature — the merits of the view. Across the river, the wind stirred the leaves of the acre's canopy at Wright's eye level.

In February 1800, Wright lined up eight sleighs on his Woburn estate, a convoy of farm families and lumbermen willing to accept his word that at the other end of a winter journey of several hundred miles there was a better life. Moving is a chore no one enjoys, but this was a chore on a scale most of us never attempt; "a new life" was newer then. In the course of my travels, I have met Yukoners who have done a similar thing: searched out their own acreage, cleared the land, dynamited out the stumps, cut and dressed the walls, grown and sold their own produce to pay for each new labour-saving possession. They would have it no other way, and their sense of place felt more acute, more fully earned, than that of southern Canadians, who mostly move from one ready-made home to another.

Wright's parade of sleighs was packed with five families and twenty-five labourers; horses totalled fourteen, and each family brought cattle. They rode over the snowy roads until the roads ran out, at Lake of Two Mountains. There they slept rough, "having no landlord to call upon us for our expenses, nor dirty floor to sleep upon but the sweet ground." Then they took to the ice on the river.

On the first roadless day, they met an Algonquin family, a man and woman pulling their child in a sleigh, coming the other way. Of the two groups, the Algonquins were the more astonished by the meeting. When his amazement abated, the Algonquin offered to guide Wright's party, using his axe to test the upcoming ice for unsoundness. The Algonquin went six days out of his way to get them to the frozen falls, then returned to resume his own trek, his stock of English words much increased.

The Wright settlers spat on their hands, swung their axes, took out some trees, and made shelter. Wright's arrival was noted by the Algonquins camped at a traditional maple syrup site nearby, and word spread to the surrounding villages. There was an exchange of curiosities: the Algonquins wanted to borrow Wright's newer-model axes, and Wright was given maple syrup and deer meat. A native delegation, including an interpreter, an Englishman married to an Algonquin, visited Wright in March, and put to him a succinct echo of Constant Penency's concerns: where was his right to take trees and land? How far was his clearance likely to extend? How would his settlement affect the hunting? Wright quoted the terms of his grant, threw in some sweet talk about how easy provisions would be to get from him, and went to Montreal and back to get Sir John Johnson to provide written confirmation of his claim, another piece of paper to wave at the Algonquins. That and $30 American got him his settlement — a bargain for what eventually became the city of Hull, though exorbitant when you consider that Manhattan was bought for a mere $24.

The five families and the single men made it through the first winter with only one trip to Montreal for supplies. After the first spring thaw, the land was surveyed, and new members invited to come live in "Wrightstown." The next year the sawmill, the engine of growth of pioneer towns, and the grist mill, the pantry, went up. The power of the falls was diverted to a water-wheel, the town was hooked up to it, and soon there was a tannery, a bark-grinder, and a smithy. To balance his expenses, Wright tried hemp as a cash crop (it was legal then) to sell to the navy for rope, but it didn't return the investment. By 1806 Wright had borrowed and spent $20,000 on raising Wrightstown. He turned to a naturally growing crop — trees — to make some income. Squared, then floated to Quebec City, they might prove salvation. In his journal he wrote, "I then agreed to get some timber ready and try it." From that little acorn of intent grew an enormous industry.

On June 11, 1806, Wright launched the first timber raft, assembled from some thousand trees surrounding the acre, on the Ottawa River. That mother raft, which Wright christened "Columbo," like a trucker naming his rig, was a flat field of around twenty smaller rafts, like Scrabble squares, stapled together with split saplings. Each square, or crib, was made up like a bed, with a mattress of seven hundred logs over which were laid sheets of staves, several thousand, and nine hundred cut boards. In the middle of the raft was a one-room hut with a sandbox fireplace, for cooking and heat; in the room, like mahouts on an elephant, lived the five men who guided the raft down the river with long boards that they wafted, galley style, to steer. It took Wright sixty-two days to reach Quebec City, too many of those days spent repairing damage caused by the river's turbulent personality. He lost one complete crib in the twenty-five days it took to get to the other side of the Long Sault Rapids, and had to go ashore and make another. He sold some boards along the way at settlements, to defray expenses.

Wright had expected the trip to take half that time; being late lost him his buyer for the boards. To rub salt in his wounded enterprise, the fledgling Atlantic Canadian timber market was already in a slump, for two reasons. One was the Atlantic Ocean, which held Britain and Canada considerably apart, and pushed up transport costs to six times the cost of getting timber from the Baltic. The other was Napoleon Bonaparte, who was heading up the latest European land-grab. The British were busy building an extra navy to defeat him, but the Baltic region was closer than Canada, and perfectly able to keep the Admiralty in spars.

It took three months for Wright's luck to change. Napoleon asphyxiated the British shipyards by shutting down the Baltic supply; Canadian timber was in demand again. A British transport ship duly arrived in Quebec (they had doors at the front like modern car ferries), and logs that six months earlier had stood near the acre were soon on their way to take part in a foreign war. Wright no doubt savoured the irony, as he took the British money, of supplying war materials to the same people he had fought against as a young man in the American War of Independence.

Eventually Napoleon was defeated, first by the Russian winter and then at the battle of Waterloo in 1815. By then, the Canadian timber merchants had lobbied hard and persuaded the British government to put a protectionist tariff on foreign timber; exports from Canada, meanwhile, got into Britain free. The lumber business rose sharply, as the trees fell. One hundred thousand tons of wood left Canada for Britain in 1805. By 1819 the tonnage was three and a half times that. Wooden transport ships with forests in their bellies moved like loom shuttles across the ocean.

Although there is no record of it in Wright's papers, his lumberjacks most likely cleared the pines and maples off the acre, the pine for ship masts and the maple for potash. Exactly when this happened, I can't say, but I can narrow it down. By 1816 Wright was sending men a ways down the Rideau River, into its tributaries in search of good trees that could be easily dragged to the water; the Richmond settlers noted the stumps when they arrived three years later. Likewise, when Colonel By arrived to start building the Rideau Canal in 1826, the trees on the present site of the Parliament Buildings had already been thinned. Further, we know the Richmond settlers had to clear trees to make camp at Richmond Landing, so Wright had not cleared off the acre by the summer of 1819. Wright supplied the settlers with wagons and food, so he may well have decided to finish the job they started and strip the landing of its profitable trees. We also know that in 1820 John LeBreton bought the parcel of land containing the acre, and that he complained about people taking trees off it. My money goes on the supposition that Philemon Wright made his money off the acre's trees in the winter of 1819.

We can imagine the labourers Wright had brought from Massachusetts arriving sometime in that winter of 1819 on the opposite snow-covered shore, and the broad axes setting to work. The axes the woodsmen used were manufactured, honed, and sharpened in Wright's own smithy. As the acre was deforested the wood chips from the axes fell where they might on top of the snow, and in springtime formed a loose floor-covering around the stumps, as though a new species of beaver capable of bringing down the forest giants had arrived. An era for the acre, an era that had lasted well over six thousand years, came to an end. Trees were pressed into service as part of the third act of the great "de-resourcing" of Canada — first the fish, then the fur, now the forest. If it is the inevitable fate of all acres, sooner or later, to be press-ganged into the service of human ambition, this acre had done better than most, holding out till 1819.

Once the trees were down, two-handed crosscut saws diced them into logs. Cant hooks, metal quarter-circles with tails on the end that grabbed the logs, enabled the loggers to pick up a log end and leash a chain on it. The logs were dragged by Wright's horses down a skidway to the river's edge, and there they were piled and parked. In the spring thaw, the ice beneath them yielded, and the river's buoyancy made them manageable as they were herded into cribs and the great raft was assembled.

By degrees, with each winter harvest of the forest, Wrightstown flourished, at the approximate rate of two steps forward, one step back. Across the river, Robert Randall made his brief appearance, and left for the debtors' prison in Montreal. By the time the Richmond settlers landed in 1819, Wright had installed himself in a three-storey stone house and started up a brickyard and the vital distillery. Potash, bleach distilled from wood ash, was being exported to Europe. There was surplus wheat in the fields. A boat named, with one eye on public relations, *Britannia* was making regular runs on the river, sharing the run to Montreal with the paddle steamer *Union*.

Wrightstown, like any settlement town, was counted here to stay the day God moved in, and in 1823 work began on the Anglican church. It was finished a year later, and old man Wright was able to say a prayer for the four members of his family who had died, three grandsons and a daughter, all within a year of one another. In 1825, Wright boasted that he took "eight hundred thousand cubic feet of timber from the King's forests." The Chaudière district, future site of the biggest sawmills in the world, was starting to have its day. But on the acre's side of the river, along the southern arm of the horseshoe formed by the Chaudière Falls, it was a slow day coming.

15

Jobs, Jobs, Jobs

ad John LeBreton come into the world in 1779 as a rock, instead of as the son of a ship's captain, he would surely have come as an igneous intrusion. In defence of his property and his reputation, LeBreton was hard as quartz to hammer off his position. Soon after he bought Lot 40 in 1820, increasing his stock of acres to nine thousand, LeBreton filed his complaint with the colonial administrators that trees were being stolen off his land at Richmond Landing. Four years later, he was mugged by lumbermen he caught looting his trees. One of them, LeBreton claimed, was Philemon Wright. After the mugging, he filed another complaint, throwing in charges of trespass for good measure — another first for the acre.

Between complaints, LeBreton was making plans to straddle a narrow southern channel that flanked the Chaudière Falls with a sawmill, and start making money. Simultaneously, he wanted to get the Town of Sherwood going by selling off lots. At this point, 1825, there wasn't much of a reason for anyone to call Sherwood home: no local industry, and the only potential work in town was going to be on the other side of it, around the canal construction. The only three takers for a Sherwood lot were a retired soldier, an American, and a Montreal merchant, each of whom opened a business selling liquor to passing lumbermen. The timber workers were now coming and going around Richmond Landing, augmented by travellers bound for Richmond, frequently enough to give rise to Ottawa's first road, a dirt path called Montreal Street. It roughly paralleled and then clipped the top of the acre.

LeBreton, however, had made an enduring enemy of Lord Dalhousie, and the pockets in Dalhousie's breeches were deeper. Dalhousie, with Colonel By as his front man, set about boxing LeBreton in. He appropriated the land directly to the west and east and earmarked it for future government use. He even appropriated the single acre holding the Firth and Berry tavern, and gave it to them; revenge is a meal best served cold. Dalhousie authorized Colonel By to use timber off the riverbank Crown land for the construction of the canal. LeBreton considered some of it his wood, and he sharpened his pen again. Correspondence began flying between the Colonial Office and LeBreton's. I remember as a kid going to the Exhibition in Ottawa, where they had a pool of water and a log laid across, a few feet above the pool. Competitors shimmied to the middle of the log from either end, pillows in hand, and tried to knock the opponent into the water. While the captain and the earl flailed away in similar fashion, the Town of Sherwood stalled, and Philemon Wright prospered and expanded.

For a time, it looked as though a bridge built across the Ottawa River at the north end of the acre might perk things up. At least the acre would have some north-south traffic, some commerce with Wrightstown. On September 28, 1826, two days after Lord Dalhousie's wife had uncorked a ceremonial shovelful of sod on Barracks Hill to start construction of the Rideau Canal, work on the bridge began; Lord Dalhousie slipped some silver coins under the foundation stone of the first span, hoping the seed-coin would grow to commercial abundance. That span, the biggest of the seven needed to traverse from island to island across the river, was finished three weeks later. At the bridge-opening ceremony, while the three requisite "Hip, hip, hurrahs!" were literally still in mid-hurrah, the span collapsed. The red-faced engineers had it quickly rebuilt, and everyone called it the Chaudière Bridge.

With a bridge up, the Town of Sherwood got off to a spluttering start, with one or two further lots sold. One of Colonel By's engineers, Lieutenant Henry Pooley, built a cedar log bridge in the small gorge beside the acre, to cut down travel time from Wrightstown to the canal site. But until there was work right by the acre, until someone built a mill, it was never going to catch up. The obstacle was the lack of investment needed to solve a major problem for the southern Chaudière region. The falls, a blessing as water-power, was also a major bottleneck for the log rafts floated down the Ottawa River.

Logs arriving at the falls from up the valley were carried overland on Philemon Wright's side of the river and reassembled in calm water further down, in Rafting Bay. This could take weeks. Some crews let the cribs rip right over the falls, a drop of sixty feet; the log bundles somersaulted like gymnasts through the white water, exploding into so many chopsticks. They were strapped together in the bay, which on busy days resembled a vast bowl of log soup. While waiting their turn to get past the Chaudière, the raft crews twiddled their thumbs in the taverns on Richmond Landing, getting up to the usual, casual hooliganism of idle, overrefreshed men. This brought some revenue to the landing, but not the kind that attracts serious capitalists.

Philemon Wright's son Ruggles solved the problem. He travelled to Sweden and Norway to study Scandinavian methods, and in 1829 scooped out a straight-sided channel, enhancing one of the narrow natural chutes the river had already engineered through the islands. The channel was just wider than a standard timber crib, with stone walls. Cribs, lined up at the end of the slide, were let go one at a time and shot through like jubilant croutons, uncrumbled. An entire raft could be disassembled one side of the falls and reassembled the other in a matter of days. Ruggles's slide was a feat of engineering, the first of its kind in Canada, and caused a dramatic boost in the amount of logging in the upper valley.

By the time Ruggles Wright put his slide in, Lord Dalhousie's term as governor-in-chief had come to an end; he was posted to India, and died in his castle in 1838. The Colonial Office held to the spirit of his feud with

LeBreton and arranged financing, in 1836, for a man called George Buchanan to clone Ruggles Wright's timber-slide on the south flank of the falls. This channel had the side effect of washing out LeBreton's plans for diverting the water down a race into his own mill. Complaints duly flew like sparks off LeBreton, to no avail. The channel went through, and the arboreal wealth of the upper Ottawa River valley began to flow around the falls like molasses. Watching the cribs go through the slides became a spectator sport for visitors to Bytown, a participation sport for visiting dignitaries, and a feature story for every passing journalist.

LeBreton was running out of time and money; sixteen years since he had bought Lot 40, and it was still a semi-vacant field. The most action it saw during those years was as an unofficial boxing ring, for the turf wars between the laid-off Irish canal workers — the Rideau Canal was finished in 1832 — and the French-Canadian lumbermen.

The Irish, less skilled as lumbermen than the French but more brutal, used intimidation tactics to make employers take them on. Their tactics included polluting wells, random muggings, burning stables, and, for some reason, cutting off the ears of horses or men and pinning them over a bar. When the French lost patience and fought back, the ends of the Chaudière Bridge became regular battlegrounds; quite a few Irishmen ended up riding the falls down to Rafting Bay. It took several riots and twenty years for the town to settle down.

Amid this civic confusion, LeBreton had to make up his steam-filled mind either to launch another lawsuit against the Crown, claiming financial harassment, which was how Robert Randall had lost the Chaudière lands in the first place, or to put down his pillow and climb back to his end of the log. While he pondered his future, the patient, determined Ottawa River was finally able to wash away, in the spring runoff of 1836, the bridge that had stood for eight years at the end of the acre. For the next seven years a one-horse-powered ferry, the horse walking on a treadle linked to paddle wheels, was the only commercial link between Wrightstown and the acre.

LeBreton's fighting spirit seems to have been washed away too. He pulled back from Lot 40 and concentrated on developing his holdings up-river, at Britannia. He started a family. He seems, not surprisingly, to have had a thing for bridges. In 1832 he had tried building one of ice at Quebec across the St. Lawrence, and for a while he corresponded with another bridge enthusiast about the idea of putting a span across the Ottawa. It was another in his series of pipe-dreams; he might have done better if he had thrown tobacco into the falls, to appease the Asticou spirit.

The bridge that stayed up across the Ottawa was built of iron in 1843; it was the first suspension bridge in Canada. It permanently joined Wrightstown and Bytown at the hip. It was also a suture between the two Canadas, which were thus no longer separated by the Ottawa River. It was christened the Union Bridge, and in the course of its construction, the land gave up a secret.

The support piers for the Union were built of stone blocks mortared together, and the sand for the mortar came from nearby, to the east of the acre. It was pure, deep sand; as the bridge builders dug down into it, they began to uncover the jumbled remains of human skeletons. Edward Van Courtland, a doctor and natural historian living a bone's throw from the uncovered grave, was fetched. Van Courtland spent two days at the burial site, but the only thing he published about the bones that still exists was written ten years later. He was maddeningly vague in stating exactly where the bones were found, but gave a fine description of what the site revealed. There were twenty bodies, arranged haphazardly like pick-up sticks, many of them children's. None of the bones showed any signs of attack, and there were no arrow heads or broken weapons. Lying underneath the bones was a crimson carpet of sand, stained by the red hematite dye the owners of the bones used as decoration. When the flesh had decomposed, the indelible stain had dropped through, or was trapped in the skulls below (as the ink from contemporary tattoos will be when this generation of body painters goes to its grave).

Mixed in with the bones, Van Courtland noted, were a two-foot-long stone club, a stone hatchet, and a beaver skin scraper. Off to the side of the other bones, Van Courtland found an intact skeleton, placed there with some care, and walled around with stones. The skeleton was, so Van Courtland wrote, "of a Chief of gigantic stature." Lying in the middle of his chest was a sandstone boulder the shape of the sun. It was, in fact, a piece of body armour, sewn into a bag and strapped on to deflect arrows. All of the teeth in all of the skulls were perfect.

What had the bridge builders unearthed? The answer is unknowable. The hard contents of the grave are lost; all that exists of them now is Van Courtland's report. Van Courtland, a man who had a habit of flicking off the caps of schoolboys as they passed him, had at one time one of the best private museums in Canada. It's hard to imagine that at the time he didn't move some of the bones across the street to his four-storey stone house. But nothing of his collection has survived into common knowledge.

I wonder if Van Courtland wasn't describing the family cemetery of the Algonquins who considered that part of the shore their hunting territory. Judging from the tools found among the skeletons, these people passed on well before the Europeans arrived with a new range of kitchen and battle ware. Other similar burial sites contained jumbles of bones, as the ossuary was repeatedly reopened and a new member added to the company of corpses. Further, this was not a mass grave for the losers of a battle, because the bones showed no evidence of wounds. No enemy would bury a chief that respectfully. Also, the site is near a spiritual centre, a powerful waterfall to which the woodlanders regularly offered tobacco in the *petun* ceremony. The sand was easily dug and redug.

What the men of 1843 found, I suspect, was an extended family plot. I'm inclined to think that some of the feet from those disinterred bones once walked on the acre. When I walked from the likely site of the ossuary, now occupied by the National Library, to the centre of the acre, it took me three minutes; a powerful sense of story, of walking in very different footsteps, came on me.

Moving On Up

John LeBreton no doubt heard of the find of old bones during construction of the Union Bridge, but it was the activities of the living, the boost such a bridge would give traffic flow across the Flats, that got him going again. He paid for two road extensions to link Pooley's Bridge with the west end of Upper Town — then the richer, more English side of town to the west of the Rideau Canal — which was filling up. To advertise his lots for sale, LeBreton tried a couple of textbook real estate ploys. One involved an auction, and the other, in March 1843, a lottery, with tickets for £15; each ticket would get you an acre, although you didn't know which one. Both these schemes collapsed like the early Chaudière bridges. Undaunted, on opening day for the Union Bridge, in August 1844, LeBreton and his agent, the lawyer Augustus Keefer, set up a tent on the acre and, while clients sipped champagne, barked the virtues of the Flats — the opportunities for growth, the views, the ease of transport away from town, much the same virtues now attributed to Ottawa.

The fact that LeBreton served champagne with lunch, and not porter, hinted at the demographic he was after as first residents of the acre. He wanted upmarket, well-heeled subscribers to a Protestant god. Bytown was indeed starting to pull in people with money to risk on a new town's growth. On the eve of LeBreton's vindication, however, his wife died, in 1847. He was in his late sixties. He retired to Toronto and died there a year later, leaving his remaining holdings on the Flats to his five nieces: Emily, Sophia, Louisa, Jane, and Elizabeth. It was they who began turning his legacy into cash.

The Union Bridge, a bridge to last, put Bytown and Wrightstown in firm communion. It conveyed steady traffic past the acre; the wheels and feet pounding between the Union Bridge and Pooley's Bridge cut a path diagonally across the Flats, and before long the path deserved a name. Road names are the pips of history's fruit, and in honour of the man whose orders had helped found Richmond Landing, and whose corpse had passed over it in a cart in 1819, this pip was dubbed Duke Street. Duke ran exactly then as it does today, the original footprints hidden now beneath generations of gravel and asphalt, like layers of weatherstain on old barnboard. Duke Street was the hem of the acre, binding it in place.

By 1853, there were seventeen houses along Duke Street, which now boasted a plank sidewalk — a boardwalk — and a multipurpose dwelling that did quadruple service as church, school, Orange Lodge, and theatre. This outbreak of inhabitation brought with it an outbreak of regulation. The laws of nature, until now sufficient to deal with behaviour on the acre, were amended by laws of order. A lengthening list of by-laws (*by* comes from the Old Norse word *byr*, meaning town) were laid on the acre. Scrolling through them in the old council minute-books is like reading a shorthand description of frontier social history; like looking into one of those busy Bruegel paintings of village life in the sixteenth century.

The first meeting of incorporated Bytown's town council, with man-on-the-make Edward Malloch present to represent West Ward, the ward the acre was in, took place March 11, 1850. It decided on the rules of order for future meetings and noted that it had the power to organize a police force, appoint assessors, purchase land, levy taxes, light the streets, keep them clean, and repeal and amend any by-laws it might pass. The first by-laws affecting the acre were passed at the second council meeting a month later. Council agreed that the free-spirited "Swine, Horses, and Cattle running at large" about town were to cease doing so. Next, they set about taxing, licensing, or regulating anything essential or fun: "Victualling and Beer Houses"; anything used to transport "High Wines, Whiskey or Beer"; "Skittle Alleys, Pigeon Holes [a game of throwing bean-bags into holes], Bagatelle Tables, Menageries, Circuses, Puppet Shows, Jugglers, Games of Chance, Livery Stables, Markets, Butchers, Gas Pipes." They bought into life a fire department (which would see much action) and a common school. They passed a by-law to prevent "Geese, Turkeys, and other Fowl from running at large," forcing them to copy their passive farm-yard cousins.

In its first four years of sitting, council passed 118 by-laws, 118 little picket fences around just about any human doing you cared to name. Then, in February 1855, the town of Bytown became the city of Ottawa, and the by-laws began to multiply like horseflies.

(On the matter of by-laws, every town, I believe, should each year allow one private citizen, drawn at random, to devise a by-law of his or her own, which council would vote on. A similar thing to the parliamentary practice of private member's bills. Mine would allow for instant fines for anyone talking during the movie in the cinema. The answering of a cellular phone call would see that patron barred for a year.)

Logged

By 1850, wood was gold in the Ottawa Valley; the wood rush was on, and John LeBreton had died just in time to miss it. Vast tracts of land, fiefdoms really, were being bought up in the backwoods in the upper valley, and a handful of resource capitalists were set to make towering fortunes. The village of LeBreton Flat (the name it bears in old newspaper ads) and the neighbouring Chaudière (the collective name for the industrial district on the islands in front of the falls) already had logs pouring into several sawmills, boards flowing out the other end like strudel, and millworkers' homes mushrooming up within walking distance. The population in and around Bytown in 1850 was about eight thousand, and the fields were growing houses at a fair clip. Within four years the town could boast a one-thousand-seat theatre, and fill it.

In the mid-nineteenth century, if you wanted to gauge a town's prospects, you counted the branch offices of the major banks. There were four in Bytown by then, a healthy sign. The Montreal, the British North America, the Upper Canada, and the Quebec had all established one-man outposts. The personality of the one man was the bank's greatest asset, and the most popular at the time was the agent for the Quebec, a Mr. Hillier Vavasour Noel, who filled the post for forty-eight years. He rented a small office in a mill just off the acre, and for several years he had no safe. Each afternoon he walked down Duke Street carrying his cashbox to his home on Sparks Street, where he slept with it under the bed.

Bytown got a new mayor in 1852, a man called Richard William Scott, a lawyer and a town booster. (Scott's descendants founded what is presently the biggest law firm in Ottawa; as if to prove that history is its own small world, my father went to work there.) By now it was clear that the Americans were not going to re-invade Canada, and Scott, knowing that a town does not survive by threat of war alone, was eager to give Bytown something major to do other than maintain the Rideau Canal. America's unarmed army, its entrepreneurs, was invited to come and grab a piece of the arboreal action.

Soon after his election, Mayor Scott got a visit from a Captain J.J. Harris of Lake George, which runs along the New York–Vermont border. Harris ran a steamer there. While in Bytown, Captain Harris was wooed as a potential investor; he was wined and dined, and promised that if he rounded up some American friends and considered purchasing "hydraulic" lots on the Chaudière, "good will" would flow. The good will was a guarantee that there would be no adverse bidding at the land auction. A sale, more of a handover really, was set up, and Harris and his fellow predatory Americans — Henry Bronson from Painted Post, New York, William Perley, and Gordon Pattee — arrived and bought lots at one shilling over the price of £50. There was no adverse bidding.

Thirty-three-year-old William Goodhue Perley promptly upped stakes and moved to Bytown, bought land on the acre at the north end — the acre's first rich man — and built a one-and-a-half-storey house. The house quickly gained a two-storey extension, making it suitably bigger than most other houses on Le Breton's Flat, as it was then called. The historical preamble in the Ottawa street directory for 1865, written with a lost eloquence, states that in 1853, there were only about twenty-five such stone mansions. The directory writer listed the various stones taken from nearby quarries thus: "The prevailing material has been cut limestone, for shops, but lately the Ohio stone has been introduced and some shops are going up of it. Black

Trenton, with Nepean sandstone dressing, for gentleman's houses, chiefly in the Tudor style, is much in vogue, and the effect is very pleasing."

W.G. Perley was already a wealthy man when he moved to the acre in 1853 from Lebanon, a thriving New Hampshire town. He had started in the lumber business as a teenage clerk, bought land in northern New York State, took the trees off it, and fed them to the busy construction industry in Boston and New York. By 1850, the best timber had been farmed out; Perley and his partner Gordon Pattee started looking around for fresh supply. That was around the time that Captain Harris offered to cut them in on the Chaudière deal. Perley and Pattee headed north and set themselves up, as their letterhead stated, as "Fine Lumber Manufacturers." Perley's timing in coming to Bytown was especially good; the year after, the Canadians and North Americans signed a deal allowing Ottawa valley lumber into the States duty-free. Perley leased some substantial pine forest up the valley, and built his mill on the Chaudière.

The river and the logs entered at the rear, the river powered the saws, and the boards were stacked like treasury bills all over the Flats, alongside the stacks of fellow mill owners John Booth, John Rochester, John Perkins, and Philip Thompson. The novelist Anthony Trollope visited the Chaudière and Le Breton's Flat in 1861, and remarked: "On the Ottawa side of the bridge there is a brewery, which brewery is surrounded by a huge timber-yard. This timber-yard I found to be very muddy, and the passing and repassing through it is a work of trouble; but nevertheless let the traveller by all means make his way through the mud, and scramble over the timber, and cross the plank bridges which traverse the streams of the sawmills, and thus take himself to the outer edge of the woodwork over the water."

The growth of Perley's lumber fortune resembled the trunk of a red pine. It rose straight towards the sunshine of large profits, and didn't branch out much. Perley put some money into orange orchards in California and Florida, perhaps for the joy of visiting them in winter, and towards the end of his life he bankrolled a man called Marshall Wheeler, who invented and patented in Europe a better light bulb that never saw the light of day. Apart from that, Perley was a textbook nineteenth-century resource capitalist; a good place to him was somewhere full of plums he could put his thumb in. He obeyed the number-one rule in achieving great colonial wealth: he got there as the party was starting, and he devoted his working life to drawing a profit from control of something people needed. Almost everything he did when he left the front door of his fine stone house was devoted to making lumber as cheaply as possible, and selling it to people for the most it would fetch, with as few obstacles to that equation as money could buy.

By 1865, the Perley and Pattee mills were churning out 16 million board-feet of lumber a year. Laid end to end (a tedious task), those board-feet could make a boardwalk that stretched from Bytown to London, England. Most of that lumber actually went to the United States, to make the walls and floors of New York's new buildings. Through ups and downs in the market, Perley's output from his mills never dipped, and that 16 million became 70 million by the time he died in 1890.

Lady Aberdeen, one of those travelling Scottish ladies from the old country who came to see how the new colony was getting along, stopped in Ottawa in 1890. She strolled on the terrace at the back of the Parliament Buildings and looked westward towards the acre. In her log she noted that she could see "thousands and thousands of huge piles of sawn planks and when you go down amongst them, you walk through them as though through narrow streets of high buildings, and you wonder how there can ever be enough demand for all this wood."

The task that occupied Perley more than any other was making sure he could get his lumber out of Ottawa. His transportation solutions were a major part of linking the acre to the rest of Bytown, the rest of the valley, and the rest of the continent. His initial problem was to get his product across town to the shipping stations on the Rideau Canal, and to the Ottawa and Prescott Railway. The railway age had begun in 1830, when the Englishman George Stephenson had sent his coal-hauling steam loco-

motive chugging at an average fourteen miles per hour between Liverpool
and Manchester. For the thirty years since then, people had been travelling faster than horses, an exhilaration that had spread worldwide. But
railways cost money to build.

Perley's solution was to form a consortium to give Ottawa its first
urban transit system, using the compromise of horse-drawn streetcars,
which ran on rails. Two horses could pull close to fifty people or their equivalent weight in lumber; after the tracks were laid in 1866, residents of the
acre got to watch the straining workhorses of the Ottawa City Passenger
Railway Company go past their windows all day, steamy breath pulsing out
of their nostrils. A year later Perley, as part of a separate consortium, solved
problem number two: getting supplies to the lumber camps up the Ottawa
valley. Perley went by water this time, and in 1868 he founded the Upper
Ottawa Steamboat Company. The early steamboats were like river tractors,
wooden sidewheelers with pencil-thin chimneys. Only one remains in service on the river today, a rich man's toy lovingly restored.

Problem number three took a bit more solving. Several Chaudière
lumber barons, Perley included, were anxious to control how their product got to the American border, at Vermont. Prime Minister Sir John A.
Macdonald's hiking of export tariffs around 1875 had miffed the barons;
they wanted to get production costs, like a well-trained dog, to lie down
and stay. The answer was to own their own railway.

By now, the railway system in Ottawa was well established. The first
train, pulled by the steam engine *Oxford*, rode into Bytown on December
25, 1854, at five o'clock. The last link, a bridge over the Rideau, wasn't
finished, and passengers took a ferry and walked into the station in the
Lowertown district, the working-class, Irish/French side of the tracks, to the
east of the canal. The Ottawa and Prescott Railway joined Ottawa to the
Grand Trunk, which ran along the St. Lawrence between Montreal and
Toronto. The Ottawa and Prescott was never a big success; it ran slowly
enough for kids to jump on and sell berries, and stopped to let people off
whenever they felt like it. It went broke, and the St. Lawrence and Ottawa

Railway Company took its place. The St. L and O ran a line to the Chaudière in 1871; at the terminal they built a passenger station on Broad Street, where it met Duke Street. Within a decade four other companies, with those wonderful join-the-places names, had trains steaming in and out of Ottawa.

To build his railway, Perley pooled wallets with John Rudolphus Booth, a Canadian and the biggest timber baron in the valley, a Vermonter called George Noble, and J. Smith, the governor of Vermont; together they started the Canadian Atlantic Railway. In 1879, four years after he had become a naturalized Canadian, Perley bought up some defunct railway charters and construction of the CAR began; in 1888 the rails reached Rouse's Point on the American border. The Canadian Atlantic Railway, with its terminal right in the heart of Ottawa, was an immediate financial success. To get to his mills at the Chaudière, Perley ran a branch line along the back of the acre, down what had been Britannia Terrace. This steel spine behind the acre was never torn up, merely buried; in the corner of the acre nearest Pooley's Bridge the rails have broken through in a thin rusted strip, like a double-underlining of a bygone era.

Perley's last hurrah was to become a member of Parliament for Ottawa, for the sole purpose, apparently, of fighting free trade between Canada and the States, which he saw as the ruination of "young nations." He favoured protectionism in general, and protection of the lumber industry and subsidy for the Canadian Atlantic Railway in particular. In the 1882 election, he lost the nomination battle for the Liberal-Conservative Party (a party named in the tradition of political oxymorons, like Progressive Conservative) to a much younger man, which rattled his branches, and he fought back. He became a shareholder in *The Empire*, a Conservative newspaper in Toronto, and used its editorial pages to push his own worthiness as a candidate. In 1887 he did get elected, and he served for three unremarkable years, making one speech to do with lumber. He became ill quite suddenly in early 1890, took to his bed at the end of March with gangrene, and died at four-thirty on the morning of April 1, in his grand mansion on Wellington Street, a few blocks from the acre and his first Ottawa home. The newspaper headline summed him up as having had "AN UNEVENTFUL BUT SUCCESSFUL LIFE."

Perley was a taciturn man; his real business was business. There is little trace of his inner life; he left a particularly thin ghost. The few details about him I could find are gleaned from the handful of bills still waiting to be settled at his death. It seems he had a liking for macaroons, and a weakness for fine French china. He was a gentleman farmer in his un-business moments, both in his native New Hampshire and on thirteen ver-dant acres outside Ottawa, on the Richmond Road. (The farm was snapped up by an archbishop after Perley's death.) He could afford the best doc-tor in town, George Logan, who advertised as a "homeopathic physician, surgeon, accoucheur [the old name for an obstetrician] and sole propri-etor of the Ottawa Turkish Bath."

Perley's funeral was described in the press as "one of the most largely attended that has ever passed through the streets of Ottawa." The papers put the number of carriages following the hearse at 2,249, an aston-ishing number that hints at funerals being a form of theatrical entertain-ment in the last century. No doubt the town was also celebrating its own municipal success, and the hand Perley had played in it. At the church his partner in the Canadian Atlantic Railway, John R. Booth, was one of the pallbearers. (Three years later Booth bought Perley's mills and rail-road holdings, making him owner of the biggest sawmills in the world. They promptly caught fire and burnt down, and did so again in 1896, 1900, and 1903.) Booth's tribute to his fellow baron was a hollowed-out log filled with flowers.

Wired

While Perley's empire had grown, and the acre had been put to work, the century around it had been reshaped by a revolution in power. The year after the steam train had chugged between Liverpool and Manchester, the Englishman Michael Faraday, the electric motor already under his belt, made working models of the dynamo and the transformer. These led to the hydroelectric power station, which in turn freed industry from its need to be alongside running water.

Across the landscape electrons began running down wires, between poles, and through the walls of factories and telegraph offices. Just as timber had been exploited for profit by the Perleys and the Booths, electricity was exploited by a new genus of capitalist. One of their number was born on the acre. In 1855, three days after the summer solstice, John and Honora Ahearn, who had moved in next door to William Perley's house at the north end of Duke Street, had their fourth and final son, Thomas. John Ahearn had left Ireland two years earlier and become head blacksmith on the Rideau Canal maintenance crew. Thomas's was one of the first recorded births on the acre, and he became the most widely known person from it. Born a hundred years later he might well have become a software baron, a high-tech zillionaire. As it was, he electrified Ottawa.

Thomas was a member of the first generation that grew up knowing Ottawa as the capital of the province, later the Dominion, of Canada. When Thomas was two, Queen Victoria was asked to settle the capital question, which had become a pin-the-tail-on-the-donkey competition between the major cities in Upper and Lower Canada. Like cities competing for the right to host the Olympics, Toronto, Quebec, Montreal, and Kingston sent lobbyists to London to turn the Queen's head. Ottawa didn't bother, hoping its facts spoke for themselves. Because it wasn't any of the other competitive, jealous bigger cities; because it wasn't near the American border; because it was a French-English mixture, and because it was on the border of the two Canadas, Ottawa, on December 31, 1857, got the job. The Americans thought it, from Canada's point of view, an excellent choice, because if they did invade again, the American soldiers would be "lost in the woods trying to find it," as one Washington newspaper editorial stated, commenting on the choice.

At age fifteen, Ahearn got his first job, in a branch telegraph office tucked away in the mills near his home. He worked for barter, running messages in exchange for lessons in keying. He became an operator, and worked in the telegraph office at the House of Commons, sending parliamentary decisions down the wire to their relevant victims. He got to rub gartered elbows with the elite he would one day join, among them Sir John A. Macdonald.

After a stint with Western Union in New York, Ahearn came back to the acre and switched wires, becoming the manager of a local telephone company. He formed an electrical equipment company when he was twenty-seven, along with the manager of a rival telephone firm, a man called Warren Soper. (They were both former telegraph operators. For amusement, they worked up a parlour trick of apparent mind-reading by winking Morse code at each other.)

The job that put Ahearn and Soper on the map — or more accurately across it — was a contract to rig up the telegraph equipment from ocean to ocean for the Canadian Pacific Railway. This took them, as it were, from playing clubs to doing stadiums. With the profits from that contract, they looked around for a niche, an embryonic technology to move into. They found not one but several, most of them based on innovative ways to employ electricity. In 1887 Ahearn rounded up a posse of investors and started an electric company that lit the first light bulbs in Ottawa. He ran a circuit of 123 bulbs out onto Le Breton's Flat, into homes on the acre. With a push of a button on the wall, corners of rooms were illuminated for the first time, and families saw each other in a different light. Taking the idea outdoors, Ahearn electrified the streetlamps.

Almost as soon as steam railways began crossing the countryside, the idea arose of urbanizing them, of running rails down the middle of city streets. Before electrification, Manhattan had a horse-drawn tramway running on raised rails, carrying forty-six New Yorkers per tram. Stage two was to run them on electricity, which a man called Ernst Siemens did in a Berlin suburb in 1881. The electrified streetcars worked fine in snowless cities, but they clogged up in northern fridges like Canada. As late as 1890, the residents of the acre were still getting about in the horse-drawn, dilapidated wagons that ran between the Chaudière and the Rideau Falls. They were operated by a conductor, who handed the reins over to a passenger whenever it came time to collect the fares.

Thomas Ahearn solved the snow problem by putting a large whirling brush like a floor polisher under the trolleys, meanwhile using the electricity drawn from overhead to heat the well-muffled passengers, replacing the woodstove and straw on the floor. Ahearn installed this apparatus on the electric streetcar service he inaugurated in June 1891. At age thirty-six, already a substantial figure, Ahearn, the mayor and council seated behind him in rows like fairground ducks, drove the lead car of the first electric street railway in Canada, the second in North America, through a tunnel of applauding citizens. Ahearn and Soper promptly went into production of these streetcars, and with each successive visit to his parents' house on the acre, Ahearn was a richer man.

The streetcars were the moving force in the redesign of cities — they made suburbs possible. Before them, the workplace and the place of residence had to be within walking distance of each other, leaving enough time between walks to get in a full day's work. The roof of your home and the roof of the factory that employed you were commonly within sight of each other. Take the streetcar, when it arrived, and work could be several miles away, unseen and out of mind at the evening dinner table. Ahearn's Ottawa Electric Street Railway Company sent its catheter-like rails out into the rural edges of Ottawa, to Ottawa South and east to the Experimental Farm, and housing divisions grew up alongside. Ahearn was one of the investors in the eastern extension — in an early example of the naming of subdivisions after the things eradicated by their construction, it was called Hintonburgh, after the farm it was built on.

As well as getting people to work, the streetcars could carry them on their days off to the rural amusement parks that became an outlying feature of streetcar cities. Ahearn's company, together with Holland Brothers, a land development company that teamed up with Ahearn to form the Ottawa Land Association, got in on this innovative way of providing both the ride, and something to do at the end of it, when they opened the West End Park on Holland Avenue in the spring of 1896. The de Champlain family, living at 79 Duke Street, might well have taken a ride out to the park that summer, as the father, Auguste, was a professional photographer. From the Booth Street tram station it was a twenty-minute journey; the avenue leading to the park was lit with electric bulbs, and arc lamps brightened the nightly acrobatic displays and band concerts. Surely Auguste, out of professional curiosity, must have tried to attend, on July 21, the *pièce de résistance* of the season: the Canadian commercial debut of Edison's Vitascope moving picture apparatus, and only the second time Canadians had seen moving pictures. Gazing up at the canvas screen, Auguste would have seen but not heard, among a variety of wonders, the Niagara Falls, waves on the ocean, and a kiss.

Ahearn pushed on to become the first Ottawa millionaire who made his money in something other than timber. He was a utilities mogul; with electricity and urban transport in his pocket, he made a Monopoly move and snapped up the Ottawa Gas Company, amalgamating it with his electrical business into the Ottawa Light, Heat and Power Company. His career never lost current after that, and he kept adding firsts to his name, as though collecting them in a trophy case. He reputedly invented the first electric stove, which he installed in the Windsor Hotel. In 1899, he drove the first freewheeling electric car in Ottawa. Leapfrogging ahead of our chronology for a moment, I can add that he made the first telephone call between Canada and England, in 1926, and the first national radio broadcast a year later, which he accomplished by calling in favours at Bell and AT&T, establishing a continental chain of radio masts, and braiding the country together with radio waves. Ahearn died in 1938, four days into his eighty-fourth year, with a fleet of directorships, a seat on the Privy Council, and a son in Parliament.

There were still streetcars in downtown Ottawa when I was a boy, in the mid-1950s. We lived in a new suburb called Urbandale Acres, and I rode my bike through the building sites on the other side of the street, out to the fields. We took a bus downtown to shop, but when we got off there was always a streetcar in view, like a runaway train carriage trying to find its engine. The last one to collect fares ran on May 1, 1959, and three days later there was a parade of all the streetcars, like circus elephants on a farewell tour of the ring, with twenty-five thousand people to see them off. A year later we moved to Liverpool, England. When I came back in 1978 to visit the places of my youth, even the rails were gone; the streetcars were extinct.

Gains and Losses

By the turn of the nineteenth century, the acre was full. In fifty short years it had gone from boulevard to strip mall, from a handful of stone-block, treed residences to a solid line of stores and trades, manned by proprietors sporting a full hand of global names, from McDougal to Sigouin to Kasouf to Mazza, all dedicated to servicing the workers whose livings were pegged to the railyards, the sawmills, and the foundries of Le Breton's Flat. The acre was lit, plumbed, and connected to the world and, as of January 1, 1889, when the neighbouring boroughs of Stewarton, Rochesterville, Orangeville, and Mount Sherwood were annexed to the ever-growing amoeba of Ottawa, it was no longer the edge of town.

The acre had gained much, but much had gone to make room for the accoutrements of progress. Trees and wildlife had backed off, reduced but not eradicated; some things were gone for good. The most spectacular extinction was that of the passenger pigeon, the long-tailed, blue-hued bird that had assisted in vegetating the acre after the retreat of the Champlain Sea. The drop in numbers was so steep that thinking about it causes vertigo; it's impossible not to see its demise as a fable for the price a landscape must pay, when humans get a taste for its riches.

The woodlanders in the Ottawa valley netted passenger pigeons simply by throwing a net into a tree in which they were roosting; it was almost like fishing upward into a school of salmon. The French and the British blew grapeshot into the solid bird mass, bagging thirty or more bodies with one blast. There are reports of settlers standing on hilltops and simply knocking pigeons down with sticks like tennis balls as they passed over. The slaughter was vigorous, but it wasn't enough to diminish the pigeon legions. A migrating flock could still take the better part of a day to pass over a rubber-necking Canadian. Naturalists' reports tell of hunters gunning down a fast dinner on Le Breton's Flat by firing overhead without even taking aim. The turning point for the pigeon was 1850, and the deciding factor was the railways.

As the cities grew, so did their appetite for squab. Squab is young passenger pigeon, considered a cheap delicacy. The railway network up to the Great Lakes, of which Perley and Booth's Canadian Atlantic was one link, provided a transport system that could bring pigeons to cities, especially New York, as fast as the cities could eat them. In one year, 1869, one county in Michigan alone shipped seven and a half million birds to New York. A quarter of a million squab left just one town in Michigan in one day in 1860. These were birds that had never reached reproductive age, and the species laid only one egg a year. The population collapsed. By 1890 they were gone from the Ottawa valley, and by 1900 they were gone from the wild altogether; a few lived on in captivity, and the last one died in 1914.

The passenger pigeon had been taken from 4 billion to zero in a single lifetime. In that same lifetime, the census on the acre had gone from zero people to close to two hundred, all packed into their coops, filling the street with their chores and pleasures.

Ground Zero

Sooner or later, every Canadian city, as it grew out of the bush, was hit by fire. A street-razing blaze was almost a rite of passage for the young towns made of wood, surrounded by woods, and serviced by lousy water supplies. Often as not, the fires were self-inflicted: the settlers burnt out tree stumps the size of dinner tables, they used fire to clear away the bush to make fields, and clearance fires often got out of hand. Domestic stoves and chimneys didn't have to meet insurance or emission standards. Nature was not above the occasional blaze herself; forest fires sparked by lightning were a fact of life for the woodlanders long before the Europeans arrived, with new ways of making an ash of things. Sometimes, just a street or two would be lost to the flames. Other times, a fiery disaster would knock the teething settlement all the way back to a charcoaled zero, and the town builders would have to wipe off their blackened faces and start again. In 1825, in the Miramichi region of central New Brunswick, a fire wiped out millions of acres, 160 people, and a Noah's ark of wildlife. Twenty years later, fire left half the population of Quebec City homeless; Montreal followed suit seven years after that, in 1852, when 1,100 homes went up in smoke.

Spring, the season of rising hopes, comes early to Ottawa in 1900; business and the trees along Duke Street are blooming. This is a special spring, the first of the new century. Just after sunrise on April 26, the northerly wind is picking up in the warm sunlight. It's Thursday, and the workers in the first shifts at the mills are coming out of the boarding-houses, out of the Couillard and Occidental Hotels, and stepping into Mrs. Noonan's and Mrs. Roy's restaurants for a cheap breakfast. At 27 Duke Street, once the home of Mr. Clairvoyant the carpenter, Mr. Fabien Robert is pausing on the doorstep, surveying the neighbours, before walking to the streetcar that will take him uptown to work.

Mr. Robert turns left into the street, giving his back to Rochon's plumbing store. The burst-pipe season is over for the plumbers, Mrs. Kipp and Mr. Rochon, but the foundry at the back of Rochon's store is wrestling noisily with heat and metal. Next door, the Venturas, as well as Mrs. Karam and the D'Amours, are banking their fruits on the boardwalk, while the rest of the D'Amour family tend to the cab horses.

By the time Mr. Robert reaches the intersection with Idol Lane, Hall the harness-maker on its corner, he has passed several restaurants and grocers; "the Flats" (as the area became known after annexation) has a high share of single, hard-worked men. Once across Idol Lane, past the conviviality of the Occidental Hotel (from which wafts the perfume of locally brewed booze), Mr. Robert can, if he chooses, outfit himself with new shoes, a new suit, a photographic portrait from de Champlain's, a fresh haircut, and a bottle of liquor. All this before he reaches the end of the street. At the far end of Duke, where it meets Fleet, the men and horses in the No. 1 Fire Station are at ease.

Gradually, towards noon, all eyes on Duke Street are drawn to the opposite side of the river, to the huge black cloud of smoke forming over Hull. The flames beneath it are feeding voraciously on the wooden houses. It's not the first hell-cloud to rise over the lumber-yards, but this is of a size to eat the world. Though the fire has been burning only an hour, word is coming back across the bridge that the Hull firefighters, official and unofficial, are already in retreat, abandoning their hoses to burn up like lamp wicks. The Hull firemen can only watch as the fire bursts through windows and doors, ignoring the holy pictures hastily nailed to the front door in the hope that divine intervention will spare the home. A gang of lumbermen, seeing opportunity in adversity, begin a heated pub crawl, taking over abandoned bars and drinking free, waiting for the heat and descending embers from the roof to drive them to the next vacant tavern.

The genie rises over the outline of the mills and the huge, sprawling lumber piles on the islands and on Richmond Landing. Behind smarting eyes, the residents of the acre realize what the strong wind, blowing into their faces, means. If the fire crosses the river, they're next.

In the early afternoon, the fire hurdles the Ottawa, hip-hopping from island to island. A blizzard of embers precedes the contagious flames, now devouring homes and businesses with the force of artillery. In Booth's sawmill, the workers fight the fire with a built-in water system, the metal tanks still bright with their first coat of paint. They save the mill, although they can see E.B. Eddy's is gone, then watch exhausted as the fire passes like a flash flood and rolls towards their homes on the Flats. The stacks of lumber behind the mill on Richmond Landing are eaten up like hearth logs, and the fire puts out the electric power stations on the islands. Parliament is in session when the power goes out, but Prime Minister Laurier adjourns it within the hour. The members unanimously note that the fire is coming their way.

On the Flats, the nightmare has come true; fire is on them, and there is no choice but evacuation. The streets are covered with panic, lost children, and mad-eyed horses. The smoke is a wind-fanned fog that consumes detail and reduces every colour to primal orange and black. Silhouettes of frantic figures pull essentials from homes and stores onto the boardwalk. These scraps of life are piled into carts, run over Pooley's Bridge and up onto the heights, the wall of limestone that might — *might* — contain the advance. Some of the refugees cannot outrun the flames and save their belongings; they let go and run, run into destitution, all those things they've worked for now caught in the maelstrom.

The men of the Ottawa Fire Department, all fifty-one of them, are surrounded and outgunned. Their entire stock of hose wagons, steam engines, and ladder trucks amounts to sixteen vehicles. Chief Peter

Provost, the city's youngest chief to date, admits that even if he had twice that number, the demon has them beat. By mid-afternoon, trains are arriving from Montreal carrying firemen, fire horses, engines, and pumps. They have made the journey in two hours. The normal end of the journey, the Canadian Pacific Railway yards and station, has fallen to the fire they have come to fight, so they disembark at the fire's edge.

Many of them are sent to defend the Keefer waterworks, just a few yards from the No. 1 Fire Station and connected to it by an underground tunnel. The city does not want to face an epidemic from unclean water in the days after the fire. The old narrow wooden bridge across the Ottawa River is gone, except for the stone pedestals; Hull and Ottawa are divided again. Someone throws dynamite at the edge of the fire, to blow it to a standstill, but the explosion just serves to blow flaming shingles into the air like kites and accelerate the destruction's forward rush.

Duke Street is now a wall of flame three stories high, from number 3 to number 97, from the McDougal hardware store to the tailor shop of Charlebois and Galarneau. Candies, half-made dresses, fresh-cut harnesses, the tools of Romain the tinsmith, the dyes of the shoemaker, the chemicals of de Champlain the photographer, the whiskey bottles of the liquor salesman, and the fresh hair cut that morning on the floor of Cleophas the barber. Ash.

Having consumed the entire Flats, the fire carries on up the low hill, Nanny Goat Hill, to the south of Duke Street and along into Rochesterville. The flames beat like mad surf against the tall limestone cliffs to the east of the acre, but don't manage to climb it; the cliffs funnel the fire south, where it takes out, among other structures, J.R. Booth's magnificent stone home and the Victoria Brewery. The fire is democratic in its appetite; the fancy stone homes and their imported luxuries receive the same treatment as the cheap boarding-houses of the millworkers. Two miles further south the flames reach the Experimental Farm on the city limits, and there bucket brigades of policemen and townspeople finally halt it, as it runs out of buildings to feed on.

Around seven o'clock the wind and the sun set down together. For a while the sunset is bright orange, invisible from the smoke-infested acre, but remarked on for its ironic shading by the crowds up on Parliament Hill, where heaps of belongings of the dispossessed are stacked. Many of the homeless, and half the relieved Upper Towners, have gathered on the cliff edge to look down into the rare sight of a city on fire. Watching through barred windows from the crowded cells of the Ottawa jail is the entire prison population from the Hull jail, which has been lost in the fire.

By nine o'clock the fire is contained; it rages on inside its blackened perimeter, a force of nature blindly reducing a fragile order to chaos. Though it reached the cliffs, and blew against them, the firestorm was unable to climb into Upper Town and reach the Parliament Buildings — not this time. They will have to wait sixteen years, until February 1916, when they will be gutted by an internal fire that leaves only the library, still to my mind the most beautiful room in Ottawa, standing.

The limits of the 1900 fire were a rectangle three miles long and half a mile wide. Inside the rectangle, more than three thousand buildings were destroyed. Of Ottawa's sixty thousand citizens, eight and a half thousand were homeless that night, including everyone on the acre. In the days that followed, the cause of Black Thursday's fire was unearthed. In one of a row of tightly packed wooden houses in Hull, a chimney had malfunctioned, allowing an ember from the fireplace to travel unextinguished from the hearth onto the roof, igniting the shingles. From one fiery acorn, a tree of fire grew and put a thousand acres of city in the shade and took seven — miraculously, only seven — lives.

Aftermath is a word we've come to use to describe the residue of war — the skeletal buildings, the sense of the vertical reduced to the horizontal, the homeless and the grieving. But in 1900 aftermath still retained another meaning, one the people of the Flats who were raised on farms would understand. The aftermath was the crop of grass that grew up after the first cut in early summer. From the cracked bricks and roasted trees a new style of Flats grew in the aftermath, built in the haste to put the

155

place back in order. Work began the next day, after an open-air church service was held in the ruins. Two buildings on the acre, however, didn't need resurrecting. The No. 1 Fire Station, by virtue of its function, was able to effect its own escape. In the process, the Couillard Hotel next door was spared. The twin refugees stood at one end of the acre, like two teeth in an otherwise well-punched jaw.

The Great Fire of 1900 was a world-class tragedy. It was reported in the newspapers of the Empire and the United States; pictures of the acre went into millions of homes. Money began to pour in, as well as food and gifts for the homeless, money from queens and commoners, $400,000 from the Empire, $45,000 of that from the London Stock Exchange. Canadians and Newfoundlanders together sent half a million dollars. In the end, the relief fund handed out $10 million to cauterize the wound the two cities had sustained.

The money went to feed the three thousand people who lined up daily for almost a month at the Drill Hall in Upper Town. An ice rink was used to warehouse the incoming gifts; it took a platoon of people two months to distribute them. The Exhibition Grounds in the south of town became a tent city for the homeless. The fund was administered with fairness and speed, and by the end of the year the Flats was working again, the freight yards rebuilt; hundreds of simple wooden homes (the rich had moved uptown, away from the timber piles) had popped up; the factories and mills were running again. And a silent, guilty prayer was added to the invocations of the congregations in the local churches. O Lord, your next fiery act of God? May it happen somewhere else.

Street Life

It is a year after the fire. Duke Street is brand-new, looking like a model railway, unweathered, all the lines of the buildings straight and true, the colours uniform and strong. A fine layer of ash has been added to the geological strata below. The veteran Mr. Robert is still living at number 27, although the building formerly attached to that number has gone, and a new one replaced it; the sawmills supplied free boards and struts after the fire, a timber transfusion that soon had the Flats back on its feet. New mills are under construction, the owners taking advantage of the damage to refit for pulp and paper manufacture. But the fire has shaken some of Duke Street's residents loose; they have moved away. The harness-maker, the cobbler, the dressmaker, and the barber are all gone. So too the tinsmith, Chabot the liquor salesman, and the D'Amours' cab stand. Likewise old Mr. William Ahearn, Thomas's uncle, who had lived on the street since 1875.

The street's business has emerged from the fire less diverse, more given to merchants' yards and less to single tradesmen. Suppliers of coal and flour have moved in. There is a physician, though, where there wasn't one before, Alonzo Martin, sandwiched between the new hotel and the lumber-yard. Of the tradesmen who have stayed, the first to re-establish himself is Auguste de Champlain, the photographer. The fire burnt especially bright in his studio, glass bottles of chemicals detonating, but he managed to flee with his cameras. Business is especially brisk, veterans of the fire sitting patiently for portraits they can hold as proof they are still here, certificates of survival. Auguste has a red-letter day in July when the Duke and Duchess of Cornwall and York pay a visit to put the royal blessing on the reconstruction. The royals come to the Chaudière, on a specially decorated streetcar, and then ride the timber-slide.

Ninety-five years after the great fire, I stand on the patch of snow where Auguste de Champlain's studio once went about its business. Nearby, trucks are arriving full of dirty snow from last night's storm and dumping it on the temporary grey mountain that grows on the Flats each winter, then reluctantly melts down to a molehill of dirt each spring. Auguste is long gone, of course, but the platform is still here, the hard ground that is as close to eternal as anything we know. In the board game that is real estate, the players come and go, but the board never changes.

It's a short drive from the snowbound acre to the City of Ottawa Archives, a schoolish, quiet building near the Rideau River. It houses the civic memory, including the street directories for the last ninety-five years. After I settle at a large, warm wooden desk in the archives, I start pulling directories down from the shelf one by one, year by year, commencing with 1901. Each year is slightly fatter than the one before it, as the city gains weight. The directory for 1901 has become a book of the dead, while the most recent directory catalogues the grid of the living. As I open them in turn to the section of streets that begin with D — Division, Dolly Varden, Dufferin, and then Duke — the directories reveal the occupants of the acre, as they came and went through history's turnstile. The street numbers, from 1 to 101, run down the side, and the corresponding names climb like a set of rungs from past to present.

It's tempting to fictionalize this dry regiment of records, as my finger runs down them. To take these anonymous names and give them lives, details. For instance, the 1910 street directory indicates that a Jean Cantin was living at 39 Duke Street. A year later the ominous description "Vacant" sits beside the same number. Murder most foul? A heart broken here and mended elsewhere? How many of these names on the page went off to world war and fell? Or did they fall right here during the Depression, the economic retreat?

Couplings and partings, illnesses and accidents, the cries of child-birth, the grunts of orgasm, the sighs of death — the acre wore these lives like changes of clothes, as it wore the successive shelters that housed them, the poker-faced, three-storey brick and wood dwellings, the ware-houses and the offices. To get at the acre's story now, we have to go through the front doors of Duke Street, for life in the twentieth century, more than in any previous century, is largely lived indoors. I love this bit of the inves-tigation, sluicing through the paperwork for clues, sitting down with peo-ple and plundering their memories; we're within range of living memory now. I feel like a detective from the other end of the century. It's the next best thing to time travel, to the land of was. It feels like the wish to step forward that comes over you when you stand on the edge of a cliff; the wish to step out into time and free fall.

1 Duke Street

As the property of the Ahearn family, the northwest corner of the acre had done long service as a provider of rents. The workers from the lumber and paper mills filed past it daily at shift change, and a succession of store-keepers drew them in and sold them necessities. The Messrs. McDougal and Cuzner spent twenty years in their corner store retailing hardware, until the 1900 fire. After the fire, the corner re-emerged for a decade as the America House. Then, in three quick years before the First World War, it sold tobacco, then meals, while a man called Michael Addleman worked up a junk business in the yard behind, between the building and the rail-way tracks. The records show that Addleman, who picked up the deed to the corner after the Ahearns let it go, sold it in April 1925 to a man called Louis Baker. From then on, for forty years, the corner was known simply as Baker Brothers.

The Baker brothers were Louis and Jankov, whom everyone called

Jake. They were born in Ukraine, in the village of Kresmestad, Louis in 1888 and Jake five years later. By the time Louis was eight, they were orphans; the Kishinev pogroms had started south of Kiev, and Jews were being persecuted in the thousands. To avoid the slaughter, the Ukrainian Jews were fleeing to North America; some settled in Ottawa. In the first decade of the twentieth century, the number of Jewish families in the city rose from sixty to four hundred.

Louis and Jankov came over on a boat in 1901, with the Addlemans, relatives from the same village. The boys had an uncle, also Louis, with a junk business on Murray Street; Uncle Louis had moved to Ottawa after an earlier pogrom, and it was he who sent them tickets of passage. Uncle Louis had taken the name Baker, and so the boys dropped the family name, Radischvetsky, and took Baker too. At first they stayed with the Addlemans, then they went to live with their uncle after Mrs. Addleman died. Jake went to George Street Public School until he was twelve, and to the shul on Rideau Street. By then, Louis had found work with a blacksmith.

Jake's first job was at the Greenberg farm, at Billings Bridge, as an apprentice. It was a Jewish community farm that provided the first wage for many of the immigrants. For the first year Jake got no wages; he worked sunrise to sunset for room and board only. In 1908, when he was fifteen, he went to live and work with the Betchermans, who had been friends of his mother. He said yes to any job that came his way, selling papers, delivering telegrams, picking up junk with a pushcart and getting twenty-five cents a pound for it, and peddling fruit with a horse and wagon. For a couple of seasons, Jake took the harvest train out to the prairies and worked alongside Maritimers and Quebeckers, getting the wheat off the vast Canadian steppes.

The Baker brothers built their savings; they had decided to go into the junk business together, and the money would buy them land. Like their uncle, and like Mr. Addleman, they saw that sooner or later everything the city bought new would come to them as scrap, the inevitable fate of objects; there was money in the end of things. In 1915, Louis Baker and Alex Betcherman opened a junk shop on McKay Street, and Jake went to work for them. There he met a woman and married her in 1919, and they started a family of four kids. There was a brief interlude while Jake left to manage another junk yard for the Betchermans. In 1925, Jake took over ownership of the yard, and in 1926 Louis joined him and they formed Baker Brothers Iron and Metal Works. They bought the corner of Duke Street, where the ground had already been rehearsed for such a purpose by Mr. Addleman. The Baker brothers worked hard, and in a few years turned the yard into the biggest scrap dealership in the city.

The Baker Brothers complex became the biggest building to rise on the acre. The centrepiece was a four-storey brick warehouse, a basement and four floors with twin spinal freight elevators running through it. Lesser progeny protruded from this master edifice. Butted against the side facing Duke Street was a one-storey dispensary of new automotive parts. In front of the auto parts store was a service station, where ever-changing car designs pulled in for gas, getting bigger with the years and sprouting fins like overfed fish, cars with names long forgotten now — the Graham Hollywood, the Packard Clipper, the Studebaker Golden Hawk, the DeSoto Fireflite, the Hudson Hornet, and the Edsel Ranger.

At the rear of the warehouse, rising over Britannia Terrace and the railway tracks, was a secondary warehouse, shorter by a storey than the main, sharing a wall with the big building. The front entrance to the whole complex faced the north edge of the acre, looking out on a road and the railway tracks. On the other side of the tracks was Chaudière Junction, a grand name for a small wooden office where a Canadian National Railway agent dispensed tickets.

The scrapyard itself, the heart of the enterprise, lay hidden behind these buildings. It was a stormy sea of metal, solid waves of it shifting shape daily. A siding ran off the old Canadian Atlantic line, now part of Canadian National, and turned into this metal sea. At the end of the siding was usually a flatbed railway car, in some stage of loading, a land barge of scrap awaiting removal and meltdown.

In the warehouse, gangs of sorters went at the never-ending task of reducing this sea of scrap into lakes of similarities, then sorting them again into like puddles. Rags and papers arrived like haystacks, and went up the elevator to the fourth floor. A large square hole in the floor provided a view of the third floor directly below. Sorted rags snowed down into a baler, the baler baled, and the neat cubes went off by train to make rag paper, the finest of papers that endures for centuries. Cardboard and newspaper were baled and dispatched for conversion to roofing tiles, to be installed over people who were, perhaps, reading the newspaper.

In the basement the copper and brass were prepared for shipment. A lot of copper came from old power lines, which were taken to a farmer's field outside town, doused with gasoline, and set alight, producing black, skunky clouds of burning insulation, and leaving the gleaming strings of reusable copper.

The lower-class metal out in the yard was manipulated by a gang of brute, thuggish machines. Grabbing cranes — magnets at the end of the arm like huge hockey pucks surrounded by closable claws, the whole thing resembling a bizarre flower from a metal planet — storked over the piles and rearranged them. These cranes were visible over the wall to passers-by. The yard also housed a set of huge steel dinosaur jaws that cut scrap sheet metal from cars into manageable pieces. The whole yard had that industrial, intimidating turmoil that fashion photographers seek out to pose models against, in risqué juxtaposition. Very large cats slept among the bales by day, and walked the yard at night with Solomon Brazzo, the night security guard, on the lookout for varieties of rat.

For Mel Baker, son of Harry, great-nephew of Jake, the scrapyard was his childhood playground, later the font of his first job. As a boy, after the Second World War, Mel would stand beside Great-Uncle Jake at the peddlers' entrance. (Mel never got the chance to work with his grandfather, Louis, who died in 1951.) Every morning at eight, Jake — a tall, thin man with a smile that never wore out — took up his station in the doorway by the scales, a pencil or a pen in hand, depending on the weather. On his shoulder, in the same place Long John Silver kept his parrot, there was always a cat. These cats were rewarded for their company with fresh salmon. For many years the favourite feline was a longhair with fur the same colour as the salmon. "In all the years I stood alongside him," Mel, a stocky, strong-handed man who's in the tool business now, recalls, "I never heard Uncle Jake swear. The only expletive he ever used was 'What the Halifax!'"

Most Saturday mornings, when Jake declared the scales open, there was already a line-up of trucks and carts stretching down Britannia Terrace. In the 1930s, this ragged line invariably included the cart of the famous junk collector "Giddy-up Maudit," so named for the phrase he used to get his horse started. When Mel started dogging Jake, there was still the occasional horse and cart in the queue, but mostly it was pickup trucks now, some with stakes stuck in the side and loaded down with the week's pickings from across town. Mingled in with the professionals, who tended to come more on weekdays, were the one-offs, the weekenders clearing out the old lawn mower, or newspapers, or boxes of old clothes, or engine parts sitting on an oily blanket in the back of the station wagon, impatient kids in the front seat waiting to see the man with the cat.

The line would caterpillar towards Jake, the boxes of scrap would go on the scale, and Jake would write a slip with a dollar value that the punter could take to the office to get his money. Big loads went directly onto the truck scale, a floating steel carpet with a scale attached that sank with the weight of the truck first full, then empty; Jake or his assistant Sid paid on the difference. Occasionally the line would yield up a rubbie with some cast-off alternator or a bag of rags he'd stumbled on, and Jake would over-pay him, give him the same smile everyone else got. While Jake was hand-ing out the slips, Mel would do odd sorting jobs and continue amassing one of the best comic book collections in the city. The unsold returns came to Baker Brothers with their covers torn off; Mel got one of each, and a few extra to swap.

As a teenager, at the end of the 1950s, Mel started working week-ends in his blue uniform. For a while he was a gas jockey, working the five islands with the ten pumps on the forecourts, pumping out the independent gas called Revo, a name his cousin Harvey had come up with. Mel's first job in the morning, one he quickly grew to hate, was using the air hose to blow up the beach balls and putting them in the cage outside, where they sat, like blowfish at a barn dance, waiting to be given away with every $3 fill-up. The forecourt was also used to sell off serendipitous bits of scrap that might bear profitable recycling. One year, the old seats from the streetcars — all taken out of service by 1960 — were sold; they ended up on cottage porches, and ringside at barbecues. It was the closing of a circle; the man who had started the Ottawa streetcar business, Thomas Ahearn, was born on the site of Baker Brothers.

When it came time for Baker Brothers to relocate, Jake was still there at the peddlers' entrance, well into his seventies, a new generation of cat on his shoulder. He didn't follow the business to the outskirts of town, but lived another twenty years, coming, in 1987, to the end of a life that had lasted almost a century, a life that started in an orphan's flight from a murderous tsar and found peace in daily communion with Ottawa's scrap collectors.

77 Duke Street

By 1900, professional photographic studios in Canada were an idea already two generations old. One of the most famous Canadian photographers, an émigré Scotsman called William Notman, had opened a branch studio in Ottawa in 1868, directly opposite the Parliament Buildings. Mantelpieces on Duke Street supported stiff portraits of the old folks, taken on the day they decided to let the future know them as they had once been, youthful and rich enough to afford a visit to a photographic studio. Prints of Canada's pet wonders — Niagara Falls, or the Rockies, or trains slicing through ravines — hung on the living room walls.

Auguste de Champlain was only three in 1868, and lived on the ocean in Pointe Saint-Pierre, in the Gaspé region of Quebec. He apprenticed as a restorer of church frescos, steady work for a young French

Canadian, but he was asthmatic and was advised to move inland. Forsaking village for town, he went upriver to Montreal. There he met and married Regina, and may well have found work similar to his trade, correcting flaws and adding cosmetic improvements to photographic portraits, with delicate strokes of a brush on the glass-plate negatives.

The smoky air of Montreal tormented his asthma, and when he turned twenty-one, in 1886, Auguste de Champlain moved to Ottawa and went into business for himself as a photographer. At first he moved onto Duke Street at number 89, operating out of a second-floor studio; he kept his eyes cast down onto the street, waiting for a shopfront to come clear.

In 1893 one did, and Auguste moved into number 77, and his livelihood was anchored there for the next thirty-five years. The fire of 1900 darkened his business, but his was the first store on the block to open up again. By 1907, when he was forty-two, he and his wife had twelve kids, including Auguste Jr., all living in the rooms at the rear of the studio. Albert de Champlain — son of Auguste Jr., grandson of Auguste Sr. — was born in 1919, and he grew up playing on Duke Street.

An older man now, rendered unsteady in body by sclerosis but unshaken in his mind, Albert found it pleasing, when I visited him, to lay out his recollections on his kitchen table, like a place setting. In fact his memories, photographs in his head, begin before he was born, with the games the generation of children before him played. Right after the fire, playing war games in the rubble, it was considered a victory to chase an unfortunate victim across the hole of an outhouse hidden by debris, and put him, literally, in the shit. Albert was also told that, as a baby, he cried every time they came back to Duke Street after a day's outing.

Albert walked me down Duke Street in 1929, the year his grandfather closed the shop and moved out west. The southern end of the street began with a bench on a small carpet of grass next to the fire station. This was a gossip and recollection post for neighbourhood veterans. This vantage point saw a lot of traffic as the streetcar stopped there, carrying people across the river to Hull, and out to the races at Connaught.

When Albert was five, two vets sitting on the bench called him over from across the street. A bus jumped forward and hit him, and he was carried into the fire station and checked for breakage. At their backs as the vets chatted was the headquarters of city garbage and snow collection, where the annual campaigns against waste and winter were plotted. The trucks were stored nearby in a long tin shed — wheels in winter, sleds in summer. Albert used to run along the shed roof, until a bulldog used as a security guard chased him and bit his kneecap.

Next on Duke Street was the Couillard Hotel, and alongside that the lumber-yard, where one day a horse-drawn wagon, fully loaded, came through the gates at an anxious, last-run-of-the-day speed. A man crossing on foot was almost flattened. He let the driver know — using, as French-Canadian Catholics do, church paraphernalia as the basis for swearing — his assessment. The driver stepped down and, despite his bulk disadvantage, did what his horses had failed to do. He knocked the man out. A bystander informed the driver that he had flattened Jacques Couillard, the efficient bouncer at the Couillard Hotel. As Couillard was now coming around, the driver abandoned his load and headed for Hull on foot.

Then came the mica store, and behind that was the Bingham factory, which specialized in brass. After that was the building owned by Auguste de Champlain — a three-storey duplex, one storey of retail, two above for boarders, with a common door. On one side of the duplex, at 79, Eugene Funk had conducted a brief experiment selling Persian cats; after that a grocer moved in. On the other side, the decorator business of Auguste Jr. had expanded to fill the space made available by the vacated photographic studio. Decorating for Auguste Jr. was a default career. Informed he had an imminently fatal heart condition, Auguste had quit his job as a bartender on Parliament Hill, a job he had held since he finished making hand grenades in the First World War in the foundry across the road.

To pass the time remaining to him, Auguste Jr. redecorated the family rooms and the store; he wanted a tidy wake. His work was admired by a neighbour, and he was invited to repaper her place. He did so, and feeling in need of a second opinion about his continuing health, walked up Nanny Goat Hill to visit his doctor.

"Did you walk up that hill to get to me?" the doctor asked him.

"I did."

"Don't worry about your heart," the doctor told him. "You'll last forever."

Auguste de Champlain Jr. promptly married a woman whose first husband had been killed by lightning. He raised a well-populated family and died in 1980 in Ottawa, a few miles from the acre, at the defiant age of ninety-two.

North of the de Champlain building was the other flank of the Mayo-Davis lumber-yard, which flowed behind it. Next to that, across the lane running back to Britannia Terrace, was a three-door row, a single and a double, which boasted a veranda on the second floor. Evoy O'Reilly, from the double, was a playmate of young Albert de Champlain. Evoy was a paraplegic who passed the clement days squatting in a wagon. From this lowly dais he press-ganged young passers-by to wheel him to the corner, and on to the restaurant by the bridge where a blind Polishman served thick soup, checking the bowl for fullness with his thumb.

On the other side of O'Reilly's there was the Purity Flour mill, which put bread on the city's tables; it butted against the brick anthill of Baker Brothers. Opposite O'Reilly's, on the west side of Duke Street, lived Mr. Bois (French for wood), the tinsmith. His son, Albert recalls, was a big lug, but he was also the best wood scaler at the Booth sawmills. He could compute, with one glance, the quantity and quality of board-feet in a load of logs with impeccable accuracy.

Rounding the corner of the acre and heading back down Britannia Terrace, Albert de Champlain, walking through memory, sees the rear walls of the flour mill and the scrap and lumber yards, much taller than a ten-year-old, breached by railway sidings. At the end of the terrace was a small hut in which sat Bob Roberts. When the trains came over the road, Bob lowered the barrier that held back the traffic, an up-and-down kind of job.

In winter, between snowfalls, this back lane would fill with activity, as the snow trucks — railway boxes bolted to flatbeds, with cabless seats and steering wheels rising up out of the engines — came to lose their loads in the gully at the back. The trucks had no hydraulics, only back ends that opened and shut like cereal boxes. To empty them of snow, a trick was used like the one by which string and a doorknob get out a loose tooth. A chain was pegged to the ground and attached to the front axle. The truck backed up at high speed onto a wooden platform built over the gully. When the chain snapped tight and pulled the truck to an instantaneous halt, Newton's law about action and reaction kicked in, and the snow flew out the back in a solid loaf. The concert of sounds as this happened was one of those real-life soundtracks, like the whir of sawmills, and the clack of streetcars, that have been rendered extinct by progress.

Auguste de Champlain Sr. kept his studio clicking at 77 Duke Street until 1929, when he left for the prairies, in his sixty-fourth year, to help his daughter try to save her farm from the clutches of the Depression. He intended to use his income as a photographer to prop it up, but the Depression overwhelmed their efforts; the farm went under, and Auguste and his equipment headed back to Ottawa on the train.

The day before Auguste was due back at Union Station, his son took a phone call from a monastery in Kenora, Ontario. Auguste de Champlain Sr. had died there on the train. Canadian Pacific had handed his body and Catholic soul over to the Dominicans, and now the brothers wondered if they should send him on, or bury him in their graveyard. Auguste de Champlain is buried in the monastery graveyard in Kenora; his equipment was sold off to cover the burial expenses.

The acre's involvement with the de Champlain family was not quite over. Auguste's sister Marie, a former nun, returned to live on the acre in the mid-1920s, and she held title to the building, renting it out for ten years. On her death, the de Champlain portion of the acre was added to the lumber-yard of the neighbouring Mayo-Davis Lumber Company. It stayed that way, stacked with the skeletons of houses yet to be built, until 1965. Family legend has it that Marie left a lot of cursed money. Some of the inheritors were drowned in a boating accident. Others were mauled by dogs while poaching apples. Still others were pinned beneath a wall as it collapsed. Curses thrive on hindsight.

When Albert de Champlain had finished his reminiscences, I asked him, "Do you have any of your grandfather's photographs?"

"No, not a one. I've met people who have, in albums, or tucked away in drawers. The name of the studio was in the bottom left corner: A. de Champlain, 77/79 Duke Street. My father had one; it was a trick photograph made by my grandfather. It showed my father sitting at every place at a table at once."

"Are you related to Samuel de Champlain?"

"I don't think so. A relative of mine, a priest also called Albert de Champlain, traced the family history as far back as 1710. Volant de Champlain brought the family to Canada sometime before that. He traded between the West Indies, Canada, and France for a while, then settled on the Île d'Orleans. He married one of Louis Hébert's grand-daughters. Hébert was the first colonial farmer, and he helped de Champlain found Quebec, but that's as close as I can get. The priest wrote the family history on the back of an Export cigarette calendar — it included a de Champlain girl who was murdered with an axe — but we can't find it now."

"Do you take photographs yourself?"

"My hobby when I was a teenager was taking train pictures. I traded with other people all over the world. I still have a picture somewhere of a streetcar, number 906, passing Chaudière Junction before the war."

"Do you ever go down to Duke Street?"

"No, I haven't been for a long time. I wonder if I would cry again, coming onto the street, as I did when I was a baby. I think I would."

101 Duke Street

The first building on the Flats was a tavern. Ma Firth's place went up around 1818 on Richmond Landing, and it had the monopoly on liquid entertainment for quite a few years. The second building on the Flats was also a tavern. And the third. As the Flats filled with customers, public houses popped up on street corners — the three-storey Russell Hotel, for instance, on the corner of Duke and Booth. Put the tavern on the corner, and the doors entice drinkers coming from two directions (and anyone exiting by one door is conveniently invisible to anyone entering by the other). Once inside, imbibers have the sense of being at the apex of the neighbourhood's flow. A tavern is a place people go to escape privacy.

The Couillard Hotel, though not strictly on the corner — the No. 1 Fire Station enjoyed that privilege but was set back from the street by the length of a fire wagon and a team of horses — occupied the regal inter-section of Queen and Duke. For a while retailers on the site had tried sell-ing boots, then nails, and then haircuts, but the spot proved most useful as a tavern. It was a full stop at the end of Duke Street, and very much part of the public life of the acre for eighty years.

In 1881, 101 Duke Street was converted to a hotel, the Canada Central, to the specifications of a Monsieur Galarneau. He lived there with his wife and daughter, Olive, and they took in boarders. One such boarder was twenty-five-year-old Jean-Baptiste Couillard, who had moved upriver from the pulp and paper town of Thurso. He got a job as a manager in T.G. Chabat's department store, then the biggest in Ottawa. In 1884 Jean mar-ried nineteen-year-old Olive Galarneau, proving that proximity is one ingredient of love, and three years later, as the son-in-law of the now deceased proprietor, he became the maître d'hôtel.

Jean and Olive changed the name of the premises to the familial Couillard Hotel. Jean, though he didn't know it then, had stamped his fate for the next forty-five years. Olive was quickly involved in the mathemat-ics of childbearing: twenty-one pregnancies, seventeen of which reached baptism, seven of which made it to adult age, four of which survived past the age of thirty. Olive died in 1921 at the age of fifty-six, having spent at least fifteen of those years pregnant.

Dolores Couillard moved into the Couillard Hotel when she was two months old, in 1917. Dolores was Jean's and Olive's granddaughter. Her younger sisters (including Pauline, who was born in 1925 in the midst of an earthquake, and who says she's been shaking ever since) were born at the hotel, and she lived on the second floor for her first twelve years. Her father, Eugène, built railings around the flat roof, her penthouse playground. From there she could look down on the fire station, or shred the sample flakes of mica that resembled petrified pastry that she got from the mica store of Stanley O'Fillion next door. On Sundays, she climbed the fence of the lumber-yard and played among the stacks. Some nights when she was older she walked across Pooley's Bridge and visited her father in his office in the Parliament Buildings, where he worked as an accountant. The noise of the trains as they slowed behind the hotel to cross Queen Street was the punctuation of her days.

Dolores lived in a honeycomb of uncles and grandparents and siblings, wedged tightly into an abundance of family in a way that has since fallen out of society. Her Uncle Émile was head banking clerk for J.R. Booth up in the north woods. He died at the sad age of twenty-seven, only three months after getting married. Her aunts Juliette, Rosita, and Évangeline were all nurses who worked in sanitariums. The Flats families were like that, big gangs in small wooden houses. As well as the many relatives, there were travelling salesmen who took rooms on the second and top floors, and customers in the bar who warned her, in a careful slur, "Fais attention" as she went into the street to play. Past the fire station and across the street was the shoe shop of Mr. Greene, and Dolores often played with his son, Lorne, who grew up to star on TV screens around the world as Ben Cartwright in *Bonanza*.

In 1930, Jean Couillard became too ill to stand behind the bar where he had pumped beer for four decades. He moved to a tuberculosis sanitarium in Quebec founded by his son Albert, a doctor. Another son, Lorenzo, took over the hotel. In 1935 old Jean Couillard died, and his son changed the hotel's name to the Duke House. By then Dolores and her family had moved out of the hotel, leaving behind the grand piano the family sang around, and the large stuffed owl that sat on it. Even when she came of age, she never drank in the Duke House, although she visited when the lumber-yard caught fire in the mid-1930s and wiped out the apartments next to the Duke. Dolores married Marcel Beriault and lived the rest of her life in Ottawa, until I went to sit with her one afternoon, and we looked slowly together through her thick "memory book." Sadly, she died two days later. How fragile a thing an old story is.

The hotel Dolores grew up in got rowdier as it got older. The men who drank there worked days bending and stacking piles of metal or wood. Their hands took a while to wind down at night, and were inclined to fist up once the beer and the boilermakers hit the rough spot. John Miles drank there and recalls that there were always exactly three fights on a Friday night, pay night, but always among neighbours. Also on Friday nights, a peddler would come in and sell fish pulled from the Ottawa River — barbut mostly, an ugly, bottom-feeding fish with a hide instead of scales, and flesh that contained several parts per million of the entire history of everything that had gone into the river.

Going into the Duke House in the 1940s involved walking past the glass-brick windows that prevented exterior identification of the patrons, then passing under the red neon sign at right angles to the wall. That put you in a cupboard with two doors. Your gender gave you a clue as to which door to use. Women had no choice; they went to the left. If you were a man who liked to drink among men, you went to the right. If you were a man with a woman, you went left. Inside, the walls were regulation green; the ornate walnut bar sat like an island in the middle of the room, serving either side. The waiters, all men, wore white shirts and bow-ties that, by midnight, smelt like the floor mop. If you were lucky, you could lift a few coins out of their aprons as they bent to empty the ashtray. Everybody smoked.

It's hard to find a bar without a TV now; they function as silent adult soothers. Back then, the first TVs on the streets showed up in the taverns. The back room of the Duke was given over to the compelling magic of the black-and-white, perched on the wall like an aquarium. On Friday nights it showed the fights to forty yelling aficionados.

Every day about five-thirty the workingmen were swept out the door. The hotel closed between six and eight so the workers could get something solid in them at home. Those who returned for the night shift had until about eleven-thirty, when the waiters would start shooing them out again. Viola Milks, who also drank there, remembers that men who found themselves financially challenged sometimes drank half a beer, then went to the Rovale bus depot across the street to pick a fly off the plate-glass window. Slip it in the beer and you might get another drink.

One night, she recalls, the Duke filled up with drinkers who usually habituated the Palace Hotel on the other side of the Flats, among them Viola's father; a boxcar had shunted off the rails that ran alongside the Palace and ploughed into the hotel. Another night Viola lost her wedding ring on the floor, and everyone got down looking for it under the tables as though it were the middle of an air raid. They never did find it, and it might be there still, in the submerged rubble.

Lorenzo Couillard lasted exactly half as long behind the bar as his father. In his turn he got old, and after seventy-two years of proprietorship the Couillard family sold the hotel in 1956 to two Polish partners, both named Paul. They were called White Paul and Black Paul after their hair colour.

The two Pauls were not cut out to be hotel managers, and within a couple of years White Paul was looking to sell out. A family of market gardeners, the Perraults, who had the largest gardens in the city, had their eye on the place. Casel Perrault knew that his sons were coming of age and wanted to get their hands out of the soil. They seemed to prefer the idea of slinging beer to cutting broccoli, so when Black Paul appeared at Casel's stall on the Byward Market and raised the subject of handing over the Duke, Casel said yes. The Perraults, Casel and his sons Gerry and Bill and their families, moved in on December 15, 1958.

Gerry Perrault, twenty that year, was keen to apply his strong back to hoisting kegs of Bradings, Dow, Victoria, and O'Keefe beers instead of sacks of potatoes. The first step was to give the Duke's well-used face a lift. The red neon sign — DUKE HOUSE — was re-gassed. The rooms were scraped down to the brick and refinished with walnut plywood, and no art was put on them. The patrons' faces were all the portraits anyone needed. The exterior façade got a marble skirt and imitation brickwork up to the roof. The ceiling was raised in the tavern, which was licensed for a crew of 112 elbow-swinging men, and likewise in the Ladies and Escorts, which was licensed for the odd number, given the room's title, of 105. They kept the square metal-edged tables and the Czechoslovakian wooden chairs. In addition to the piano, Casel brought in an organ, and for many years it was played expertly every Tuesday to Saturday by Dorcas Farn, from Chinatown. The waiters kept the dicky bows and the white shirts, and they were called Paul and Marcel. Marcel, in his time, escorted a few ladies of his own.

Casel Perrault was an unlikely landlord for the final years of the Duke. The switch from irrigating onions to pulling pints never sat well with him; it brought him into contact with fresh varieties of humanity he hadn't anticipated meeting. He abetted them in their sojourns with the booze, but kept his family together. Casel was an honourable man who tried to run an honourable hostelry. He had a halo of hair bordering a bald, infertile area, and when he first heard women swear in his bar, his son Gerry remembers, Casel's bald patch turned as red as the beets he used to grow. He wanted no transactions of a hot nature on the premises. Casel ran an old-fashioned neighbourhood inn, in an old-fashioned part of town, even after the rest of Ottawa started getting nice and serving beer in pints, not quarts, with waiters who hoped you had a nice day.

The Duke never really calmed down, even when it turned eighty in 1961. By then the gallonage of beer (pub success stories are measured in gallons) consumed annually by the Duke's patrons had risen tidally from eleven thousand in 1958 to thirty-six thousand. Big old claw-foot bathtubs used to hold thirty gallons, so that translates as twelve hundred bathtubs full of beer. That level of enthusiastic consumption inevitably led to the odd punch-up, but Gerry Perrault had established himself as a fighter who won a lot more than he lost; he usually herded the brawlers out to the "sandbox" as he called it — the back yard — where the testosterone would drop back to reasonable levels, and new bloodstains would mark the old stones.

In 1962, Casel Perrault received notice from the National Capital Commission, the federal agency devoted to making Ottawa a nice Canadian place to visit, a sort of Maple Leaf City, that the Duke was going to be expropriated. His era — and the era of Le Breton Flats as the working-class district of Ottawa, the place where things got made — was soon to be over. By now Casel's sons had moved on to taverns of their own. But his tenants in the rooms above were still there, the vets and the widowers, some of whom had lived at the hotel since he took over. Casel decided to go on until the bulldozer drivers called in for one last drink before they knocked the Duke down.

The swan song for the Duke House — alias the Couillard Hotel, alias the Canada Central — came on St. Patrick's Day, 1965. By then the Flats was almost completely devoid of buildings; Duke Street, converted to one-way traffic, was the lone hold-out. St. Patrick's Day, though no more than a passing headline in Ireland itself, a trip to mass and a shamrock in the lapel, is still an almighty shindig in parts of Canada where the descendants of Irish immigrants, cut off from the well, have been reduced to cartoons. There is an outbreak of leprechauns, and green cars at reduced prices are moved to the front of the lot. Anyone who feels Irish that day, whatever their nationality, heads for the pub.

The Duke filled to bursting March 17, 1965, with 250 people crammed in, many of whom used to live a beer-glass throw from the hotel, people whose houses had been expropriated and whisked away. The Johnson family, as always, went and got their instruments, and "Paddy's Lament" was sung once too often. It was a joyous wake. Five months later Casel shut the doors for the last time. By the first snowfall the Duke was gone.

Burn-out

Buildings cease in various fashions. In cities, they mostly yield to younger ones; not many urban dwellings are allowed the graceful rottage of the abandoned farmhouse or the moulting barn. Some go out with a bang, levelling themselves in seconds in a noisy cloud of rubble. Some are there one day, gone the next time you drive by. It is given to only a few to pass on with a sense of irony.

The No. 1 Fire Station was built in the winter of 1886, to replace the old one, which had to move when the Canadian Atlantic Railway went through. J.R. Booth paid for it, at a cost of $3,145. It looked like a house: gabled roof with dormer windows, and stable doors where the front door should have been. In the fire of 1900, remember, the No. 1 Fire Station at 103 Duke Street and Couillard's hotel next door were the only survivors in the area. Two decades later, the station smoothly made the switch from horses to horsepower. The platoon at No. 1 were still there in 1916 to fight the fire that brought down the Parliament Buildings.

One day, I stood on Duke Street with Harry Munro, a small sickly man with an invalid wife. He had moved onto Le Breton Flats as a boy in 1918. Harry remembered Sergeant James Humphries, the five-hundred-pound policeman with the reinforced car whose beat was Duke Street; nobody ever bested him in a fight. And he remembered the fire station horses. When the alarm sounded, he told me, the mares, with the discipline of synchronized swimmers, quit the stalls of their own accord and shimmied into position beneath their harness. A pull on a lever and the harness flopped onto their backs; straps were cinched, and they were out the door like rodeo steers.

For sixty-two years, through the Second World War and beyond, the firefighters in No. 1 fought the memorable blazes of Le Breton Flats. The next-to-last fire the station handled was on Booth Street, at the home of the Gagnons, on the morning of February 5, 1948. Like many of the families on Booth, the Gagnons were in double digits — eight kids, six of whom were at school. Mrs. Gagnon had gone into the cellar shortly after getting everyone out the door, using a paper torch to light her way. The torch, after she had shaken it (almost) out and gone upstairs, led to the gutting of the lower floor, driving the family out.

The No. 1 fire engines had to travel only two blocks to get to the Gagnons'. Two policemen also drove up, but they were not and headed back uptown. With the smoke of the Booth Street fire still in their rear-view mirror, they noticed that smoke was also coming out the open doors of the empty No. 1 station. They went through the hall to the door at the back. Behind the door was the kitchen — and a dragon's breath. Caught in the wrong profession, the policemen did the wrong thing and kicked in the door. The blast threw them all the way back to the doors they had come in by.

The alarm was in to headquarters now, and two rigs from No. 2 and a pumper from No. 11 turned out. Right behind them, in hasty disbelief, came the prodigal No. 1 platoon, a newspaper reporter clinging to the back of the truck with his notebook still out from the first fire. By high noon the fire was feasting on the sixty-two-year-old timbers, and every exit was a flaming mouth.

Fireman Don Fraser, from No. 8 platoon, appeared at a second-storey window. Stepping back, he kicked out the window (one of the few that the fireballs of gas hadn't yet blown out) and sliced his foot in the process. A policeman told him to jump, quickly, and Fraser did, falling twenty-five feet, bouncing off the policeman, and landing on the lacerated foot. Dozens watched Fraser's leap, and hundreds more quickly turned out to enjoy the unique spectacle of a fire station burning down.

In no time the flames were coming through the roof, and the blackened, red-faced men below knew their belongings on the second floor were gone. They turned their attention to blocking the fire's progress along the wood-lined tunnel that ran under Queen Street from the station to the waterworks. Having a fire station and a waterworks burn down would be a little too much irony for one day. They halted it, and by one-fifteen they had control.

There was an inquiry, but the results weren't made public, and there was no mention of the fire in the 1948 Fire Department Report. The speculation in the Duke House was that either the range in the firehouse kitchen or the furnace had set the thing going. The black husk of the station stood for a few days. It was decided to remove it, and not rebuild — a foreshadowing, sixteen years early, of the fate awaiting the rest of the street. A romantic might suggest that the No. 1 Fire Station, instead of waiting to be demolished, decided to commit edificial hara-kiri, and go out in a blaze of glory.

Tumbling Walls

Cities have always been cannibalistic. They eat large chunks of their own pasts, chewing up landscapes and buildings and regurgitating them. This municipal mastication implies a kind of hunger, the hunger to replace then with now, to recycle stale visions of a city with fresh ones.

Civic vision is a variable thing; it changes from town to town. Older towns are generally long-sighted, eager for their former glories to be on display. They cherish architectural souvenirs from their former status as seats of world power and commercial prowess. Think of Utrecht, or Venice. Younger ones, the colonial towns of the Americas, were almost all born short-sighted. They are architecturally myopic, unwilling to look back into history. The future is the place to be, and their sanctums of business and government reflect that vision, even as their towers reflect each other in mirror-glass walls. The young cities of the world feel their glory years are yet to come.

A handful of Canadian towns, the older ones in Quebec and Nova Scotia for example, have managed to be bifocal, keeping some aging quarter down by the river in focus, if only as flypaper for tourists. But for newer cities like Ottawa there is no looking back. History in Ottawa is an element in a theme park. What happened to the acre in the 1960s was the result of a steamrolling civic vision. It is perhaps the premier example in the country of the haste to reach glory, to be world-class, overwhelming a parochial sense of community.

What happened to the acre was, if you apply the sad wisdom of hindsight, inevitable. For most of its life the acre was subject to no vision but its own. It buckled and settled to the forces of geology, to internal stresses and strains. It harmonized with the elements, was shaped by competing engineers — the plant and animal life, from bacteria to giant beaver, that took up residence. With the arrival of the lumber barons, the sawmill capitalists like Perley, the acre became a shop floor, and a dormitory for the industrial side of town.

The "plan" for the acre was haphazard. There was just growth, the product of a simple equation; labour in, money out. But there was a plan unfolding elsewhere, and it had a definite moment of ignition. It was launched by Queen Victoria's decision, on the last day of 1857, that Ottawa was the spot on Canada's chest where the medal of capital city should be pinned. The vote in the Canadian parliament ratifying the royal decision was close, sixty-four to fifty-nine, but it went through, and at that moment the city underwent a seismic shift in vision. Like a train on a turntable, it began to swing slowly away from capitalism and towards being a capital city. Just as the citizens of Ottawa's leafier districts now dress up for a visit to the National Arts Centre, an act of display and high culture, Ottawa itself began to dress as a capital city should.

Big City Dreams

Even as the street life of the acre flourished, it was always overshadowed by the Gothic peaks and towers of Parliament Hill. After the capitalizing of Ottawa, the two areas drifted further apart. Parliament Hill became a national figure, the centre of the country's adolescent ego. Le Breton Flats became Ottawa's back door, the tradesmen's entrance to the city, the wrong side of the tracks. Both parts of town, the Flats the older by twenty years, were fixed in their personalities early on, and never outgrew them. The Flats was a community of labour, the Hill a community of management, the management of the country. They dressed accordingly, the one in the architecture of manufacture, in buildings like soiled overalls; the other in the architecture of government, in buildings like tailored suits. In the end, one vision outgrew the other. The suits won.

The role model for Ottawa, the city it aspired to be, was not London — except for its parliament buildings — but Washington. Ottawa has long had edifice envy for Washington and its Grecian institutions divided by ceremonial avenues. Both cities were founded on rivers, both as compromises: Ottawa on the historical division between Upper and Lower Canada, Washington as a port on the Potomac, close to the historical North-South line. (The port idea never succeeded; the river was too silty.) Washington had a head start in planning itself, although Ottawa had the jump on the American capital for natural beauty.

From the start, in 1800, Washington was a law unto itself, an island of federalism in a sea of states. Sixty-nine square miles of territory was set aside to accommodate the parks, forest, and broad avenues, and the business of running America. For a while, seventy-one years in fact, it was stuck in the mud, considerably more magnificent on paper than on the ground. Then control passed from a municipality to a commission with federal financing, and the American capital took off.

Meanwhile, Canada had only just become a confederation four years earlier, on July 1, 1867. When British Columbia joined, in 1871, Canada became a union of provinces equal in size to the United States, but very unequal in its attitudes to its seat of government. Canada's seat of government, in fact, kind of sat there, a small city between two big ones, though with some fancy stone buildings hogging the best view in town. As the bureaucracy grew with the country, at the quietly astonishing rate that dust collects, extra buildings were added, some of them no grander than barracks for housing rows of desks.

In Ottawa, the urge to play catch-up grew stronger as Washington flourished. Prime Minister Laurier held an outdoor meeting in 1896 (they were still in fashion then) and told the crowd he wished to make Ottawa "the Washington of the North." By 1913 the need to match Ottawa to its status was getting hard to ignore. A commission was the obvious answer and one was duly set up, chaired by Sir Herbert Holt, a bank president from Montreal. The commission hired an American, E.H. Bennett, to do the redesigning.

Two years later, in 1915, the Holt commission turned in its plan. The Holt Report is a fine, elegant thing, coming out of an era that in turn echoed the baroque of Louis XIV. Holt's team saw a corridor of power-buildings stretching west from Parliament Hill to the limestone bluff overlooking the acre, a promenade of stone châteaux like a receiving line at a wedding, roofs raised high and blocking the view up the Ottawa valley. The acre, and the Flats in general, remained unscathed in the plan, apart from some tinkering with the railways and a plan to send the streetcars down Duke Street. There were no recommendations about housing; this was a report about style, not content.

The Holt commissioners did ring a few bells whose notes did not die away. They recommended a vast park to the north of the city, peopled by "simple farmer or hunter folk" who could be converted to wardens, and that happened. More ominously, the Holt commission underlined the need for "control of the city by a body of expert federal commissioners." This would lead, they were sure, to the "drawing ever nearer of a dignity and beauty in Ottawa which will fit it to rank among the notable capitals of the world." They cited London, Paris, Berlin, and Rio de Janeiro as older sibling capitals worthy of emulation. The itch to be world-class, to be a player, was getting deeper.

The first serious step towards co-opting the acre into the national vision was taken in the head of William Lyon Mackenzie King, which was a fascinating place. King, the grandson of William Lyon Mackenzie (the man who had fought to get the acre back for Robert Randall), was certainly a visionary: he believed he could see beyond the grave into the future. When he became prime minister for the third time, in 1935, he started to implement the visions he had for the capital of his country. He had been walking the streets of Ottawa since 1900, having come to the city as a deputy minister at the age of twenty-six.

King decided a world-class city needed a world-class designer.

In 1936, he went to France to walk the site of the upcoming world exhibition. There he met the exhibition's chief architect, Jacques Gréber. Gréber worked under the Ruritanian title of "General Inspector of Reconstruction and Town Planning" in France; more important, he had just finished remoulding part of Philadelphia, where he had displayed his penchant for parkways, and getting railways out of city centres. King asked Gréber to take a swing at part of Ottawa. Gréber did so and in 1938 he put in a report for the "District Capital."

Then came war, and Gréber's plan went into suspended animation. In August 1945, two days after the end of the war, he got a note asking him to consider a major redesign of the whole city. The war, too, had gone to King's head. He saw Canada's tough and brave record (quite rightly) as separate from the British involvement, a turning point in the country's opinion of itself, something to be taken note of in a monumental way.

To make sure that whatever Gréber came up with could get off the planning paper and into reality, King solidified an idea that Holt had recommended thirty years earlier. The week before King wrote to Gréber, Canada got its own District of Columbia. With the Peace Tower on Parliament Hill as the centre pole, the National Capital Region was staked out like a groundsheet, nine hundred square miles on either side of the river. The fiefdoms within it, the cities and villages, kept their mayors and their councils, but chains were rattled. A higher authority, the National Capital Commission, had been turned on, with the ultimate right to expropriate.

After five years of planning, Gréber, shuttling much as Champlain once did between France and Canada, had his plan ready. In 1950, together with a choice selection of worthy citizens, he stood, pointer in hand, for the press cameras before a vast model. Laid out like a toy railway, the model portrayed the new National Capital. Mackenzie King was not there among the worthies; he had taken ill in 1948 and resigned as prime minister. He lived long enough only to see the depopulating of Le Breton Flats on paper, and died in 1950.

Looking down on the model acre, you saw only grass and a couple of tiny trees. All the people, all the buildings, were gone. A major road swept over the Flats, which was bedecked on the model in false, perfect grass and fake, perfect trees. Gréber, true to form and to Mackenzie King's sentimental fondness for arranged nature, had given the prime minister a ceremonial parkway along the Ottawa River, a showcase for Canadians to view through the windows of their motorcars. In fact, the main thing about the plan was that it declared the age of the railway dead in Ottawa and hailed the new era of the motorcar. Gréber had designed a requiem for the community that is train travel, and a fanfare for the individuality of the car. It had been easy enough for him, working to a higher vision, to take up pen and paper and erase the homes and businesses of three thousand people, substituting a manicured park motorists could look down on as they swept over his bridge to Hull.

The best-laid plans of prime ministers and foreign architects can go awry, however, and by the end of the fifties Gréber's "parkification" of the acre had yielded, as plans do, to compromise. The acre would not be a mannequin in a gentrified national shop window. Instead it would provide ground support for one of the ghastlier forms of architecture: the government complex. The acre and fifty others would be seconded, as a letter to his bosses from Lieutenant-General S.F. Clark, chairman of the National Capital Commission, stated, "at a building density which would yield about three million square feet of office space." The cars of the people employed in those square feet would disappear for the day into underground garages; the roofs of the garages would be paved terraces and gardens. Thirty-one adjacent acres would be stuffed with government buildings, high-rise apartments, and office buildings.

As George Orwell wrote in *Nineteen Eighty-four*, published only thirteen years earlier, describing the four ministry buildings that ran Peace, Truth, Love, and Plenty, "The Ministry of Truth was startlingly different from any other object in sight. It was an enormous pyramidal structure of glittering white concrete, soaring up, terrace after terrace, three hundred metres into the sky. The Ministry of Truth contained, it was said, three thousand rooms above ground level, and corresponding ramifications below."

On April 19, 1962, the two local newspapers published a reworking of a press release issued by the National Capital Commission. The headline in the *Ottawa Journal* read: "Gov't Takes Over 150 Acres of 'Flats'" (actually 154, including 60 acres of railway yards, 12 acres of streets, and 53 of private dwellings). The National Capital regionnaires had been secretly working up the expropriation notices for years, and on this day they had filed them. The acre would become part of a "transformation into a dazzling new annex to Parliament Hill," the *Journal* said, whereas before it had been "rail-yards, junk and scrap piles, garages, tractor-trailer sheds and largely down-at-the-heel row housing."

The rationale for these momentous changes came from Public Works Minister David J. Walker, who spoke to the press that day. Walker wanted the people of Le Breton Flats to know that one day, what was about to happen to them — their houses would be torn down over the next two years and they would be relocated — was going to feel like a "godsend." It was amazing, Walker assured them, "what the Central Mortgage and Housing Corporation could do to put people in new and better surroundings."

Walker led the Le Bretoners to a vision of the new order, the concrete altar on which the sacrifice of their homes and businesses would be made. "It simply didn't make sense that there should be Parliament Hill here, and directly to the west this incredible eyesore," he said. "Something had to be done, and we are doing it. It is the translation into steel and stone of the prime minister's vision of Ottawa as a great and beautiful world capital." And then, because all visions need something to focus on, he injected urgency and said he wanted as much as possible to be accomplished by 1967, when Canada would celebrate its hundredth birthday.

Send in the Lawyers

"Owning" land is a myth. Ownership of part of the earth's crust is really no more than leasing, with the option to sell the lease. Expropriation is always possible, by an act of government or an act of violence. In the acre's case, Chapter 106 of the Expropriation Act of 1952 gave sanction to the unhousing of the 2,800 people who lived and worked on the Flats. The buildings and lives on the acre were officially part of a dying community. It was to be an ordered death, an act of state-sanctioned euthanasia that would take two years to see through and be attended by a team of lawyers.

One thing lawyers know how to make is documents, and there were enough legal documents relating to the "taking of the lands" (as one of the documents called it) on Le Breton Flats to fill a bay. Indeed, nearby Nepean Bay, the other side of the Flats, was being infilled by the direct process of dumping the city's garbage into it to form fresh land. The conversion of water into land in Nepean Bay continued even as the buildings came down, as though a hand were pushing down on Le Breton Flats and the displaced soil were coming up in the bay. Over five years, twenty-nine acres of land was reclaimed. The plan was to put a road on a dyke across the new land, giving commuters fleeing their government jobs in the new complex a way back to their suburban nests. There was talk of building a beach at the edge of the garbage infill. Refuse Beach was suggested locally as a good name for it.

The first legal document that the Le Bretoners saw was an expropriation notice. It went out en masse the day of the newspaper announcement; it laid out, without apology and in straightforward terms, how expropriation comes knocking at your door. After "Dear Sir or Madam," the opening sentence read: "This letter will advise you that on April 18, 1962, the National Capital Commission filed a Notice of Expropriation covering the property owned by you at [address]. This property is required as a site for government buildings and for the further development of the Ottawa River shoreline."

Homeowners were told that solicitors would soon be visiting with more details. For now, "It is important to realize that the Notice of Expropriation having been filed, title has been automatically transferred to the National Capital Commission." This was to warn the owners that they might want to reconsider any improvements they had been planning. No point fiddling with the wallpaper while Rome was being demolished.

The remainder of the notice contained information and advice from the commission. After the solicitors, it said, there would be appraisers, who would appreciate cooperation in deciding how much your home was worth. The commission wasn't going to come and get your house or business for two years, so you had lots of time to find somewhere else to live. If you had fire insurance, cancel it, because it wasn't your property any more. But go on paying your property taxes, and they'll be included in the eventual settlement. You can apply for an advance against settlement; pay off the debts on the property with it, then lease it back from us until you have moved away. Two weeks before you move away, give us written notice if you are a householder; a month if you are a business. The notice was signed by the director of property and planning.

Le Breton Flats was by no means the first "unsightly" part of a Canadian city to suffer the expropriate-and-demolish routine. In 1961, an entire district of Halifax had been bulldozed to make way for a cleaner view. The district was called Africville, and as the name implies, it was the black side of town. It had been populated since the 1840s by blacks who had fled north after the War of 1812, been granted some crappy land they couldn't use, and then moved into the city. It was a haven against the certain and persistent racism that beset them. The city neglected Africville to the point where it was able to condemn it.

Le Breton Flats was largely working-class French Canadian, two-thirds in fact. Most people owned their own houses on the Flats, and the National Capital Commission admitted in its study that while most were slums, some of the houses were well kept, most of them were run down but not condemnable, the sanitation was vintage but serviceable, and the sewers were holding up fine.

Two years after the Le Bretoners got their notices, Mr. G.G. Steele, secretary of the Treasury Board, got a letter from Lieutenant-General Clark saying that the expropriation and subsequent demolition were going well.

Clark, after reminding Steele that the Flats comprised "an unsightly mixture of industrial development, slum housing and railway yards," reported that compensation for the "slum residents" was proceeding rapidly. There had been 204 owners and 20 leaseholders; all but 56 of them had got their money. The bill looked likely to come in at $15 million. Consider the renovating they could have done with that in 1964, without moving people away; but that, of course, was not the point. The point, Clark restated, was to clear the decks so that "the foreground to Parliament Hill, when viewed from the west, will be greatly improved."

As for the statistics of demolition, Clark wrote that, as of May 1964, "the Commission has been able to demolish seventy-five buildings, which may contain as many as twenty-five families, out of a total of 215, and the balance are being removed as quickly as possible." He went on to say: "As is characteristic of local residential districts, when about 40% of the properties are vacated, the occupants of the balance of the housing leave voluntarily. This seems to be caused by the break-up of the social community and the remaining homes, due to their proximity to vacated housing which is subject to vandalism and to other annoyances. As a result, most of the occupants of residential properties in the Le Breton Flats have now left." You can almost hear the wind blowing through that last sentence.

Painting It Out

It is the job of the arts to record, maintain, and reincarnate stories; artists, with their singing, painting and writing, are the job's appointed mechanics. Often at the root of their artistry there is a description of land, of the meaning of place to the tribe. It's there in the songlines of the Aborigines of Australia; in the rhythms of the griots of West Africa; in the recitations of the Algonquin; in the libraries and galleries of Ottawa.

Harold Vail was not an artist, he was a businessman. Among his enterprises was a laundry on Wellington Street, a couple of blocks south of the acre. Vail was aware that a special part of the story of Le Breton

Flats was about to go under, including his laundry, and he wanted it preserved. Knowing he couldn't do the job himself, he phoned a friend, the art teacher from a local school, a man called Ralph Burton.

Burton knew something about disappearing communities, since the one he'd been born into in 1905, Newington, Ontario, was not far from the seven villages that were buried underwater at the bottom of the St. Lawrence Seaway in 1958. As a student, Burton had studied with a Parisian professor in Ottawa before the Second World War, and made money from his paintings, which appeared on such things as sporting goods calendars. In the exploding fields of Europe he got plenty of practice as a war artist, rapid-sketching the ruins of homes and people.

In 1947 Burton took himself to the Banff School of Art. There he met and befriended the famous landscape painter A.Y. Jackson, one of the Group of Seven, that most famous ménage. They took the groundwork of the Impressionists and adapted it to the unpopulated, as-is landscapes of Canada, substituting tough fir trees for umbrellas and vast lakes for the Parisian waterways.

By the time Harold Vail phoned him, Burton had travelled enough with Jackson — the two artists perching themselves on some of the finest vistas in the Ottawa River valley — that something of Jackson's style had rubbed off on him. Never bold, the thick bands of Burton's muted colours marked out components of the landscape in chunky blocks; it always seemed to be an overcast day in his oil-based world. Details were few. There was a sense in his work of nature shrugging off attempts to straighten it out; fences sagged, the edges of fields were unruly, power poles were beginning to curl. What mostly came across was the land's indifference to the artist painting its portrait.

Beginning in December 1963, but mainly in March 1964, Burton went down to Le Breton Flats in his car, and in a series of nineteen paintings he recorded the last days of this chapter of the acre's story on birch boards measuring ten inches by thirteen and a half. The boards fit snugly into the lid of his sketchbox, held at the corners by tiny metal propellers.

The lid had two arms on the front that allowed him to prop it three-quarters open on his knees, so it looked back at him like a laptop screen. When one painting was finished, after a couple of hours, he moved it to the front of the box, in the slot provided. When the second sketch was done, he headed home.

It was cold work, done in a sombre mood of requiem mixed with the underlying pleasure of doing what he had always wanted to do. Burton was a year away from sixty, getting less tolerant of winter, so sometimes he painted in the car. He was fond of cars anyway, having sold them in New York State when he was first married. He'd sold a make called Peerless. The job hadn't lasted long, and that was when he had come back to Ottawa.

As he painted, Burton smoked his pipe, out of habit saving the matches as shims to separate drying stacks of paintings when he and Jackson went on their trips. The car filled with the perfume of paint and pipe smoke. He was unconsciously messy, dabs of colour escaping onto the upholstery, his coat, his sandwich, and his forehead. He came back from his expeditions looking like a self-inflicted Jackson Pollock.

The Le Breton series of paintings are silent now, hanging in municipal offices or stored in the city's art archives, but in the background as Burton created them was the sound of bulldozers. Put your ear to the paintings and you can hear them. The nineteen windows on the past he left behind and later donated to the city are the only artistic legacy of the mood and the personality of the community that surrounded the acre. In one painting Burton was parked at the bottom of the acre, a little down the street; behind the dispatch office of Red Line Taxi you can see the roof of the Duke House, and the little hut that controlled the railway crossing on Fleet Street (renamed Queen Street West). In another, a wall of Baker Brothers still stands, the name high up on its shoulder.

The mood of the streets rises off the paintings. Queen Street West, Lett, Oregon, Duke, Booth — all seem to know their fate. The roads are riverbeds, almost dry; the slushy snow is like stale white-out. The lines of the buildings are sagging, submissive; no legionnaires of gentrification are going to arrive to straighten things out. Even the street signs are twisted by time, as though time were a prevailing wind. There are no trees. The few people we see, a bent man leaning on a bent stick, a woman listing to the tug of a child, all look as if they are trying to get out of the picture.

Look at all of Burton's paintings for a while and you see there is no light source, no shadow. It's forever overcast. The sky, the street, and the buildings are kin in colour, all fading like clothes washed too many times. The tenement doorways, some wearing rickety wooden umbrellas, are only one long step from the road. In the leafy districts of Ottawa, the houses are set a full lawn shy of the street, but here on the Flats everything was everybody's business, space was a commodity, and no one had the cash to buy elbow room. Up on the second storey, through windows no wider than a factory worker's shoulders, you could watch the world go by — the little kids from big families; the lovers, rough hand in rough hand; the established couples out on Saturday, at least one of them looking to drink the wage packet dry. Now they are outside the frame altogether.

A Level Field

The last building to come down on the Flats was the Duke House. The demolition order was signed on October 27, 1965, the day the Beatles received their MBEs at Buckingham Palace. As with almost all the other buildings on the Flats, the brotherly firm of Cohen and Cohen, who called themselves "the Happy Wreckers," got the demolition job.

A dozen young men working for a buck an hour came down to do the deed, packed national-guard style in the back of a truck. They set up a perimeter fence a body-length from the building, and all kinds of people came to watch the work-in-progress, and the end of something. The street people had set up a temporary dormitory in the empty building. Their evidence was removed, but they came back each night during the demolition, the Duke's final clients, and were gone before the men got there in the morning.

First, as always, the windows were knocked out. Then the fittings and fixtures were stripped, including the fine curved stairs and the aged wood strips from the floor, each step and strip worn down by the slow sanding of time. As they had done when they erased the seventy-four other buildings from the Flats, the Cohens set up a trailer outside as a temporary stall, and the fixtures were sold off as they left the building. One or two items were saved by the Perraults: the safe from the Duke House, manufactured by the Gary Safe Company of Buffalo, is still in service in Gerry's new bar, the Chez J.D. When I visited him, I asked why he had not called it Chez Duke.

"J.D. was the name of one of my racehorses. He won me enough money to pay for the renovations of this place when I bought it."

"Do you have anything else from the Duke besides the safe?"

"Yes, the guest book, and an old picture of the inside. But they are both a little waterlogged: burst pipe in the basement. In the guest book, the companies that drank there signed in the front — Curie's Transport, Bill the Mover — and at the back, there were pages for Individual Patronage. We had lots of that."

When the inside was down to a bare-walled hive, work began on the outside. The outer layer of house-skin was only one brick thick, veneer brick, easily brought down. A sledgehammer banged out the bottom few rows, and gravity brought an end to a century of sedate verticality. The bricks, five hundred to a pallet, were sold off-site at a nickel a brick.

At the end of the first week, the shovel came in. The more knowledgeable work-watchers, who had attended other Le Breton demolitions, passed the word along. The crowd swelled. Among the onlookers were members of the Perrault family, wearing the faces of a bedside family around a dying relative. (They had received $250,000 in compensation for the Duke, calculated from their annual gallonage, but dollars cannot replace a stolen future.) The shovel started up and, like a lobotomized boxer, knocked the building to its knees, then scooped it up and dropped it in a circus line of trucks. The Happy Wreckers had already checked in the cellar for nasty hazards; the basement was filled in with rubble — the million stories, whispers, and songs mixed in with it — until the hole was gone, and there was just level land. The Duke was down. The Flats was flat again.

The rubble from the Duke was taken across town to an area called Riverside and added to the dump there. A few years later, that part of the dump was levelled and used to support luxury condominiums. The weight of the towers bore mightily down into the earth, and somewhere underground the broken bricks from the Duke turned in their grave.

Days of Speculation
1966–1996

Put out the eyes, forbid
the drama of exits,
entrances; somewhere
in the rubble a mechanism
leaks time,
                    no place
familiar for a fly
to land
on

GARY GEDDES
FROM "WHAT DOES A HOUSE WANT?"

Whatever Next

With the demise of the Duke House, the Flats became an open book, two blank pages divided by the spine of a deserted Booth Street. The wind coming off the river blew without interruption, deprived of the sport of chasing hats down the street, drying work-soiled washing slung between houses, and pushing the summer mosquitoes away. The snow that fell in the winter of 1965 fell, for the first time, in an even, smooth blanket.

The previous text on the pages of Le Breton Flats, which had begun to scroll out a mere 120 years earlier, had been erased by bulldozers at the bidding of the National Capital Commission. The lives, and the livings, that had grown up in the thin soil had been cut and pasted elsewhere. Now the NCC was to be the author of the new, revised edition of Le Breton Flats.

The acre had been laid off as an industrial park (a modern oxymoron), the part of town that made things. It became instead a word forge, an opportunity for a thousand shackled bureaucrats and free-range consultants to have their say, and bill for it. I've read most of the stack of probes and reports the acre was subjected to; they would fill it an inch deep in paper. By September 1963, the vague official intentions for Le Breton Flats had solidified into a probable certainty. Word was that the acre was going to be drafted: it would become part of the country's national defence headquarters. The old headquarters consisted of thirty-five tired buildings scattered around town like an occupying army. The nation could be better defended from one big building.

Consequently, at the end of August 1964, an air vice-marshal, a colonel, and a captain went to visit the ever-busy Mr. Eric Thrift, the aptly named general manager of the NCC, to ask if they could put their big building on the acre. The acre would serve as the roof of the underground car park and would donate 43,560 square feet at ground level as part of the 1.6 million square feet making up the whole building. The complex would cost $48 million, and then some — three times what it cost to expropriate the Flats. Work would start in 1965 and take a decade to complete. Surrounding it, on thirty acres, would be enough government office space to meet requirements till 1985.

Already, in the memos circulating around the NCC offices, there were signs of the new word order. Once the acre had absorbed the bilingual babble of the Duke House, the timbre of the lumber-yard, and the scatology of the scrapyard; now it was part of an "initial skeleton schedule of action required through to completion of the building, in the rough form of a critical path analysis chart."

In fact, the acre was never drafted into the military. Its contours were checked, its bedrock punctured, and the health of its soil diagnosed by a squad of traffic engineers, soil specialists, landscape architects, and real estate consultants. After all that, for a reason I can't discover, the decision was made in 1973 to leave it to devices other than defence of the realm. Defence headquarters was eventually housed in a downtown building of overwhelming ordinariness alongside Colonel By's canal. The scuttlebutt (a word that originally meant a naval drinking fountain) among ex-Le Bretoners was that a military headquarters on the Flats would have been insecure. Anyone with the right equipment could have spied into it from the high-rise apartment building overlooking it on the limestone bluff. Remember, this was during the Cold War, and Le Carré had just published *The Spy Who Came In From the Cold*. It was a serviceable, durable rumour; several people told it to me straight-faced when it came up in conversation.

After retreating from the military option, the planners went back to the drawing board and began a process I can make sense of only by turning to the myth of the Hydra. Scaled tail at one end and nine heads at the other, the Hydra was one of many bad-tempered serpents that plagued the ancient Greeks. It lived in marsh alongside a river, had a taste for crops and sheep, and was known to have homicidal halitosis: with one breath it could kill. If attacked, it employed a frustrating defence: if you cut off one head, two would spring up in its place. It was eventually defeated by the enterprising villagers it picked on, who burnt down a forest, cut the heads off one by one, and cauterized the stumps with red-hot poles. The final head was buried deep in the marsh.

The acre was once a marsh, later forested. The fatal breath of change blew across the Flats and wilted the community. The acre was at the mercy of a mini-Hydra with three heads of relative ages and sizes. The oldest was the City of Ottawa, the smallest head with the least teeth. Next was the Regional Municipality of Ottawa-Carleton, a misshapen head of many lumps, with large grinding teeth of its own. Finally, dwarfing the others, was the National Capital Commission head, the one with the sharpest vision and teeth capable of chewing up whole buildings in one bite. The NCC led the attack on the acre, coming up with plan after plan, each of which was decapitated, whereupon two would spring up in its place.

The latest head began growing in 1986. The planners got serious about something called, in the new word order, Core Area West. Core Area West would straddle the Ottawa River, a sort of bilingual meadow with francophone acres on one side, anglophone on the other. Core Area West was a collective name for the cleared Le Breton Flats, the gaggle of islands in the river festooned with historic remnants of the lumber industry, and, on the Hull side, a pretty, modest tributary of the Ottawa known as Brewery Creek, whose waters were used in ale-making as early as 1844.

The acre was part of the Le Breton/Bayview portion of Core Area West. Bayview was the neighbouring acreage to Le Breton, on the west side, with a view of Nepean Bay, which is now partially filled in with city garbage but minus the projected beach. The LeBreton/Bayview project was a word-mill of wondrous proportions, rivalling in output the board-feet production of W.G. Perley's sawmills. Wading through the library of project briefs (why are they called briefs if they're so long?), explanatory brochures, public consultation reports, status reports, graphical compilations, environmental impact assessments, feasibility studies, and master plans, you get lost in verbiage. It all seems an exercise in making sentences, not fashioning a living landscape.

Eventually, by the end of the eighties, the planners had herded the words and the drawings into five separate pens, or concepts. These described a handful of ways to juggle three things: citizens, parkland, and history. These three headings broke down further. Which citizens? What ratio of rich to poor? How should we mix and match the low-rent types with the retired types with the cell-phone types with the civil-servant types? How much, and what sort of, retailing should we integrate? Should there be chic restaurants along a terraced canal, or video stores at the bottom of office blocks? Parkland comes in three varieties, like paint colours: wild, manicured, and pastoral. Should the park be by the river or in the middle? Should the history be Disneyesque, in other words "themed," padlocked in the past with reconstructions and cheery guides; or should it be unlocked and incorporated, the old buildings and waterways renovated and put to new use?

The juggling of these elements in five different ways — two parts manicured parkland, say, to one part Disney history, to four parts low-density housing — added up to five distinct philosophies. Each philosophy was given a title, and the three main elements — citizens, parkland, history — lined up behind it, according to rank. The vocabulary describing each philosophy is difficult to penetrate, but by squinting hard, hacking away at the syllables, and jettisoning the ballast, the outlines can be discerned.

• Concept One was aimed at "Consolidating the Capital." (Fanfare of trumpets.) The strong odour of theme park rises up from this one. Government would grab the big share, with federal buildings and manicured parkland ringed around a few acres of national park, the "National Oval." People would go to the oval to feel Canadian. Much of the acre would disappear under a lake adorned with boaters in the summer months, skaters in the winter. Homes and shops would be kept as far back from the river as possible. The designers came up with a clever designer phrase for this mix-and-match urban planning: "Town and Crown."

• Concept Two was dubbed a "Symbolic Bridge," *un pont symbolique*. This meant lots of roadless parkland along the river, mirrored by parkland on the opposite bank, and another national park for letting off official fireworks and meeting other Canadians (an activity done more and more in Ottawa by émigré Pacific Rim families, out on extended picnics, and people sporting the latest fashion pet, a ferret or a pot-bellied pig). The symbolism referred to bridging the old fiefdoms of Upper and Lower Canada, French and English. Architecturally, this meant squishing the federal facilities and pavilions up by the river, and having a large chunk of shops and offices in the middle of the Flats. The acre would have a multiple personality: part office building, part federal enclave, part road, and part parkland.

• Concept Three had the least cheery title of the five, "Multi-use Node." The west half of the Flats would be given over to a low-density (read "upmarket") village, the east half to a pastoral park. One quote from the planners is worth mentioning here, as an example of low-density wordage. "These elements establish a community structure within which specific uses can take a variety of forms." Quite so, but what does it mean? The acre was to be pastoral in nature, with a polygon-shaped, ornamental pool at the foot of it. On the former site of the Duke House and its contented patrons, there would be contented ducks.

• The fourth concept had the mystic label "Creating an Urban Capital." Lots of open greenland here, and symbols of national culture in expensive architectural flourishes. The national park, to be called Exhibition Park, ran either side of the canal behind the acre, leading to the old waterworks. One of the main islands would also be nationalized.

Otherwise the bulk of the Flats would revert to homes and shops in a wide block all the way to the riverbank. Mixed residencies were to be the order of the day, different ages and economies living cheek by jowl, with a premium paid for river views. The acre would be schizophrenic, half exhibition park, half housing. The planners' hearts didn't quite seem to be in Concept Four, but they enlivened it by twice describing it as "urbane" when they meant "urban." Urbane, of course, refers to well-bred politeness, a commodity for which Ottawa is famous.

• Concept Five was, drum roll, "An Agora for the Capital." Apart from a fat T shape of stores and restaurants in the middle, covering half the acre, the centrepiece would be a cheese-wedge-shaped national park in the middle of the Flats, to bring on that Canadian feeling. The thin end of this wedge lay on the acre. Most of the riverbank would be "a stage for cultural and institutional buildings," all strategically placed to make sure there was a clear view from Parliament Hill west up the Ottawa River.

The winner, the NCC plan voted most likely to succeed, was Concept Five, "An Agora for the Capital." It was promoted to the rank of "Preferred Concept." Over the next five years it was refined, and refined again, bits added, bits taken away. The bits added were offices and residences; the bits taken away were park.

The Preferred Concept remains, until the concrete starts to pour, a figment of the planners' imagination. The only way to visit this imaginary version of the acre is to take a virtual reality trip — virtual realty — into the drawings of the Preferred Concept, the way real actors now step into animated films and move about.

There is a sheaf of these drawings, black pen and ink, lying flat on my desk, printed on sheets of extra-large paper. The sheet nearest me is the "Overall View." Looking down on it, I might be in a hot-air balloon, floating above the acre, a mile east of it and a couple of thousand feet up. Below me is a paper world that hasn't been built yet and may never be. The wind is behind me, pushing me towards the acre. The sky is pure white; so is the water in Nepean Bay off in the distance. There are tiny black cars, only a few for so large a city, on the white roads. They are all of the same design. The buildings are super-clean, there is no dust, no birdsong, in the bright clean air. It's completely silent.

From up here, the Flats looks like a large dinner plate, with a wedge of white, short grass stuck in the middle, the thin end of the wedge towards me. There are tiny trees, like the tops of Q-tips, along the sides of the wedge, and a curious tower at the wide end. On either side of the wedge the dinner plate is covered with streets and buildings. None of the buildings is taller than five stories; most are four-storey rectangles, like kids' building blocks, or miniature museums. The sloping roofs do look Greekish, in keeping with the Preferred Concept, "An Agora for the Capital." I can see the intention for the acre.

The cartoon balloon loses height when I tell it to, comes down on the wedge of grass. I've moved over into another drawing, labelled "The Common." People of the future are using it; I imagine the year must be 2010, all building completed. There are three hot-air balloons, two aloft and the one I arrived in tethered to the ground. I jump out of the basket onto the white grass. The curious tower I could see from the air turns out to be a rotunda, housing an eternal flame. Caricatures of people engaged in common activities are dotted over the Common. Ottawa seems to have returned to being an ethnically challenged town; everyone is white and happy in these architectural drawings.

Over here, there's a family picnic; Dad's about to put the cooler down, Mum's already got the hamper open and is serving a salad of shredded paper. Others are seated politely nearby as though singing "Kumbaya" around a fire in front of a fake castle gateway. A troop of cross-legged Boy Scouts is listening to the silent rallying speech of a man in shorts with no features on his face. Another crowd, a huge, older one, is seated in deck chairs listening to what I hope is jazz, while behind them automatons with an infinite disposable income are passing down a row of tents labelled Japan and Romania: some kind of international consumer fair. They are static and inanimate as I walk past them towards the acre.

It's as if someone clapped his hands and time dropped into neutral.

I cross a street easily; some plague has wiped out all but a few hardy motorists. The white grass at the thinnest point of the wedge is perfect. I'm on the virtual realty acre now. Looking left, towards the river, then swivelling my head to the right, I can see that the acre has been gentrified, just like millions of other urban acres, another nudge in the global push to make all acres dress roughly the same way in one vast homogeneous culture, where only the language on the road signs lets you know where you are.

Fancy That

While the NCC was thinking ordinary planning thoughts, other minds were firing in more exotic ways. A blank piece of land the size of Le Breton Flats is a great exciter of the imagination. Cities all over the world have them now, these urban meadows, the result of clear-cutting poor communities. Heads of state, mayors, multimillionaires, and capital city planners tend to get Pavlovian about empty acreage. When they look at something like the acre, they see a bad case of arrested development and get all determined to build their sandcastles on it.

Back in the fall of 1986, a gang of local politicos, members of Ottawa's city council, went to a nice house on a nearby lake called Meech. They sat around a big table and talked about Le Breton Flats. They divided roughly into two camps. In one camp were the "Disney on the Ottawa" types; they favoured decorating the Flats with a museum full of interactive stuff, or a place they could call Canada Place that would be full of Canadian stuff, spider-webs for tourists. In the other camp were the pragmatists. Never mind museums, how about an incinerator on the Flats, or a housing development?

The big ideas hatched at Meech Lake duly floated away; nothing came of them. Five years later, a local business consortium suggested dropping $100 million, only a tenth of it theirs, on a convention centre, as a centrepiece of the Flats renewal. The city already had a new convention centre, squashed in downtown alongside the new national defence headquarters (the one originally supposed to go on Le Breton Flats). But that convention centre was too small; it couldn't handle the really big trade circuses. In fact, it must have been designed specifically not to handle them, since large trade fairs were a known thing in the world when it was built. Uncounted dollars duly went into consultants' pockets to see if it might be feasible to build a centre the right size on the acre.

Maybe the acre was suitable, maybe it wasn't; that big fish got away too, a very expensive lure stuck in its mouth. Meanwhile the public had got in on the act. A local playwright suggested inviting architects from around the world to submit plans for economical, attractive low-income communities, and building a sample of each on the Flats, an international showcase.

In 1991, the mayor of Ottawa, Jacquelin Holzman, a woman for the times, a fiscal conservative lacking in renown as an orator or as a cultural visionary, did a political U-turn. (There was plenty of room to do one on the Flats.) From an emphatic, pre-election promise of "no mega-projects for the Flats," she went in a single week from shelving the trade centre idea (estimated cost $100 million) to replacing it with a terminal for a high-speed rail link running from Windsor to Montreal. Estimated cost for the Ottawa section: $1 billion. The project would involve tunnelling under the acre and across town to join this new fast-track daydream to the old Union Station in the heart of the city, which hadn't seen a train arrive in forty years. There are anglers in Ottawa who have hooked sturgeon at the bottom of the river weighing as much as three hundred pounds, impossible to reel in. The mayor had got a hook in one of those.

Six months after the rail-link terminal idea got terminated, it was announced, after two years of planning, that plans for a $70-million aquarium on the acre had also floundered. It had come closer than most to reality, but the seed money from the city just wasn't there. The head of the aquarium corporation was left gasping. "It would have created a tremendous locomotive for the economy," he said. "It wouldn't have been just a tank for the tourists." One of the highest-priced items needed for the aquarium was twenty acres of land to build it on. The gang behind the aquarium had hoped to get it for a dollar an acre, but the NCC's asking price was a cool $1 million per.

As I write, the latest dream for the Flats has just died. In 1967, Canada had a world's fair in Montreal called Expo that for many marked Canada's coming of age. In 1986, Vancouver also had one, which didn't generate the same proud swelling in the Canadian chest, but it did teach an awful lot of people where and what Vancouver was. Another gang, the toughest yet, had decided that Ottawa should bid for the 2005 world's fair, and mount it on Le Breton Flats.

If you wanted to buy your very own world's fair and put it on Le Breton Flats, it would cost around $700 million, 1995 dollars. This project got as far as a report, made with a $70,000 grant from the Hydra heads, which proved how feasible it all was, naming Core Area West as the dandiest site in the city for it. The worldwide deadline for submissions seeking consideration as a world's fair host, June 1996, came and went with no bid from Ottawa.

All the acre has ever got was words — great heaps of them, in report after report, plan after plan, each erased to make way for a new one, like a giant Etch-a-Sketch pad. More than thirty years' worth of words, as I write this, millions and millions of words, and not one serious building has been built there. The Flats is still flat. Babies born in houses torn down in their youth are now taking their children to see the spot where Mum and Dad were born. The acre has remained vacant through all this, going about its own business while people stared at it, planned, consulted, and dreamed. Perhaps the reason that nothing has ever happened was that anything could.

Dancing Backwards

When a community is wiped off the map, the map is never wiped clean. The acre's blackboard was blank, the traces of the lives that crossed it were gone; but they left their dusty mark. After a century of habitation on Le Breton Flats, there remained, in the ground, lingering evidence that people had passed this way.

In the years following demolition, there was a revolution in our attitude to the land. Our home and native soil became, along with the air and the seas, part of the environment. There had always been an environment, of course — the parts of the earth we didn't make — but now its degradation, preservation, and restoration were taken up as a cause. The Great Lakes were a sewer; the ozone layer was turning into Swiss cheese; forests — as the acre knew all too well — were being farmed out, their experience destroyed; the rain was acidic; the earth was slowly heating up like a vast kettle. A groundswell of people sensed that we had become a serious threat to ourselves, in unhealthy and unpoetic ways. Frankensteins with fridges and Fords, we'd created a monster; the monster was loose, seeking revenge. "Nature is the witness of all our follies," wrote the Mexican novelist Carlos Fuentes.

As it grew from a mood to a movement — in the mid-eighties, the environment came out on top in a poll of Canadians' political concerns, although it would soon be superseded by deficit dread — environmentalism took on the force of a religion. The movement brought God down to earth and made the environment, the ecosystem, its roofless church. It gained disciples, and it identified its martyrs, its warriors, and its punishable sinners — the protesters run over in passive blockades, the knights of Greenpeace mounted on Zodiacs, the regulation and token fining of industrial polluters.

The acre had no idea, after so many static years, that it was part of a movement, any more than the stones of a church know that they house religion. While people were using it, the acre mutely received their by-products; the crap went in the ground, and chemical catastrophes and plagues of pollution ran through the subterranean ecosytem, in mute acknowledgment of the human bustle up above.

By the 1990s, environmentalism was an established religion. The genesis of all religions is self-interest: they're a way of getting around death. Environmentalism was no exception. It grew out of self-interest, too: environmentalists wanted to prevent a predicted hell on earth from coming any truer than it already had. The reason for the hellish state of affairs, I've come to believe, is simple lack of respect for the land beneath our feet. While everyone was looking the other way, the ancient, honourable business of respect had given way to a more modern and less honourable respect for business.

The state of the river and the soil around the acre was proof of that. When it was industrialized by the steam engine in the 1850s, the Chaudière sawmill industry began throwing off sawdust, edgings, the general garbage coming from a factory site. As early as the 1860s, the nuisance value of these clots in the river's flow was recognized, and the Rivers and Streams Protection Act was passed. The mills ignored the act — it was bad for business — and in 1873 a commission was appointed (sound familiar?) to study the problem. The manager of one of the local mills sat on the commission. The mill owners appeared at the hearings and gave their concerted opinion on regulation: thumbs down. An order-in-council was passed shortly thereafter exempting, for two miles either side of the Chaudière Falls, the mills from the protection act. The problem thus grew, and in 1886 a boat-house operator on the Ottawa reported "hideous deserts of saw-dust."

A century later the acre had its own problems. Sooner or later, they would have surfaced, but the combination of demolition and the urge to redevelop the Flats, plus the political fascination with environmental impact assessments — the secular result of environmentalism's sermons — led the NCC to start prodding and probing the Flats, to map out the toxic ghosts of a hundred years of industry. In 1991, a consultant's report summarized several previous studies, and did some digging of its own. It's interesting how much like a medical report parts of it read.

"The most significant environmental impact related to the redevelopment of Le Breton Flats/Bayview concerns the contamination of soils and groundwater throughout the area due to the areal extent of this contamination and the presence of unacceptable levels for some of the identified contaminants." The report went on to mention a 1988 study that used historical documents, plans, photos, and visits to investigate sites throughout the city with a potential for hidden nasties. Most sites, the authors decided, were "deemed to present little or no environmental risk."

However, two spots on Le Breton Flats were among those in the city where "the probability of residual wastes was judged to pose a higher risk of environmental impact." One of them was Baker Brothers; the report said it had been "the site of bulk oil storage facilities and a waste material warehouse. Also on site were two gas stations and an oiling pit. Since demolition of these facilities, the vacant site has been used as a snow dump. The risk associated with storage facilities was the leakage or spillage of petroleum products which contain hazardous chemicals (benzene, toluene, xylenes), other aromatic compounds and occasionally lead." The other hot site was the home, for sixty-seven years, of the Ottawa Paint Works, just west of the acre. The rock below there was contaminated with heavy metals — red and white lead, cadmium, chromium — and haunted with hydrocarbon waste.

The Flats had also been dumped on periodically since the Depression, with snow and garbage. The garbage dumps — two of them, one eighteen acres, the other nineteen — were as deep as a basketball player in most spots, and as deep as one player standing on another's shoulders in others. The acre had also shouldered its fair share of dirty snow sucked up from the city streets. All this meant that there was methane percolating in the old garbage dump sites, in some spots in concentrations "well over safe limits," and a "high lead content" residue beneath the former snow dumps.

The consultants wrapped up their report by looking at the "significance of soil and groundwater contamination" in the places where, according to the "Agora for the Capital" plan, there was going to be disruption. "On all the sites studied," they decided, "the results indicate the presence of a range of heavy metals in concentrations that exceed the Ontario Ministry of the Environment criteria for the projected land use." In the soil, "the potential for significant environmental impacts is widespread, particularly during the construction period. There is also significant risk of long-term environmental impacts." In the groundwater, "the possibility of migration of contaminated groundwater towards the aqueduct or the Ottawa River, in itself, constitutes an issue of environmental concern. The groundwater in the area of Le Breton Flats is not to be used as a drinking water source."

I don't envy the NCC, which has inherited this Pandora's box. If the commissioners want to build on the Flats, they are going to have to lift the lid. It's going to cost them — which means us — a large fortune to rid the acre of its accumulated afflictions and bring it up to modern standards. The better course may be to disturb it as little as possible, while cleansing it as much as possible.

As I write, the NCC has asked companies who specialize in the cleanup of toxic leftovers — the modern hired dragon-slayers — to name their price for dealing with the ground around the former site of the Ottawa Paint Works, thirty years after the factory was demolished. The NCC considers this site a priority, to prevent the mingled toxins below, which are spreading in a "plume" (the NCC's word) towards the Ottawa River, from reaching it. Remedies being considered include skimming off six feet of topsoil and taking it somewhere else, or drilling drainage holes straight down into the earth to speed up "natural decay."

Our degrading of the earth is not new; it began, like the weathering of mountains, as soon as we were lifted up. The excavated sites of the earliest cities in the Near East show that they sat on extended piles of garbage. In 312 B.C. the Romans built their first aqueduct to carry in fresh water — they'd decided the Tiber was too polluted to use. Strabo, a Roman from the sixth century, recommended chimneys for lead smelters, to carry away the deadly gas. The burning of coal was banned in London in 1307, but nobody took any notice. In 1912, Chicago had to deal with the disposal of ten thousand expired horses.

Those earlier crises aren't a patch on recent developments. The panoply of homicidal pollutants our twentieth-century ingenuity has spawned is amazing. The astonishing variety of tools in our box has made the modern city possible, but it has dismantled, not built up, our respect for the land the cities stand on. The deeper we draw on our wits to prop up the modern city (Seoul and Mexico City are already past 20 million; the greater Ottawa area is one of the fastest-growing metropolitan regions in Canada), the dryer becomes the well of respect.

The key to stopping the erosion of respect is ritual; I'm certain of it. The rituals of respect for birth, marriage, and death are still around, but the rituals of respect for the land beneath our city feet have faded. North American environmentalism, when it was taking its first steps, had no stock of rituals on hand to stoke up respect — so it went to the First Nations, and borrowed theirs (even ones they weren't using themselves). The fascination with native ceremonies, music, and philosophy was rejuvenating, but in the end it was nostalgia for something that, for the majority of Canadians, who live in cities, was never theirs.

A fresh set of rituals, urban rituals for urban acres, is what's required, to revive the idea of stewardship — we have inherited the city and its foundation, we are guardians rather than owners, we are fleeting parts of something more vast and encompassing than we allow. It's fine to fight for the cute parts, the rural acres and the wilderness, but the ugly metros are also in need of redemption. Respect can be infiltrated into our cultural rituals — movies, plays, books, songs, even a TV series — as Yves Beauchemin did in his novel *Juliette*, about the desecration of historic Montreal. Some other possibilities for ritual: on each new building, include a picture and the story of the one it replaces. Teach local history in schools on CD-ROM, but then take it outside. Institute an annual welcoming festival, a ceremonial greeting for new citizens.

There's a chance that some day we'll exhaust the land with our nagging energy and our growing numbers. A revival of respect, and the rituals that go with it, could govern our worst tendencies. The acre, meanwhile, neither knows nor cares if we respect it. If and when we are gone, it will swallow what we've forced down its throat and then fall to the task of repair. It is to our benefit to perform the rituals, to use our resourcefulness to understand and maintain the acre's resources.

The Sermon on the Flats

In the absence, year after year, of imposed progress, the acre defaulted to rituals of leisure. The city's squad of hot-air balloonists, who knew a flat space when they saw one, held several festivals on the Flats. There aren't many sights more glorious than a hundred balloons — tigers, beer cans, castles, horses, and dozens of the regular light bulbs — drifting like dandelion seed through a summer sky. Cirque du Soleil, the famous Montreal circus, came to town and pitched its animal-free big top on it. Dogs took their owners for their ritual walks across it. And in 1984, a more spectacular ritual came to town.

When a pope comes to visit and wants to hold a mass, the first problem is where to put him. This was a pope, John Paul II, who had considerable mass appeal. He wasn't Italian, he was Polish, and a controversial reactionary. He had been admitted to the select club of world leaders who have been shot and survived. His twelve-day tour of Canada, in September, was due to wind up in Ottawa with an outdoor communion and message to the world. Estimates of the expected crowd went as high as three hundred thousand souls. If Pope John Paul was going to break bread with a congregation of that size, right downtown, there was only one place to stage it.

If you opened the gates of a field and asked three hundred thousand people to walk in and sit down, the field would need to be forty-five acres large. Forty-five acres of Le Breton Flats was duly roped off. Because the acre had a raised lip in the northeast corner, and the parkway and the aqueduct valley provided a natural limit to the Flats on that side, that corner of the acre was chosen as the site of the altar. In front of the altar, in the six-thousand-seat reserved section, separate but adjacent, would sit the handicapped and the privileged members of the church and the community. There was also to be a large delegation from Wilno, a dot on the map west of Ottawa that is Canada's oldest Polish community. Elsewhere on the site the various needs of any huge-scale event were catered to — stalls for the reporters who would bestow secular blessing on the proceedings, a hospital tent to repair the inevitable human damage, and, most vital, a Pentagon-shaped maze of toilets on the site of the old fire station.

The altar-makers moved onto the acre a month before the Pope was due to commune, on the same ground where the peddlers and the junk collectors, Ottawa's lowly, had come to have Jake Baker judge and reward their heavy loads. The altar was dedicated to an ancient piece of spiritual theatre Jesus Christ had scripted: wine for blood, wafer for flesh, the taking of spirit within. About the time that last supper had unfolded in Jerusalem, woodlanders had stood alongside the Asticou waterfall and hurled tobacco into the foam, in their own act of communion.

A week before the Pope would mount it, the altar was finished. Originally, altars were places of simple sacrifice (the word *altar* comes from a Latin term meaning to burn up) but this was a contemporary ritual, designed to allow a modern multitude, schooled in the ways of celebrity, to hear and see a spiritual pageant. It was showbiz with soul. Thirty feet above the stage a big bouquet of white umbrellas sheltered the highest of the Catholic hierarchy from the elements, and lit them with theatre lights. The biggest sound system Ottawa had ever heard would spread the papal word over all forty-five acres. And a giant TV screen would broadcast close-ups of the Sermon on the Flats.

All week the pre-communion show was rehearsed; the night before the mass some of the hardier faithful camped as near to the stage as they could. A few local camping stores had been offering See-the-Pope! discounts. A soap bar called Pope-on-a-Rope was a brisk mover. The day before the mass you couldn't buy a deck chair in Ottawa, even if you offered up your first-born. The campers mingled merrily and watched gangs of volunteers set up chairs, drive in the metal posts, and string the red ribbons that would divide the crowd into corrals of five thousand.

At five the following morning, under a sky cloudy and full of rain, the early birds began arriving. They filled the corrals nearest the stage, then worked their way back. It was the greatest weight of humanity the acre had ever felt. By mid-morning fifty-three corrals were packed tight. In among the quarter-million were hundreds of ex-Le Bretoners; people recognized one another and talked of now and then. Everyone sat through a two-hour video of the Pope's Canadian tour. They sat through an orchestra, two choirs, and the inevitable square-dancing. The price of the souvenir program was dropped by half, to $5, and still forty thousand of them didn't sell. Then the sky made good on its threat and the huddled mass sat through a short, fierce rainstorm the Pope was powerless to prevent. Umbrellas bloomed like crocuses, and the sound of rain on canvas hid the crowd noise that tracked the Pope's approach. He was late, but dry and visible inside the bulletproof bell-jar on the back of the Popemobile.

Three-quarters of an hour behind schedule, Pope John Paul II travelled down Duke Street, waving his arm. The crowd chanted and waved gold-and-white flags at him. The Pope then looped around behind the acre, disappeared into the changing room at the back of the stage, and emerged in a crocodile line of bishops. The sun, of course, came out.

Those receiving mass directly from the Pope's hands included a hundred locals and twenty of the nine hundred people there in wheelchairs, a disparate tribe parked in front of the altar. A Polish heart-transplant patient had the health of his three-month-old second heart inquired after. The Pope's message, which condemned physical violence on a grand and personal scale, was telecast across lands and oceans; for a brief moment, the acre was seen in millions of homes. By early evening, the Pope was on a plane back to Rome and the clean-up began. Three days later, the acre was back to its normal state of limbo, awaiting a decision on the exact nature of its reincarnation.

A year later, in the fall of 1985, three men sat in Fuller's diner on Bank Street, in the south of Ottawa: John Albert, Tony D'Amico, and Armand Vanasse. They were all born on Le Breton Flats almost sixty years earlier, within a year of each other. They had grown up never more than a street apart, had swum naked together in the "52," the deep part of Nepean Bay that went down that many feet, had run out over the log rafts, brave and fearful of getting rolled under, and had been handed a Catholic education. They had watched the older boys catch strange-looking, wormy fish in the aqueduct, then throw them back. To make a quarter, they'd scavenged for scrap — an old tire, copper wire, a stack of newspapers, rags — and taken it over to Baker Brothers; Baker Brothers had sponsored their hockey team, which played in the park by the western end of the aqueduct.

When the three boys ended up in separate grade schools, Tony, eight years old, walked out of Saint-Jean-Baptiste and down Nanny Goat Hill to Sainte-Famille, the two-room school that first put the books to generations of Le Bretoners. While Armand watched, Tony told the teacher he'd been demoted and would have to rejoin his friends. It was the first of many little routines Tony would work up in his life. He was the comedian in the trio, but he could knock a home run farther than anyone else on the Chaudière softball team, then relive it and add a few yards afterwards.

The three men, then in their mid-thirties, were all still there when they got the notice of expropriation; Armand and John lived opposite each other. (Armand still needles John about the time John's sister called the cops on Armand, for playing music too loud — "she should have just crossed the street.") John was building a basement extension for his family of six kids, out under the summer kitchen, when the notice arrived in the mailbox. "To hell with that," he told himself, and left the hole half dug. All that remains of his home on Sherwood Street is the two elm trees he planted in the fifties; the bulldozers went around them. The Alberts moved April 1, 1963 — a sunny, sad day — to a bungalow on a crescent in suburbia; likewise the Vanasse family. The Alberts actually bought the bungalow in 1962, but stayed on the Flats for one last Christmas.

John and Armand worked in the post office till retirement, and stayed busy after it. Tony went into the army, came out, tried a few businesses, didn't have the knack, and became the manager at the navy club on Victoria Island, in the last bit of the Flats that still looked like the old days. When the Pope came to town, some secular sense of communion moved in Tony, perhaps the communion of shared memory. It was in his genes, too; his dad, a musician, had helped Italian immigrants find their feet in Ottawa, and taught several of them to play.

At the diner table, a year after the Pope's visit, the three men talked. Tony, balding now, with a curtain of white hair around his head, started a couple of stories the way he always did: "You know so-and-so? Well," and off he'd go, gossiping at a slow canter. Then he asked what they thought of a Flats reunion. A dance, for as many people from the old place as they could unearth. Get a committee going, work the phones. A night to remember. A night for remembering.

The idea clicked, loud and hard. They tracked down one ex-Le Bretoner from each of the old streets, got them to call former neighbours; the mailing list grew to a hundred, two hundred, three. They got formal about it, and appointed a president — Tony. Fay Charron, bless her, did the secretary work; she had a computer at her office. Notices went in the paper. They settled on a place — the church of Saint François d'Assise, the patron saint of ecologists — and a date — third Saturday in April.

Invitations went out, starting "Dear Friends." A separate committee worked on the program, winkling out businesses that used to operate on the Flats, or tracking down ex-Le Bretoners now self-employed, getting them to chip in for an advert to cover expenses: Gilbey's Distillery, Convention Signs, Touch of Europe. Someone was dispatched to the library to research the history of the Flats, and they boiled the past down to five dates, so it would fit on one page: 1818, the Richmond settlers; 1820, John Le Breton buys the lot for under £500; 1900, the fire; 1959, the population on the Flats reaches 1,320; 1962, April 18 — expropriation begins.

On the day of the dance, the committee spent the afternoon making sandwiches at the navy club. They figured four hundred people would show, so they piled up enough ham and cheese and egg salad to feed an ark. When they drove over to the hall, in the basement of the church, the DJ was setting up — the stage was directly below the altar — and Roger Fournier was stringing signs clear across the room like Main Street on Canada Day. There was just one bar. They opened the doors at six-thirty, and the ex-Le Bretoners and their families poured in, the way logs used to jam up and then burst free at the Chaudière Falls bottleneck. A hundred, three, five, seven hundred people, a few cops among them who would have had to be blind — and deaf — not to know that some licence violations were evident here.

"They shrugged and smiled in an off-duty sort of way," John Albert said, sitting at his kitchen table with Armand Vanasse and me. (Tony D'Amico died four years ago, of cancer.) "Tony managed to hush the noise down and say a few words of welcome, and remembrance, and the night began."

The applause after Tony never died down; it just blended into the noise of words and music. Everyone's tongue did a few laps around the old days, and tried to follow the trail of as many lives as they could. The former sports stars — footballers Mose Siegel and Billy Collins — pulled out the old glories. Couples bumped hips on the dance floor, sang off-key in each other's ears. Photos got passed back and forth like cards at a whist drive.

"The smoke was like a fog," said John Albert. "Every now and then a loud toast would go up at a table. People worked out on their fingers the last time they'd seen each other."

They kept it up past midnight, past one o'clock, and stacked up the chairs around two, still talking. It was a ritual of memory, almost an orgy. As I talked to John and Armand ten years later, a snatch of a poem I'd heard once, on a bus tour of Ottawa's literary highlights, popped in my head. I didn't feel safe reciting it from memory for them, but I looked it up. It's by Clive Doucet, writer and poet laureate of an Italian restaurant, from his epic poem "Before Star Wars." Doucet used to play as a kid on Le Breton Flats, and remembers:

Acres of childhood.
Childhood's supposed to be magical or golden.
I remember it mostly in streets and acres.
I remember Le Breton Flats
Before the government demolished it.
Men and women drinking beer
on stoops in the summer heat.
The streets cracked and worn.
The old, red brick houses leaning
against each other for support.

The ghosts of demolished buildings are not in the habit of reappearing. But it wouldn't have surprised anyone at the dance if, walking home in the chill April moonlight, past the cleared acres, the outline of a stoop had appeared beside a cracked, abandoned street, and the clink of beer bottles had come echoing over the grass.

Never Surrendered

What is history? It's an ever-growing collection of events past their due date. It's leftovers, the crumbs of something time ate. It's a shoebox stuffed with facts, waiting to be sorted out. But putting those facts in the right order is not always easy, because facts have hidden personalities.

Historians, meeting new facts, never take them at face value. It's the same with particle physicists: hard at work in a different part of the fact factory, they've concluded that the observer is not aloof from the experiment. The observer is actually a variable, able to affect the outcome. Change the observer and you change the result. Historians have long known this to be true. Just who happens to be looking at a set of historical data (in this case me) has a considerable effect on the story of what happened; someone's paradise gained can be someone else's paradise lost. It's a matter of perspective. This dual nature of history — part fact, part interpretation — has led to such sayings as "History is written by the winners," or "All of history is gossip," or, my favourite, "History is a set of lies agreed upon." None of these is strictly true, but they all serve as useful taps on the historian's shoulder.

Consider the fact of the acre's ownership. The answer to the question of who, in fact, has title to the acre is not as cut-and-dried as it might seem. Certainly, the winners — the British — having defeated the French, considered themselves the title-holders from 1759 on. The fact of the matter for the British is that they won Canada fair and square, in the deadly lottery of battle. As victors, they went through the motions of buying the land from the natives, then moved in with the speed of beavers, customizing the landscape as they went.

In the spectacularly ugly Court House, an anthill for lawyers in the centre of Ottawa, known to locals as Fort Court because of its military appearance and judicial function, the chain of owners of the acre is written down in large books in the provincial Land Registry Office. Opening them is a two-handed task; each page is the size of a small desk. On the pages relevant to the acre, the entries for the title-holders of the acre's several lots begin with John LeBreton and pass to his flock of nieces. From then on the list of people who have called some part of the acre their own divides out like a family tree. From branch to branch money changes hands down through the generations in swelling amounts. Each list comes to an abrupt halt, with the line "NOTICE 17 APRIL 62 NATIONAL CAPITAL COMMISSION EXPROPRIATION WHOLE ETC." After this line the acre has, in effect, a second childhood. It becomes again what it once was: Crown land.

But during all of those 175 years, there have been ghosts in this list, invisible to the legal eye. The ghosts are the Algonquins, who, despite fighting alongside the British, had a forced history lesson from them in the ways of property, when they learnt the hard fact that land can be bought and sold. The Algonquins became strangers in their own land, aliens in a world of property values, of grants and treaties. When the registry books were written, the Algonquins were left out. But the Algonquins have a list of their own. It's a list not of entries in a land registration book but of petitions to the British royal family, hoping at least for the same treatment that other Canadian native bands received: the right to say Yes, we give you title to our land. Or No, we don't. The right to be asked nicely.

The first monarch of Britain to have a petition addressed to him from the Algonquins, as we've seen, was George III. "Farmer George," a king at his happiest away from cities, was a busy man, losing and gaining colonies, dealing with difficult children, eventually going blind. Although he sat on the throne for another forty-eight years after the Algonquins, in 1772, had requested he honour the terms of the Royal Proclamation, they got no reply. George III died visionless and mentally loose the same year the acre was sold to John LeBreton.

The next George, who remained faithful to the mathematics of monarchy — George IV — was king for ten years. Several petitions were sent his way, but he was too preoccupied with entertaining, dressing up, and supervising extravagant confections of architecture like the Brighton Pavilion to consider a request for native rights.

In 1830, the British royal family took a break from Georges and had a William, also the fourth. As a prince, at the age of twenty-one, William had visited Canada, the first member of the royal family to do so. He was sixty-five when he took up the crown, and he wore it only seven years. He was an honest man, somewhat palace-bound; he never replied to Constant Penency's request for some quiet land, away from the canal-building tearing up his hunting territory.

Then Victoria, at age eighteen, in 1837, began her era. She oversaw one of the greatest land-grabs in history, staining huge portions of the world's map Empire red. When she took the throne, Victoria could count the number of her subjects living on the acre on one royal hand. She died in 1901, as the acre was repopulating itself after the fire of 1900. It was about midway through her tenure that the stream of Algonquin petitions to the kings and queens of their conquerors dried up.

By the 1850s, most of the remaining Algonquins were living north of the Ottawa River. In 1857 the Lower Canada Algonquins were granted, as though they were settlers arriving late, two parcels of land, postage stamps on the envelope they had once wandered. On the southern side of the river, in Upper Canada, a handful of Algonquin families had been funnelled onto land on the south shore of Golden Lake. Golden Lake is about a hundred miles west of the acre. The five families were weary of shifting; they didn't want to move again. So, with deliberate irony, they asked for the same two hundred acres each that the original British settlers had got — settlers who were still buying up land all around them.

The request took seven years to reach Ottawa. Finally, in 1864, the Ottawa government took $1,561 out of the Indian Affairs budget, bought 1,561 acres on Golden Lake from the Upper Canada government, and settled most of the remaining Algonquins on it. The Algonquins accepted this patrimony by default, even though they were certain they had never signed a treaty with either government. They believed they were right — the Royal Proclamation of 1763 still held legal sway, but the British had never kept to their promise. "No strangers, my Children, have a right to establish themselves on your hunting ground," Farmer George had told them, but there the strangers were, at the very edges of the reserve, looking in.

The last petition was sent to Victoria on July 21, 1863, the year Abraham Lincoln declared the American slaves free. The Algonquins had sent twenty-nine petitions; although addressed to the Great Father or Mother, they never left Canada. The governor, more likely his staff, handled them, and never replied. The original petitions are stored in the National Archives, on the site of the burial ground discovered during construction of the Union Bridge.

A hundred years later, when the acre was still being considered as a site for an Orwellian government complex, the interest of the Algonquin Golden Lake First Nation in what had happened to the title on their lands was revived by their chief, Chief Dan Tennisco, who asked a simple question. What was a railway doing running through their reserve? Had they ever sold any of their land to a railway company? Research into that question turned up a bigger question. Have we ever, in fact, sold any of our lands to anyone? Surrendered them? Signed a treaty of cession?

All the research the Algonquins did pointed to the answer no. At the end of 1982 every adult on the Golden Lake Reserve was canvassed; all agreed that they should claim back title to their lands from the federal and provincial governments. They had no wish to wind back events until they became once again the rightful stewards of the entire southern watershed of the Ottawa River, an area of 8.5 million acres. History moves only forward. Rather, they wished for their title to those acres to be acknowledged, and some form of compensation to be computed and handed over. They wanted to talk about how land was taken, and where the taking led to, and whether the descendants of the original takers felt history could be repaired. They wanted to get the story of their land straight.

When they wrote up their 1983 petition, the Algonquins, wise to the PR power of tradition, used the same language their ancestors had. The petition opened with the phrase "since time immemorial our Nation has occupied and enjoyed the territory." The Algonquins spoke of "great promises" that were "only promises and so light that they were blown away by the first wind," and said that "innumerable squatters" had "destroyed our magnificent forest, abused our ancestors, and forced them into pitifully small tracts of land in abject poverty." They ended by praying that discussions would soon begin. They addressed the petition to the "Personal Representative Of Her Majesty The Queen Elizabeth The Second," the great-great-great-great-granddaughter of the first monarch they had asked to keep a promise, 220 years earlier.

The land the Algonquins wanted title to was a fair slice of Ontario. If the shape of Ontario can be said to resemble a mukluk, then the Algonquin title dispute was the heel. By disputing the title to a swath of land that size, the Algonquins, if they ever reached the negotiation stage with their petition, would need a three-sided table — themselves on one side, the Ontario government on the next, and the federal government on the third. With a fine sense of historical irony, the area included the capital of Canada. There were jokes in the press, including some from politicians, to the effect that the Algonquins were welcome to it.

On February 2, 1983, with the classically worded petition in a briefcase, four men from Golden Lake drove off the reserve and down the hundred miles to Ottawa, pulling up at Rideau Hall, the home of Queen Elizabeth's personal representative in Canada. One of the men was Greg

Sarazin, who subsequently became the chief negotiator for the Golden Lake First Nation, and the acre's most recent champion. Sarazin wore a buckskin jacket into the plush receiving room, where the men handed over the petition to Governor General Edward Schreyer. Then they held a press conference. In effect they were nailing the petition to a maple tree, and waiting to see what happened.

Can We Talk?

Lots of nothing happened for four years. Sarazin, meanwhile, had become chief (as well as chief negotiator), and after five years of silence from Her Majesty, he turned up the political decibels. It was a time of native unrest across the country, a series of fires breaking out after smouldering for too long. In 1988, the road into Algonquin Park, named after the people from whom it was usurped, was blockaded on the Labour Day weekend. Politicians and others going into the Houses of Parliament in Ottawa were reminded that they were on Algonquin land. "As chief," Sarazin said, "I was always there on the steps, welcoming to Algonquin territory any aboriginal people who went in to visit Parliament, and giving formal sanction for them to be there. Then I'd make a speech about Algonquin rights."

The Algonquins now had some luck. In 1990, in a surprise election result, the government of Ontario swung left, to a party that had included in its election platform the promise of resolving native land claims. It was a small promise compared with the one George III had made in 1763, when he forbade any individual to "appropriate to themselves a single particle of your hunting grounds," but it was a promise. On June 15, 1991, the Ontario government and the Algonquins signed an agreement to begin talks. A 220-year silence had ended. Eighteen months later, in December 1992, the federal government, the party with the acre in its suit pocket, took its place on the third side of the table.

Two and a half years later I travelled west from the acre to the Golden Lake reserve, to ask Greg Sarazin how the talks were going. I followed the river for an hour, then cut inland. Land that only two centuries earlier had been a dense fur of woodland was now cleared and cultivated, a web of fences and fields, the population moving like a slow wind off the fields and into the city streets.

You know right away when you have driven onto a reserve. The houses become more basic, more similar, and the urge to manicure nature is less pronounced. Cars that would be dead if Detroit had its way are still running. A third of the remaining thousand Ontario Algonquins live here, and only eight of those speak fluent Algonkin. The reserve is slightly bigger than it was in 1873 — 1,745 acres — and it's still the only Algonquin reserve in Ontario.

The Makwa recreation centre, at the heart of the reserve, is like any other small-town arena. It was in the main hall on the ground floor that the Golden Lake First Nation celebrated in December 1992 when they finally got a federal reply to their petitions. There was a drumming grand entry, a sweetgrass ceremony, speeches and songs, eating and drinking, and a reading of the wampum belts by their keeper, Chief William Commanda of the Maniwaki reserve, beneath the large papier-mâché bear paw on the wall.

Greg Sarazin's office is on the second floor of the Makwa centre. As in many similar administrative offices in Ottawa, there is native art on the wall, including a painted deer skull. The difference here is that Sarazin shot the deer himself, one shot, and knows the man who painted it, Norman Knott. The Pope, the Queen of England, and Prince Charles also have examples of Knott's craft. Sarazin is a compact man whose eyes narrow down when he smiles. He isn't voluble, and waits a moment before he speaks, as though polishing his words before releasing them. I doubt he flusters easily. He carries behind his pacific face as much knowledge of the history of the Algonquins as anyone can, and he has been talking about the past and future of the acre, and the other 8.5 million acres in the title dispute, for fourteen years. It's what he does. Every two weeks he sits at one of three tables — one in Ottawa, one in Toronto, or one of the trestle tables in the hall below. He and his assistants face the chief negotiators of the other two governments and their assistants, eighteen people in all. "I sit about as far apart from the other chief negotiators as that guide you mentioned did from Champlain in the canoe in 1613. We talk nation to nation, from a position of equality."

Hour after hour, the two nations try to sort through the facts in the shoebox. One of those facts is the acre. The negotiators have come together down different historical paths; somewhere ahead is the single path they can leave by, and they proceed towards it by putting one word in front of the other. There is no discussion of history; by agreeing to talk, all parties have agreed to move towards a settlement. They talk instead about the 2 million private homes pinned to the 8.5 million acres under dispute. The Algonquins, aware of how it feels, have no wish to pull the rug out from under those families. They talk about Crown land and how much, for the sake of argument, it might be worth. Such divers establishments as the Houses of Parliament, a Canadian army base, all of a brand-new national gallery, an arts centre, and a museum of civilization packed with native artifacts stand on Crown land inside the disputed area. The Algonquins look for enough money, in lieu of taking back the acreage they never did cede, to become financially secure as a self-governing people; the other two governments, primarily the provincial government, which controls most of the title dispute, look to make "enough" as little as possible, and be fair to their taxpayers. The modern ones.

The acre is part, then, of something as simple as a custody battle. It was, the Algonquins have declared, snatched from them, raised by surrogates and turned out to work. Its true lineage has been recently discovered; who will claim its allegiance from now on? There is a day in the future when the dispute will end. Not this year, not next, but hopefully sometime, surely not never. (Another swing in government in Ontario, this one back to the right — about as far right as Texas — has dropped the talks into a lower gear for at least the next five years.) Till then the acre is in limbo. It may cease to be Crown land, and become Algonquin territory, its welfare a matter of Algonquin concern. Or, if the price on its head is agreed and paid, the NCC may get to keep it. The NCC seems to be proceeding as if it's a done deal.

Before I leave the reserve, Sarazin takes me to a workshop behind the house of his father, Dan. It's the size of a standard one-car garage, with a view of Golden Lake through the back window. On the floor, where the car should go, there is a half-finished canoe — a birchbark canoe, its method and materials of construction identical to those that went into its ancient forebears. Dan Sarazin is famous for his canoes. This being July, it is time for Dan to go into Algonquin Park and harvest the birch bark used to cover the two or three canoes he produces each year. Algonquin is one of the few protected wilderness areas left near Golden Lake that have birch of sufficient quality and girth.

When the canoe is finished, a short walk will carry it to the Sarazins' dock. Travelling across Golden Lake and down the Bonnechere River, it could reach the Ottawa River at a wide stretch called Lac des Chats. From there, with a couple of minor portages, two long days' paddling would bring it to shore at the foot of the sharp slope under the Parliament Buildings. A short walk along a path brings you to the Rideau Canal. Cross that, walk up the slope to Nepean Point, and you come to a larger-than-life statue of Samuel de Champlain.

In the pose chosen by the sculptor, Champlain is taking a reading with his astrolabe, a hand-held navigational device that helped him work out how far north he was. (The sculptor has put the astrolabe in Champlain's hand upside down. Had Champlain taken a reading as posed, he would have wondered how he had come to be so far south of the equator.) The explorer's pose is heroic, his clothes are immaculate. He is facing upriver, gazing along the route he took in a birchbark canoe in 1613, when all the land at his feet ceased being Algonquin hunting territory and became Nouvelle France.

At the foot of the pedestal supporting Champlain, on one knee, with a bow across his shoulder, a leather skirt, and a feather in his headband, is a generic, life-size Indian. The Unknown Indian. It's the only statue portraying a native in Ottawa, and it's a footnote, literally, to the prominence of Champlain. The Indian's gaze is also trained upriver, across the acre and towards the land he once knew as his partner in survival. I like to think of it as a statue of Constant Penency, as yet unacknowledged and awaiting transfer to a pedestal of his own. It's Constant I imagine making the journey in the canoe built by Dan Sarazin.

If the Unknown Indian were to come to life and turn his head, he would see a city that includes an Algonquin Hotel, an Algonquin Animal Hospital, an Algonquin Auto Body shop, an Algonquin Careers Academy, an Algonquin Commercial Collection Agency, and a company called Algonquin Moving Systems. It's become a habit with natives to drape a blanket over the statue — not to blind him to the city, but to remove him from his position of minor billing to Champlain — until he gets a pedestal of his own. I've an idea where the pedestal could go.

Sunset
JUNE 21, 1996

It is not the land
that spells the end of things.
From the bones we lay
forever in the earth,
at the urging of sun and wind
something grows
something rises to the light
and has its say.

LORNA CROZIER
FROM "TIME TO PRAISE"

Internal Memory

A thin woman walks a Great Dane past the acre, some exercise between rain showers. Pointing my deck chair towards the intermittent sun, I take a seat under the young Manitoba maples planted on the site of the old fire station. The three trees are now the biggest thing on the acre. The ground cover around me is waist high in goldenrod, ankle high in clover. The rest of the acre I've come to know so well was recently mowed; the wild flowers are just coming back. A breeze off the river bends the yellow flowers to the west and plays with the clover's strong, sweet aroma. I watch the woman and her dog as they walk out of sight over Pooley's Bridge.

Three years ago to the day, on June 21, 1993, I sat here under the trees in a feeble drizzle, waiting for the contours of the acre to rise out of the dark; waiting for this story to begin. Now I'll watch the acre slide into night, at the end of this year's summer solstice: the end of the story. For the moment, the sun sits over the acre's northwest corner, yellowing out to blood red.

Another dog-walker passes, this one with a collie. Her jogging pants are the colour of thistles. She has some dog turds in a plastic shopping bag: politically correct canine defecation. When I close my eyes, white noise comes from the traffic on all sides; buses pulling away, car wheels on summer tarmac. It's as though they've been hired to just drive round and round, striving to keep the decibel level constant. The cars and the nearby running water sound similar. The birds can hardly get a note in edgeways.

The last time I was down here was a week ago, when the biggest women's march in Canadian history arrived at Le Breton Flats and set up a tent city on the acre. It was a march against encroaching poverty, against the two nations inside a single border — the rich and the poor — that Canada is becoming. The Bread and Roses caravan had started a month earlier, from each end of the country, and met in the middle. Two thousand camped out on Le Breton Flats. Ten thousand left from here the next day to snake through town to Parliament Hill for a rally.

I biked down and arrived as the marchers were crossing Pooley's Bridge. They were singing their way across, a bunch of different protest songs all at once, as though someone had pushed all the buttons on a juke-box. They were not unhappy, they were glad to be heard, and their certainty of injustice was infectious. The segment nearest me sang:

As we come marching, marching, unnumbered women dead,
Go crying through our singing their ancient songs of bread
Small art and love and beauty their drudging spirits knew,
Yes, it is bread we fight for — but we fight for roses too!

After they had passed, I went onto the acre. It was covered with tents, eight of them along Duke Street's east side, three large ones behind; it was a working acre once more. There were that many tents again on the other side of the street. With the crowds temporarily absent, the acre resembled a country fair that had been evacuated. Each of the eight tents on Duke was devoted to a different category, as the stores along the street in the 1870s had each had a different corner of the market. The signs outside read: Disabilities, Women of Colour, Lesbians, Healing, Aboriginals, Unions (two of these), and Creative Strategies. One of the big tents was a food market, another was a kids' playground, the third a meeting hall, with fresh bread and roses on the front of the stage. In the meeting hall there was a quilt hung up, made of four-inch squares of colour, each with a handwritten message — "The Language of Silence is Getting Louder" was my favourite. I looked down at the soil beneath my feet, but couldn't hear anything except papers blowing off a table.

I fell in talking with a woman who had started her own business that day, selling hot dogs and hamburgers from a little cart. It was the first new business on the acre in thirty years. She had sold out, and was happy and tired. I told her the story of the Richmond settlers, who had camped out like this 187 years earlier, who probably also put up a food tent and a meeting tent in the four months they stayed here. We paused to imagine the scene, then someone cranked up the sound system to test it, and the spell was broken.

As I relax a week later, in the leathery heat on the empty acre, it feels like a single day has gone by, three years long. In my hand, in a small metal box with a padlock, I've got a three-and-a-half-inch computer disk. On the disk is a copy of the text of this book, minus this last chapter. In effect, I'm holding the acre's memory, stored on silicon in one megabyte. I'm going to bury the disk in the acre, under one of these trees. Buried memories. The interment — the implant — will coincide with the moment of sundown, which the newspaper says will happen at 8:55. I've got half an hour before I start digging.

Joggers, cyclists, bees, hot-air balloons, and mosquitoes all arrive and depart at random intervals. Between these blips of activity, while the crickets sing, I doodle in the cork-covered notebook that's accompanied this project. I write *acre* several times at the top in different handwritings, then notice it's an anagram for *race* and *care*, which perhaps signifies nothing but the mischievousness of words. Below that, I draw an x and y axis for length and width, and mark off a model acre, with stick people standing on it. Then I draw the z axis, time, through the point where the x and y intersect. I drag the z line down to the bottom of the page, start drawing little people from the same stick nation standing on each other's shoulders. By marking off the z axis in decades, and drawing lines across at each decade, I've created a timescraper, a building rising high into millennia.

233

Interesting, I guess, but not what I'm after. Too modern, too drab. So I draw something like a wheel of cards, each card an acre, a fan of acres pinned in one corner, each acre representing a different era. I look at this arrangement, as I slap a mosquito, and realize I've come to hold the acre's history like a village in my mind. It isn't a village of area — it's a village of time; a village in which all the acre's eras are adjacent. All the people who have lived here, paused here, or passed by, all the myriad events that have happened here, are part of a community; a neighbourhood of years I've come to think of as Acreville. In Acreville, Time has taken time off, and history has collapsed into a single, unending day. An old piece of graffiti from a university wall pops in my mind: "Time is nature's way of making sure everything doesn't happen at once." In Acreville it all happens at once: Constant Penency and Greg Sarazin walk the trapline together; old man Perley takes a rowboat out on the Champlain Sea; Robert Randall and John Stegmann sit on the bench and talk over old times; Étienne Brûlé puts his feet up in the Duke House and tells Ralph Burton tall tales of life among the Indians.

Over the three years I've been coming here, people have been added to the population of Acreville, people I've invited down to walk the acre with me. Ken, the bearded TV interviewer, who looked up when I told him that whales used to swim above our heads. Sally, from the women's poverty march, who strolled the perimeter in sympathy with women settlers. Peter, the landscape artist, who listened patiently in the snow while I poured history out like mulled wine, and his son sledded alone behind us. Dan, the campaigning naturalist, who told me a man called Sir John Richardson had probably stood here in 1827, when he travelled with the famous explorer Sir John Franklin. Franklin was returning from an expedition up north and had dinner with Colonel By. Richardson was the foremost natural historian in North America at the time (there is a squirrel named after him); it would be a pleasant miracle to chat with him, to see the acre through his eyes, to tell him all that has passed since he stood here.

A peripheral movement catches my eye, puts me back in real time. One of the campers from the campsite has trudged over to the phone booth that sits forlornly on the opposite corner. I watch the camper talk, without being able to hear her. Opening the notebook again, I write today's time and date down as a continuous series of numbers. 2035 21 06 1996, then divide it up like a telephone number: 20-352-106-1996. Next, I scribble the same time and day, but in 1959, the year Ottawa street directories started listing phone numbers. 20-352-106-1959. The "20" is obviously the country code for the past. Then I add from memory an actual phone number from that year, the number of the Duke House: 234-1812.

I have a recurring fantasy about phones. I wish they weren't trapped in the present tense, and you could dial any phone, anywhere in time. You don't know till you try. When the camper leaves, I cross Duke Street, step into the booth, and fish in my pocket for my phone card. I start dialling the past. After four numbers I get a recording telling me to put a "one" in front. Makes sense; the past is undoubtedly long-distance. On the next try, the phone starts ringing before I dial the five in 1959. A woman on her little acre in West Hartford, Connecticut, assures me that this is not the Duke House, June 21, 1959. We disconnect.

This abstract silliness, of course, still has one place left to go: the future. What is to become of the acre? What if I dial a date yet to come? Ten years from now, or as long again into the future as the acre has been unpopulated, thirty years. Would it just ring and ring, the acre still vacant? Would some householder take the call from a luxury terrace, the low sun coming in through the window turning the river golden, while her children play in the park out front? I'd probably get an answering machine.

Over the past three years, of course, I've developed my own best wishes for the acre. I want it to be part of a park. Penency Park. Ottawa is a town whose citizens cannot meet outdoors in large numbers. Over the years, apart from its infamous cleanliness, it has earned a reputation as a city that is easy to get out of. Ottawans say it to each other, usually in February, when they rehearse the reasons why they stay in such a shocking climate. And it's true. Twenty minutes in the car and you are back in the trees, a native for a day.

But that is also a good reason to put a park inside the city, to allow the urbanites the chance to get a quick fix of parkness without leaving the perimeter. It is part of being a Canadian to feel like you are living in a vast park, with the terrors of America to the south and the endless snowdrifts to the north. The country feels like one big park, with the acne of habitation sprinkled over it, worse in some places than others. This is a country where city people occasionally have to deal with moose trapped in their swimming pools, and bears sometimes shove aside raccoons to get at the garbage. This is a young country in an old land.

What better symbol, in the centre of the capital of a country that thinks it's a park, to have acres devoted to that concept, alongside a major river. Make it big. Decorate it with chess tables, weekend art markets, statuary to commemorate ancient burial sites and vanished communities. Add a concert bowl, a skating and skateboard rink, riverside cafés. Then popes and assorted potentates can visit as they wish, outbreaks of patriotism can enjoy a proper width of spectacle, and that most wonderful of inventions, the festival, can bloom like a well-planned garden throughout the year, within sight of the seat of governance, alongside the waterfall that was the magnet that initially aligned human filings here in the first place.

Besides, as we know, the soil beneath the acre, all over the Flats, holds some nasty secrets better left buried. There's a Pandora's box of environmental pus under the skin of the Le Breton acres, and any development is going to have to break that skin. The cost of dry-cleaning the Flats, perhaps involving carting away (to where?) tons of contaminated soil, may be one of the reasons the Flats has sat idle all these years. (Another reason is the simple maxim that the more people you involve in a decision, the less likely you are to get one.) It may be best to leave unwell enough alone, and settle for a park, a reminder that we are not the only architects at work on the landscape.

I return to my chair, pick up my shovel and the box with the computer disk. Fifteen minutes to sundown. Time to start digging. Stepping back into the trees I notice a groundhog at the entrance to his hole. I could touch him with my shovel. His nose is pointing down into the warren, but his eyes are glancing sideways at me. He knows my type and is suspended between caution and curiosity. He must be, I figure, the biggest resident of the acre. One step forward and I cross an invisible perimeter in his head. In a fur-flash he forsakes the grassy porch for his earthen hallway, but keeps an eye on me.

Beneath the trees, half hidden under some torn-off grass, I spy a briefcase. Its contents are spilt out in a white nest, a bunch of meeting notes, envelopes, phone numbers. A bag-snatcher has come here, evidently, to sort through his grab, the rewarding part of the profession. For his pains, all he's got is some worthless government documents. Crime hasn't paid. The papers reveal that the owner is an archivist, which is pleasantly ironic. (When I phone the archivist later, I learn that the case had been taken from her car that day. It hadn't even been missed.)

At ten minutes to sundown I begin digging. The roots resist the shovel, then give way like turkey bones. I dig at an angle to decoy raiders. The sun has already gone out of sight behind the paper mill, but I wait until exactly five to nine. Then the box, the acre's story — so far — goes underground. Terra interruptus; terra firma. Two campers arriving for the nine-o'clock closing of the Le Breton site glance my way. When I was here at the same time last year, a dozen Algonquin street kids, tired of sleeping at the mission, where they are the lowest of the low, had put up a temporary village in the camping grounds. People gave them tents and food. One night they were attacked by local morons who had decided they were "cleansing" the neighbourhood. One of the Algonquins was put in hospital with a head wound. The land they slept on is still, of course, subject to a native land claim.

My little ritual has come to a conclusion. I know more about this piece of land than any other on earth, and more than anyone else on earth, I imagine. The acre went from woods to words in a blink of history's eye, from dense forest to procrastination project. The history of Ottawa can be summarized in a sticker, FROM LUMBER TO LEGISLATION; the acre's history is a perfect microcosm of that. Comparing my small mound of knowledge with all that the acre has seen and felt, I realize I know next to nothing, though I know enough to feel respect.

I fold up the chair and walk again around the acre, my head a flood of facts, back to where I started three years ago, to the former doorway of the Duke House. In the twilight, two ducks pass over the far end of the acre, where the Richmond settlers made camp. The ducks circle round over my head and divide, one flying over the river, the other heading inland. One last step and I'm off the acre — and onto the next. As I walk away, one of the ducks turns back the way it came, as though it has forgotten something.

Index

Index

The text of this book is set in Bodoni Book,
a typeface based on a 1787 font cut by the prolific
Italian printer and type designer Giambattista Bodoni.

The headlines are set in Meta, a typeface designed by
Erik Spiekermann and issued by the Font Shop in 1991.

Book design and typesetting by James Ireland Design Inc., Toronto

Line drawings by Franc Van Oort

Detail from "A Bird's Eye View of the City of Ottawa," ca. 1876,
reproduced with permission from Natural Resources Canada